The Physician Employment Contract Handbook

Second Edition

A Guide to Structuring Equitable Arrangements

Maria K. Todd

CRC Press
Taylor & Francis Group
Boca Raton London New York

CRC Press is an imprint of the
Taylor & Francis Group, an **informa** business

A PRODUCTIVITY PRESS BOOK

Productivity Press
Taylor & Francis Group
270 Madison Avenue
New York, NY 10016

© 2011 by Taylor and Francis Group, LLC
Productivity Press is an imprint of Taylor & Francis Group, an Informa business

No claim to original U.S. Government works

Printed in the United States of America on acid-free paper
10 9 8 7 6 5 4 3 2 1

International Standard Book Number: 978-1-4398-1316-4 (Paperback)

Visit the Taylor & Francis Web site at
http://www.taylorandfrancis.com

and the Productivity Press Web site at
http://www.productivitypress.com

Contents

Foreword

Responsible medical schools would make the *Physician Employment Contract Handbook* a required text. Prudent physicians would keep their copy and refer to it as necessary throughout their careers. This book is that important. The practice of medicine and the business of practice are two distinct disciplines. Mastery of the former and neglect of the latter nearly guarantee an unhappy and unfulfilling professional life in medicine.

For many new physicians, their first employment agreement is a near-mystical document representing the end of many years of grueling medical education and the beginning of their careers as doctors and healers. As many new physicians begin their careers with significant medical school debts to repay, the employment contract also represents a means to repay these debts and to lay the foundation for a successful career. More experienced physicians, too, often view employment agreements simply as a means to an end. This view, while understandable, can be perilous. Todd's book provides anecdotal evidence of misunderstood or casually reviewed employment agreements that have gone terribly wrong. It does not have to be this way.

Over the course of my legal career, I have had the opportunity to review, draft, and negotiate literally thousands of contracts. Some of the most sophisticated, complex, and therefore often-litigated agreements are related to the business of healthcare. Physician employment agreements, of course, fall within this group. As the business of healthcare grows more complex daily, physician employment contracts are particularly susceptible to misunderstanding because physician education and training prepare one to treat patients—not to skillfully negotiate an employment agreement necessarily laden with federal and state laws, rules, and regulations directed to the many legal aspects of practicing medicine in the United States.

This is not to suggest that physician employers, be they hospitals, managed care organizations, or other physicians in private practice settings, are intent on exploiting their colleagues or leveraging their bargaining position to extract unfair concessions from the unwary or ill informed. Of course, some employers do take advantage of their experience and access to expert legal resources when developing and negotiating physician contracts. The employer's legal counsel typically drafts employment agreements, and employers typically have much more experience dealing with employment agreements. The agreement's "default" provisions will almost certainly favor the employer, and the general tenor of the agreement will be tilted in the employer's favor in almost every instance. However, you can and should take steps to shift this balance of power in your favor.

In my experience, the biggest mistake many physicians make is presuming these agreements are nonnegotiable. Notwithstanding an employer's seemingly superior negotiation position with respect to physician employment agreements, the careful physician would do well to approach every employment agreement as an opportunity to clarify critical issues dealing with day-to-day practice expectations, long-term career planning, and compensation arrangements that are often quite a bit more complicated than one might expect.

This book helps physicians make sense of some of the complex topics and issues they will need to master in order to ensure their contract negotiations are meaningful and beneficial. There can be no negotiation without information and understanding. If you do not understand your employment agreement, you will lose the negotiation every time, and the results of this loss could impact your entire medical career. Too many physicians enter into employment agreements not fully understanding the complicated terms and conditions, and as a result, some physicians become trapped in unhappy environments. Others, even more unfortunately, must deal with the devastating financial consequences of not understanding their promised obligations.

What makes this handbook so invaluable, and why I am so happy to have been asked to provide this foreword, is that it not only walks physicians through the key agreement provisions they are likely to confront in almost every physician employment agreement, but it also takes the time to carefully and plainly set forth the legal and regulatory framework dictating the need for many of these seemingly arcane employment provisions. It is one thing to know what to expect in terms of the language, compensation formulas, and practice issues, and quite another to become proficient at understanding these provisions in context. Physicians who take the time to understand the legal and regulatory context of these provisions will be very well prepared to negotiate the terms of their employment agreements on an equal footing.

Let's consider a few examples. After reading this book, you will understand the noncompete provisions in your agreements and, more importantly, you will understand which provisions are enforceable and which are illegal. State law governs these provisions, so it is important to consult with an attorney in the jurisdiction where you will be practicing to understand how they will be construed in your state. If you accept a contract with a burdensome but enforceable noncompete provision, you could find your ability to practice medicine in your chosen discipline severely compromised in your geographic region for a very long time. The medical marketplace is increasingly competitive, and employers are vigorously protecting their practice areas.

For many physicians, partnership opportunities are an important incentive for picking one employer over another. Practices should be willing to explicitly describe the path to partnership in clear terms. Practices not willing to spend the time to explain your partnership track should be carefully scrutinized. Your employment agreement is an important tool when it comes time to make your argument for partnership. If you do not understand the path from here to there, or if the target seems like it is always moving, take the time to ask questions and negotiate terms that are fair. Once you have read and mastered the material in this book, you will know which questions to ask and what the answers need to be.

Perhaps you are a specialist. Does your employment contract guarantee access to the equipment you need to flourish? How will equipment be shared between practitioners in practice groups? You need to ask these questions before there is an issue, and there is no better time than before you have signed your employment agreement. Make sure you have the tools you need—when you need them.

Much has happened recently at the federal level to curtail the use of corporate dollars to subsidize continuing medical education (CME). Does your employment agreement clearly set forth how much you are entitled to receive in CME dollars? How about work-related travel to important conferences or critical memberships in important medical societies and groups? Again, after you have signed the agreement is no time to start discovering that you will be largely required to pay your own bills—especially as practices are tightening their belts in a troubled economy.

Of course, these are just a few of the many elements of your physician employment agreement that you will need to carefully understand before you sign. An employment agreement can be one of the most important and effective tools in setting the foundation for an effective and prosperous medical career. Take the lessons provided in this book to heart, and do the work necessary to ensure a successful employment contract negotiation.

Gary D. Wimsett, Jr.
Attorney and Counselor at Law
Gainesville, Florida

Preface

Medical group practice administrators and physicians are challenged with the responsibility of tending to details regarding physician employment. Much has changed in the last few years regarding compensation, financial incentives, compliance with federal regulatory requirements, ever-increasing fraud and abuse prosecution, and the enactment of the Omnibus Reconciliation Act, known as Stark II.

Physicians nearing the completion of their training have many opportunities to contemplate and may not have reviewed basic contract concepts and matters of regulatory compliance before being thrust out into the real world of actual medical practice, either privately or in a group setting.

In the last decade, we have seen a proliferation of physician practice management firms that trade in physician practices like any other stock on the publicly traded market. Their attitude is not always the same as the physician but is instead more focused on the bottom line and is performance driven.

A new breed of physician has also been identified—that of medicine as a job—with a different quality of life demanded by the physician and his or her family. Ask any administrator what it is like to hire this new breed of physician and their eyes roll back. The demands of the new physician are tough to meet and sometimes almost surreal. Gone are the days of joining one's father's practice and carrying on the family tradition of being the town physician. It is a rare occasion to find a newly graduated physician who will agree to accept night calls, make it in a private practice, or even grow a practice slowly.

In many cases, the newly graduated physician has already come to the conclusion that he or she will work for someone else. The realization that many health maintenance organizations (HMOs) and preferred provider organizations (PPOs) have closed panels and will not allow newcomers into the fold, paired with the fact that they control most of the steerage of patients, means that the new physician is probably right. In order to have access to patients, the new physician will probably work for someone else who already has access to contracts. The only new physicians who may have it different are cosmetic surgeons who have a cash trade.

This idea of working for someone else is assumptive of the fact that the contracts they hold with the managed care entities allow for new physicians joining an established practice to become credentialed and contracted with the plan. It is essential, therefore, to understand the mechanism of contracting, the similarity between contracting formats, and all the nuances that make life as a new physician interesting.

This book was created for those physicians and administrators who wish to prepare themselves for the contract and employment decisions that lie ahead of them. There can be no substitute for experienced legal counsel, but this book is designed to help you get more out of that consultation. After you have finished this book, you should be able to ask more meaningful questions of legal and accounting counsel. Physicians will be able to do a preliminary review and analysis of the agreement offered and even compare what they have been presented by a prospective employer to other standard agreements without endangering anyone else's confidentiality agreements.

Administrators will be able to design standard text and save some time and money on legal fees by having their corporate counsel review and add the final touches to their agreement contract drafts.

Remember that all contracts are a documentation of an agreement. They declare that there has been a meeting of the minds. If your contract is not crystal clear upon its completion and signature, how will it stand the test of time? Contracts were designed to be the only documentation remaining that can be depended on by a third party in the event that the relationship breaks down. When we think of breach of contract and unfair dealings, we think of the phrase "I'll see you in court!" This is not necessarily so these days. The contract may have a requirement to be submitted to a dispute resolution mechanism such as arbitration or mediation. Chapter 11 provides a basic understanding of that process.

Employment contracts are not the only contracts you will face as a new physician. Managed care, with all its acronyms, will also play a role in your initiation into the delivery system of healthcare in America. Chapter 12 was written to help with the understanding of many of the more popular managed care entities that may become a part of your professional life.

Before attempting to review any contract, it might be helpful to spend some time reviewing the basics of contract development in Chapter 8. Remember, just because a contract might make sense to your brother who is a general practice attorney, healthcare provider contracts have so many regulatory overlays that the basic contract may not be legal or enforceable for physicians. Hence, I added a review of basic concepts in fraud and abuse, corporate practice of medicine, and antitrust concerns in Chapter 4.

We need to rely on others who are trained in healthcare law to guide us beyond basic knowledge of these issues. One resource for finding such counsel is the American Health Lawyers Association (1120 Connecticut Avenue, N.W., Suite 950, Washington, DC 20036; phone: (202) 833-1100; fax: (202) 833-1105; www.ahla.org).

Another source is the Internet. Simply choose a search engine and enter "health law." You are bound to find an exhaustive list of references to law firms that have different areas of expertise in this broad category of law. You can also search "employment law" and find firms that offer both. The material in this book should be limited to advancing contract development techniques, finding ideas, preventing problems, and strengthening skills. The opinions and thoughts are those of the author and are not a substitute for legal counsel.

Acknowledgments

Many years ago, prior to the authorship of this book, I received a call from Dr. Lawrence Cowsill, the Director of the Primary Care Program for the Michigan State University Consortium of Graduate Medical Education and Training (COGMET). We decided to develop an educational program for the residents and fellows in the Michigan COGMET on managed care issues and touch on physician employment contracts as a combined subject area for a multiday mandatory attendance program. What we learned as teachers surprised us, as well as the presenters and sponsors. Nowhere was there a current manual for those new physicians to review for guidance for one of the most important decisions in their new careers. The first edition of this book provided one, and now it is updated again through this second edition.

In 1998, I proposed the book to Kris Rynne (now Mednansky), who was then with McGraw-Hill Healthcare Education Group, and soon the wheels were in motion for the first edition of this book. The first edition was published in late 1999, in cooperation with the Healthcare Financial Management Association (HFMA) and the Medical Group Management Association (MGMA). Today, this book is the product of updated information and research into the subject matter as a second edition. Kris is still there, now with a different publisher, and we are both 10 years older and wiser.

As in my first book, I reached out to friends and colleagues to help me update certain sections, including many wonderful and generous attorneys who are always there for me to bounce off ideas, answer questions, and even take a few calls from my readers.

I want to take a moment to thank them for their kindness and generosity. Also, I thank the many office managers, administrators, and physicians who graciously supplied specimen contracts from their own files for me to review and compile as models for the book.

Last but not least, to my loyal and patient spouse, Alan, who fed the cats, made dinners, and kept the house running for me while I rushed to finish my five books under contract this year. Without his patience and interest, my successes would be hollow.

Maria K. Todd

About the Author

The information and techniques provided in this book come from the author's experience of more than 30 years in practice management and healthcare administration and work as a hospital administrator, group practice administrator, Independent Practice Association (IPA) executive director and revenue cycle manager (operations), and a national health maintenance organization (HMO) provider relations coordinator (the "insider" aspect of contracting with health plans). It also has strong overtones from her work as a health law paralegal (research and due diligence process) and her work as a certified mediator (negotiation techniques) in dispute resolution.

Mixed into this, she also brings her understanding of the realities of a physician's need for autonomy, work–life balance, and a commitment to high-quality care delivery from her days on the clinical side of healthcare. In all her books, articles, and white papers, Todd shares tips and techniques from the trenches, student questions and insight from more than 2,600 previous presentations, and lessons learned from process improvement exercises and medical practice development with thousands of consulting clients over the last 30 years at hospitals, clinics, private practices, and other provider settings, both in the United States and abroad.

You can visit her Web site for additional tools, tips, and techniques as well as view the schedule for webinars and live presentations at http://mariatodd.com.

1 Introduction

OCCUPATIONAL OPTIONS FOR PHYSICIANS

First, let us examine the options for physician medical practices by setting. Categorically, we can divide these into

- Research
- Academia
- Clinical practice in an office setting
- Hospital-based physicians
- Staff model health maintenance organization (HMO) physicians
- In-house company physicians
- Administrative physicians
- Consulting physicians

Within these categories, we can subdivide them into more specifically designed roles within these types of organizations. Research physicians work in a number of settings, including but not limited to

- Pharmaceutical and genetic research laboratories
- Private research interests
- Research foundations
- Government settings
- Hospital and university settings, and so forth

If you are interested in these types of positions, you should add a consultation with an intellectual property attorney in addition to one well versed in employment law.

MANAGED CARE IMPLICATIONS

As managed care extends its reach across the United States, physicians are increasingly concerned about potential reductions in income and loss of clinical autonomy. Managed care's emphasis on cost reduction—together with its logical consequences—is forcing physicians to seek new organizational structures that will allow them to compete in this changing healthcare environment. Physicians realize that participation in some type of integrated delivery system is necessary to decrease the operating costs of their individual practices as well as to provide them the means to compete for the managed care contracts that are increasingly channeling patients into prepaid medical care.

The number of options available to physicians is ever increasing. Complicating the choice of an appropriate model is the fact that one's peers, depending on age and employment experiences, all seem to have differing opinions as to which choice is best. Making the correct decision becomes even more difficult in light of the fact that some of these options include big dollar buyouts, the sacrifice of lifestyle choices, and sometimes the sacrifice of clinical autonomy.

Management services organizations (MSOs) are a primary mechanism for assisting physicians. First, not all MSOs employ physicians or purchase their practices. They provide access to the economies of scale available to larger organizations. Depending on the particular model, MSOs typically provide physicians with capital, management, staffing, marketing, planning, research, and systems support. In return, physicians pay the MSO a percentage of collections. If the MSO has purchased a physician's practice, the physician receives a base salary with potential for a bonus. Types of MSO affiliations range from the simple merger of physician practices to complete buyouts by hospitals, other physician groups, or publicly traded equity organizations. Sometimes mergers do not even occur, and physicians simply economically integrate at the MSO level without resigning their independent business unit. At that point, the MSO is more of a joint venture option.

For physicians, knowing which option is right for them depends to a large extent on their expectations, their goals for the future, the level of autonomy they are willing to relinquish to the affiliated organization, and the degree of risk they are willing to assume to consummate the deal. Before entering into any affiliation agreement, physicians should first ask themselves the following questions:

- What do I expect from this affiliation?
- What aspects of my practice do I want to separate from the other entities represented in this decision?
- Is this decision to integrate physician or purchaser initiated?
- Is integration a short- or long-term strategy?

Despite these questions and concerns, the decision to move beyond the current organizational structure can be a positive and strategically correct move. The difference between a successful and an unsuccessful affiliation rests upon the amount of effort one puts into it and the extent of self-appraisal that precedes the final decision.

Fortunately, there are a wide range of affiliation options available to meet physicians' varying needs. These options include but are not limited to

- Hospital-owned MSOs
- Group practice without walls, or "integrated health systems"
- Open physician hospital organizations
- Closed physician hospital organizations
- Comprehensive management services organizations
- Equity management services organizations
- Foundation models
- Staff models

Although each model has a distinct purpose, all try to focus on controlling costs and capturing enrolled lives in managed care contracting environments. It is a little like "widget" design and manufacturing. Despite the number of options available, there is no one perfect solution that represents an ideal fit for each situation. The correct organizational structure is unique to each physician or group and can only be arrived at after an in-depth comparison of expectations against available options.

HOSPITAL-OWNED MANAGEMENT SERVICES ORGANIZATION (MSO)

In this model, physicians purchase practice services from the hospital subsidiary at fair-market value. Physicians retain complete clinical and financial autonomy from the health system and each other. This model was originally created to assist physicians with their billing operations. It was popular with hospitals as a way of bonding and, in more progressive environments, a way of establishing databases of comparative practice information. In addition to billing, services typically include practice administration, purchasing, long-range planning, and physician recruitment. The hospital seeks to gain physician trust by demonstrating its ability to increase practice revenues with improved collections and reduce the practice's operating costs through efficient management.

In many cases, the hospital-owned MSO never reaches its true potential, because it is run by hospital administrators who are relatively unfamiliar with the operations of a physician practice, physician capitation methodologies, and billing nomenclature. In addition, the risk of alienating the physician through reduced cash flow brought on by poor collections has caused many hospitals to rethink their commitment to this method of bonding. However, the concept remains a viable one if the supporting organization retains an experienced MSO administrator who can provide results. Prior to entering into this type of affiliation, physicians need to assure themselves that the MSO has a successful track record and can actually produce what it promises.

The hospital-owned MSO allows for quick network expansion and maintenance of physician independence, because the physician is selecting services on an a la carte basis and is not surrendering autonomy or decision-making authority. However, this model does not address the fundamental issue of physician lockout from payer networks. Most hospital-based MSOs focus on management and administration of practices and not on the marketing of the managed practices for contracting purposes. As an MSO gains experience, its parent company may expand its role to include contracting. Usually, this aspect is handled by some other entity within the healthcare system, such as a physician hospital organization (PHO). The hospital-owned MSO is recommended for the physician or physician group that wants assistance in practice management but expects to eventually move on to a more complex integrated delivery system.

GROUP PRACTICE WITHOUT WALLS/CLINIC WITHOUT WALLS/INTEGRATED HEALTH SYSTEMS

Physicians in a group practice without walls yield limited authority to the larger group. With Stark II, these arrangements became illegal, although physicians still saw the need for consolidated ancillary service providers, particularly in geographic areas where many of these ancillary services were unavailable. The creation of group practices without walls allowed a group of physicians or practices to affiliate while maintaining separate locations. This model was established as an initial response to Stark II legislation (Stark Law, §1877 of the Social Security Act), which is aimed at stopping referrals from physicians to ancillary providers with whom they have a financial investment. Prior to Stark II, it was common for a group of physicians in a geographic area to invest in laboratories, imaging centers, and other service providers and then refer their patients to these entities. By ensuring a steady stream of patients, the entity was usually very profitable, and a percentage of these profits was returned to the physician investors. By using one provider number, they met the restrictions of the Stark II legislation. But by maintaining their own separate locations, they retained most decision-making authority within the local office. This loose alliance can be effective in the sharing of overhead costs and the negotiation of payer contracts and requires no hospital involvement. However, physician autonomy is maintained at a price, because this model is more effective at managing costs than in obtaining managed care contracts. Physicians who want to benefit from the economies of scale that come from consolidating overhead operations, such as billing and administration, while maintaining a high degree of independence, may want to explore integrated health systems.

OPEN PHYSICIAN HOSPITAL ORGANIZATION (PHO)

The open PHO is a joint physician and hospital structure that accepts all members of a hospital's medical staff. Its primary function is to negotiate managed care contracts. If the PHO is successful in obtaining contracts and acts as the entity that accepts insurer payments, it may then have to expand its structure to process the premiums paid by the insurer. The open PHO is typically a shell organization and is lightly staffed. Physicians retain 100 percent ownership of their practices and usually contribute annually to the PHO to fund operating expenses. The advantage of this model is that, for a relatively modest investment, the physician can be part of a larger contracting organization. The disadvantage is that the PHO does nothing to fundamentally change the physician's practice; therefore, physicians are not necessarily any more competitive than before joining the PHO. Even if the PHO obtains managed care contracts, the loose structure of the PHO does not provide a mechanism for managing the cost of care. Many PHOs establish bonus systems to reward physicians who meet predetermined care standards within acceptable financial limits. Many physicians join open PHOs in response to pressure from the sponsoring hospital seeking to obtain the largest physician pool possible.

CLOSED PHYSICIAN HOSPITAL ORGANIZATION

The closed PHO functions like an open PHO except that membership is offered only to a select group of high-quality, cost-effective physicians. To ensure that it is attracting and maintaining only those physicians who provide care within the parameters required by its managed care contracts, the closed PHO usually establishes more comprehensive mechanisms for credentialing physicians than its open PHO counter-part. Sometimes these data come from the managed care organizations. Other times, data are provided within the PHO. With its focus on exclusivity, the closed PHO is an effective way to build an elite primary care physician base. However, it can act as an irritant to the specialists on the medical staff because it is not all-inclusive. Those physicians not allowed to participate often leave the sponsoring hospital. The closed PHO is primarily a contracting vehicle and typically does nothing to improve the management or efficiency of the physician's office. Consequently, over time, physi-cians tend to gravitate to models that do. At best, the closed PHO represents a transi-tion to a more advanced model.

PHYSICIAN PRACTICE MANAGEMENT ARRANGEMENT

The physician practice management (PPM) arrangement is formed when an entity pur-chases a group's assets, manages its medical practice, and negotiates its managed care contracts. Included in the purchase are the practice's hard assets, including medical equipment, furniture, real estate, supplies, and information systems. Services provided to the practice include nonclinical personnel management, administration, group pur-chasing, office leasing, and contracting. The physician group maintains a separate legal identity that hires nurses and other clinical personnel and retains some ownership of its revenue stream. This model is currently quite popular because it allows the physi-cians to turn over all the headaches of management to the PPM while retaining control over physician compensation and governance. The PPM provides the management of the office, usually through employees that previously were on the physician's payroll. This model is used extensively by venture capitalists in response to competition from hospitals and other MSOs. Because nonprofit organizations cannot bid up the purchase of a group's goodwill beyond a fair-market value, they find it difficult to compete head-to-head with PPMs. By purchasing only the hard assets of a group, they are able to provide some infusion of cash into the practice while still allowing the physicians a higher degree of independence than is found in hospital-sponsored MSOs.

If the PPM is successful in providing effective management services to its physi-cians, loyalty to the company is increased. Nevertheless, this model is still viewed as transitional. Physicians tend to move on to more advanced models that integrate their practices, allowing them to better negotiate and manage risk contracts. During the early to mid-1990s, many physicians abandoned early PPM arrangements. The physicians were unhappy and felt that the venture capitalist mindset misaligned with their medical practice, personal goals, and objectives. In other words, although it may have appeared appealing at the onset, in reality, the numbers and the culture of the physician groups did not really mesh. The trend is regaining some momentum as physicians wrestle with the apprehension associated with healthcare reform initia-tives and the burdens of the administrative processes such reform may bring.

EQUITY MANAGEMENT SERVICES ORGANIZATION

An equity MSO is a for-profit, private, or publicly traded organization that purchases a group's tangible and intangible assets, manages its medical practice, and negotiates its managed care contracts. PhyCor and MedPartners were two popularly cited examples of this setting from the 1990s. The revenue stream, which used to belong to the physician, was now directed to the MSO, which either took a percentage off the top for its services or paid the physicians predetermined compensation and kept the rest. The physician group would retain a separate corporate identity or become W-2 employees of the MSO or parent company. There are still many states that enforce a corporate practice of medicine prohibition where physician practices prohibit business corporations from employing physicians (corporate practice of medicine) so that a separate professional corporation might be established. This organization is owned by and then employs the physicians but is contractually bound to the MSO for management services. This contractual bond is strong and essentially gives the MSO control over the professional corporation. The equity MSO provides the physician with an alternative to unilaterally affiliating with a single hospital or healthcare system.

Equity MSO provides the advantages that come from economies of scale and broad-based experience. By the time the equity MSO is ready to acquire a practice, it has usually developed a track record for successful management of physician organizations. The disadvantage of this model is that the equity MSO can be a risky option because the MSO is subject to fluctuations in the stock market as well as to mergers and acquisitions occurring within the industry.

FOUNDATION MODEL

The foundation model is a truly integrated model. This large-scale, fully integrated entity involves a nonprofit subsidiary of a health system that purchases the tangible and intangible assets of a physician's practice. Physicians remain employees of a separate professional corporation but sign a professional services management agreement with the foundation. This model is often used as an alternative to direct employment of physicians, which some states prohibit under corporate practice of medicine laws. The main difference is that the physician becomes affiliated with a health system that can negotiate for both hospital and physician services.

In many respects, this is the nonprofit institution's alternative to the buyout of a physician's practice by the equity MSO. Both tangible and intangible assets of the practice are purchased by the foundation. Through ownership of the physician's practice, the foundation can invest liberally in the practice and allow physicians a share in the resultant revenue growth. Because 100 percent of the group's revenues come from the health system, physicians tend to support a shared destiny. Physician autonomy is retained to the maximum extent possible, but there is the potential for physician infighting. This is typically found in models that are heavily dependent on specialists but whose ultimate business objectives are focused on building a primary care delivery system. Because the model depends on tight integration, individual physician needs are sacrificed for the greater goal of the foundation.

This model is excellent for those physicians who are committed to hospital and physician integration as the way to control costs and obtain managed care contracts. When joining a foundation model, the physicians in many respects are moving beyond the limits of a physician organization and into the arms of an integrated healthcare system.

Many changes are occurring in the way hospitals and physicians collaborate. The driving force for such change is the integration of economic interests and services to make the most of shrinking provider payments. New partnerships span a wide spectrum of opportunities and assume different venues from loosely defined collaborations to hospital acquisition of physician practices. Further complicating these transitions are changes in reimbursement, hospital market share concerns, regional and national specialist alliances, for-profit company practice acquisition and management, primary care versus specialist tensions, and general physician uncertainty about the future.

In reading a first-year report by David J. McCombs, MHA, and Joseph R. Halperin, MD, of the Moses Cone Health System in Greensboro, North Carolina, a 1996 merger of a private medical oncology practice and hospital system was successfully completed due to several key factors:

- Mutual vision of a new healthcare delivery model
- An effective merger process
- Creative negotiation of key issues
- A unique collaborative management structure
- A jointly developed physician incentive program

Not simply enhancing the economic position of either party was fundamental to the success of this endeavor. The goal was to create new value in cancer services for the community, which the hospital and physician integration was able to accomplish.

The first task was to hire an outside consultant to evaluate several collaboration scenarios using financial and statistical data from both parties. Considered scenarios included continuing a full and separate relationship, creating a joint-venture operation with practice management services provided to the physicians by the hospital, and using a full employment model. These scenarios were modified to reflect current and projected changes in the managed care environment and governmental reimbursement. The conclusion of all parties was that the full physician employment model produced the best financial and services alignment. This model would best position the merged program to make the difficult decisions necessary to achieve its long-term vision.

Underlying the actual negotiation of the merger was the fact that the medical oncologists were seriously considering a proposal from an investor-owned, national company. From the start, it was clear that the hospital could not provide the same financial arrangements for the physicians as would result from an acquisition by an investor-owned, publicly traded company. Nevertheless, because both sides shared a mutual vision and commitment to the community, creative opportunities to craft additional benefits of a merger were sought in addition to direct payment. This was key to the success of the merger. Careful attention was paid to strictly follow Internal Revenue Service (IRS) and regulatory guidelines, and a mutually agreed-upon third-party practice evaluation expert, plus diligent experienced legal review, was used to ensure this objective was achieved. Additional benefits that the merger would provide to the physicians included the following:

- Commitment by the hospital to provide resources to build a new freestanding cancer center
- Availability of resources for cancer program development including research, patient support systems, nursing (maintains important structure of each physician having a designated nurse or nurses), and ambulatory chemotherapy
- Long-term employment contracts with stipulated renewal parameters
- Support of system-wide continuing medical education
- Vacation time
- Fringe benefits such as insurance and retirement
- Maintenance of competitive physician incomes based on an agreed-upon construct, including overall program success
- Regional alliance building

One pivotal principle to which both parties subscribed was to do whatever necessary to maintain the entrepreneurial and patient care success of the medical oncologists' private practice model. This meant taking the new entity out of the traditional, cumbersome hospital management structure. To accomplish this task, a medical management board was established. The board, which would report directly to the hospital president, included the medical director as chairperson, two medical oncologists, the executive vice president, and the new position of practice/ambulatory center director (ex-officio). This board's responsibilities would include overseeing all financial matters, planning, and program elements that relate to the practice and the ambulatory center (including the chemotherapy suite).

To ensure integrated services, there are dotted-line relationships to the other cancer center structures with broad representation by medical management board members on all appropriate cancer center committees. The medical management board represents the physicians at regularly scheduled monthly meetings as well as on an as-needed basis.

In addition to salary, both parties agreed that an incentive compensation program would be appropriate. The formula takes into account the overall success of the program by tabulating the total number of new patients seen in the cancer program and the number of new patients seen annually by each physician. Satisfaction of patients and referring physicians—not the volume of procedures—is another important indicator of success that would be tabulated and used as a basis (although less heavily weighted) for incentive compensation. Patient satisfaction would be determined by a survey crafted by the medical management board. Another important incentive included physician service components, such as research, teaching, community oncology activities, and committee membership, to be selected by each medical oncologist with input from the medical director.

Both parties agreed to fulfill the mission of serving a large arena of cancer patients by encouraging efforts to increase market share and serving the needs of the local community and region.

In the years since the merger was accomplished, all outpatient professional and technical services previously located in the hospital were physically consolidated at a site adjacent to the medical oncology practice. The integration has met both the hospital's and the physicians' goals. Projected financial and program goals have been exceeded, and patients have benefited from a consolidated delivery site and new program elements, such as nutritional and pastoral counseling, pharmacist presence, social services support, and an expanded patient and family education program.

STAFF MODEL

In the staff model, physicians are direct employees of the acquiring entity. They sign employment contracts, earn a negotiated salary with perhaps a performance bonus, and usually work on a negotiated schedule. This model offers more direct control over physicians by the employer through management of salaries and the ability to intervene one on one. However, physician productivity can suffer if appropriate productivity and incentive compensation plans are not put into effect, particularly for a physician who has spent extraordinary hours working to build a practice. Once he or she has sold that practice to someone else, the incentives are usually to enjoy the proceeds of the sale and develop a more stable personal life. This must be key to the physician's decision to select this option. Putting it bluntly, medicine as a life is no more, and it is more of medicine as a job. This model works well for someone who wants only to care for patients, is not interested in becoming involved in the management of the practice any longer, or is approaching retirement and sees this as a way to transition out of the practice. It is not right or wrong, only different, and may be excellent as a choice for many good physicians.

CONCLUSION

As healthcare costs skyrocket, employers and insurers are searching for ways to provide more cost-efficient models of care. Organizations are springing up to provide the skills and data management systems necessary to compete, and physicians are flocking to them. Which model the physician selects is more than just a matter of personal preference. It is the result of a detailed, well-thought-out approach to the future of one's practice. With proper planning and a clear understanding of both short- and long-term objectives, physicians can move into the future and take advantage of the opportunities that this revolution in healthcare is creating.

2 Working with Search Firms

Search firms do not market you, they work for employers and usually only have specific "job orders" or "contracts" with those employers to help fill certain positions. Do not waste time in your job search by thinking that recruiters will go to work for you and find you a job. Instead, send your résumé to hundreds of search firms in hopes that one or two or more of them will be currently handling positions that fit your qualifications or career goals. Do not think that you should limit yourself to contacting only recruiters working or living in your region. Often, the recruiters that handle the best jobs in your area do not live or work in your area. Local recruiters rarely handle top executive and professional positions. In the age of plane travel, fax machines, e-mail, and the Internet, it is not at all necessary or even true that the recruiters you work with should be located in your town. Recruiters and search firms will handle your résumé confidentially. They will not present your name or résumé to anyone without your specific permission. It is a good idea to cultivate a handful of good relationships with recruiters that you will maintain throughout your career. To find recruiters, you will want to use a directory. Many are found on LinkedIn and remain active in the groups in which they are likely to encounter physicians.

Although recruiters are adept at reading and understanding résumés, they cannot read your mind. They may not know what position you are seeking, what area of the country you would like to live in, or what your career goals are. Even the well-formatted résumé can leave out important information. The cover letter is your opportunity to seem more human, more personal, more authentic. If a recruiter has the sense that you are a real professional, the recruiter is more likely to think of you when an appropriate position opens. Cover letters provide both a personal and professional touch. Cover letters have the most impact if you use the name of an individual. Avoid sending letters "To Whom It May Concern."

PREEMPLOYMENT ISSUES

The physician's curriculum vitae (CV) is designed similar to a standard résumé, but it has some differences. For all practical purposes, unlike a regular résumé, all that is necessary is a synopsis of the physician's medical education, employment history, and basic personal information. A graduating resident or fellow will, of course, omit employment history unless it relates directly to the medical field.

There is no set formula for writing a CV, but the following guidelines seem to be the best received by those professionals who hire physicians.

CURRICULUM VITAE: DOS AND DON'TS

- Format it neatly with 1-inch margins at the top, bottom, and sides of the page.
- Be sure that the type is clear, easy to read, and dark enough to reproduce well when copied or faxed.
- List well-spaced, major categories for name, address, and telephone number. Medical education should usually come first for physicians, with a few exceptions.
- Be specific about the name of your medical school, the city and state where the medical school is located (address is not necessary), your degree, and the year of completion.
- Include internships, areas of specialization, facility, city and state, and year completed.
- Follow with residencies, fellowships, specializations, facility, city and state, and year completed. With a resident/fellow who is still in school and beginning to seek a practice location, the beginning date should be listed, along with the date of anticipated completion (rather than "to present").
- List undergraduate degrees last, and only elaborate if the degree was in a field related to the medical profession.
- Include any certification information, listing boards, and national exams taken, with appropriate dates.
- Include licensure, listing states and years in which you are currently licensed.
- Include employment history. Begin with your present or last employment, stating your status (partner, associate, staff physician, medical director, etc.), name of clinic or group (or solo or private practice, where applicable), admitting facility or facilities, city and state, and specific beginning and ending dates (or "to present"). If confidentiality is a factor, it is permissible to give a general idea of what your current status is without giving specific facility names, and so forth. Just say "group practice," "partner," and so forth, and your city and state.

Employment should be continued in reverse chronological order, always stating beginning and ending dates, along with other pertinent information. The personal information category is optional and should contain only very basic information.

DO NOT DO THIS!

- List references. Just add to the bottom of the CV, "References and additional information available upon request." The additional information can include abstracts and publications or any other related data.
- Give military background unless it is part of your medical employment history.
- Include an objective, practice preference, or compensation information in the CV.
- Make the CV longer than two pages, three at the most.
- List hobbies and outside activities unless they relate to your profession. These things are best discussed in an interview.

THE PHYSICIAN RECRUITMENT PROCESS

Because there are so many more variables and considerations when a physician decides to make a career change, the process generally takes more time than in other job searches. If the physician has a clear understanding of the progression of stages involved in the recruitment process, he or she can become better prepared for the events to unfold.

On many occasions, physicians have specific ideas about what they want in a new position. Their needs may be financial, geographic, or situational. Others are vaguer in their assessment of their ideal situation. They simply know a change is needed. Some introspection may be necessary before venturing out in the job market so that the weeding out of those "not just right" opportunities can be better directed. It is always beneficial to get as much information as you can about the practice opportunity before continuing with an application.

THE SCREENING PROCESS

The initial contact between the physician and the hiring facility is vitally important. Generally speaking, the CV is the first communication between the two parties and should be presented in a format that is in a classic style, conservative, and easy to follow. Hiring facilities will check the CV to ascertain that the physician's qualifications and credentials are consistent with the practice requirements. Often the CV will be reviewed by both administrative and clinical personnel before contact is made with the physician. During this stage, the most important variables are historically the physician's training, background, and geographic upbringing. Quite often, physician candidates are disregarded during this stage because of specific requirements mandated by the current physician staff and the practice environment. The main priority during the screening process is to identify the candidates best suited to achieving a long-term relationship. Once candidates have been identified, the interview process begins.

THE INTERVIEW PROCESS

Unless a physician is interviewing in his or her own location, the interview process generally begins with telephone conversations between the applicant and administrative or clinical personnel. This gives all parties involved an opportunity to discuss their specific requirements and determine whether to continue further discussions. Scheduling interviews is the largest obstacle encountered during this phase. It is recommended that telephone conversations be prearranged, allowing all parties an opportunity to speak freely and without interruption.

The next step is the site visit. This stage can be equally as frustrating in terms of scheduling. Interview expenses are nearly always covered by the hiring facility. On occasion, the physician may choose to make the necessary arrangements himself or herself and receive a reimbursement check when he or she arrives for the interview. Over the course of the interview, the candidate can expect to get a tour of the facilities, meet with other physicians on staff, meet administrative personnel, meet real estate agents, and be briefed on local school and community information. In general, the client will make every effort to give the candidate all the facts he or she needs to make an intelligent and accurate evaluation of the opportunity.

At the conclusion of the interview, an official offer may be made to the candidate. Of course, the candidate will be given time to consider an offer—no one expects or wants a rash decision. However, do not assume that all is not well if an offer is not made before leaving. In many cases, the opinions of the staff who met with the candidate need to be gathered and discussed before an official offer is made. Contracts will have to be prepared, and negotiations can slow this process. The candidate should, however, expect to hear from the hiring facility with their decision in a timely manner. If a deal is not reached, the process for the physician begins anew, but perhaps now with better focus on what he or she wants in a new position.

SUBMITTING YOUR CV TO SEARCH FIRMS

Although a small percentage of search firms are now accepting résumés through e-mail or Web sites, do not limit your contact to this method. When you send your résumé by e-mail, it is best to "copy and paste" it as plain text added to the body of your e-mail. You should include information about what type of job you are looking for, why you are contemplating a change, what location, and so forth. Many people try to attach their résumés to e-mail messages as Microsoft® Word® or WordPerfect® documents. Although they may look better this way, many recruiters will be unable to download them in that format. Further, many recruiters are reluctant to download those attachments due to fears about computer viruses. So, it is wise to simply "copy and paste" your résumé into the e-mail itself. Recruiters often ask for résumés by fax. This is okay. It is in your best interest to mail résumés and cover letters, following your faxed or e-mailed copies. They look better, they copy better, and they leave a more positive lasting impression with the recruiter. A follow-up package sends the message that you are a true professional.

Recruiters only work on specific positions from their clients—the employers. Recruiting offices receive hundreds of résumés by mail and numerous telephone calls every day. Usually, search firms have excellent procedures for cataloging résumés and matching them to appropriate positions. It is not necessary for you to call. In fact, sometimes search firms will become annoyed with telephone calls. This further emphasizes the importance of a well-written résumé and cover letter. Feel free to call search firms if you have moved and want to update them with your new address, or if you have an urgent need. It is also okay to call recruiters if you are trying to get a mailing address. Before you call a recruiter to talk about your job search, it is best to get a résumé in the recruiter's hands first, either by e-mail, fax, or postal delivery.

The recruiter has a responsibility to the employer. He or she is, in fact, representing the employer's interest when you are interviewed. Treat the recruiter with the same respect, integrity, and professionalism that you would want to present to a prospective employer. Be honest, positive, knowledgeable, and confident. In many ways, you will want to be more straightforward with the recruiter than you usually would be with an employer. You will want to treat the recruiter much like you would a confidant, because the more the recruiter knows about you, the easier it will be for him or her to find the right position for you. Recruiters make great advisors and mentors. With their knowledge of the industry, familiarity with current industry changes, and contacts, you may also learn much to assist you in your career decisions and career planning.

The recruiter makes his or her salary by successfully filling a position. Usually this means that some or all of the expenses incurred are the recruiter's responsibility. Time is important to recruiters and so is their relationship with employers. Be sure not to waste the recruiter's time or money by stringing him or her along if you are not really interested in a position. Also, this will maintain your positive regard with the search firm, which makes it possible for them to contact you many more times in the future when they learn of other opportunities. Do not burn any bridges!

Once you make initial contact with a search firm, keep them informed if your status, location, or job changes. It is really helpful to simply send an update letter, revised résumé, or postcard to the recruiters when your information changes. We advise professionals to do this immediately after every job change.

Sometimes search firms locate the best candidates for jobs through leads and referrals. Even if you are not interested in a job change, you may know someone who is. Go ahead and call recruiters back when they call you. You should keep track of recruiters and let them keep track of you. In doing this, you are not being disloyal in any way to your current employer. This is simply a necessary part of your career planning. Many times, when professionals are happily employed, they think that they do not need to talk to search firms and, in fact, they may feel some guilt when recruiters call. So, out of loyalty to their employer, they cut the conversation short and do not write the recruiter's name down. Big mistake! Then, as things go, 6 months later, there is a downsizing, a new boss who is hard to get along with, or a need to move to another location for family reasons. Then, those professionals kick themselves for not having kept the names of those recruiters who had called them. Do not let this happen to you. It is smart to maintain your relationships with them throughout your career. Let them send you a business card or brochure that you can copy and give to your colleagues and file away for a day when you may need the services of a recruiter. This is called networking, a key for success in any career.

Different recruiters know about different positions. They do not usually know about the same ones. This is particularly true with retained firms. By sending your résumé out widely, you will be placed in many different confidential databases and be alerted of many different positions. If you send your résumé to only a few, it may be that none you send to will be working with positions that are suited for you. Throw your net widely. If you change jobs, it is also wise to send follow-up letters to the recruiters and alert them of your new career move. Many search firms follow people throughout their careers and enjoy being kept up to date. It is a good idea to have your résumé formatted in plain text so you can copy and paste it into e-mail messages when requested to do so. Then, follow up with a nicely formatted copy on paper by postal mail.

Some people estimate that only 1 to 3 percent of all résumés sent will result in actual job interviews. So, if you send only 50 résumés, you may have only two interviews, if that many. Send your résumé to as many recruiters as you can. It is worth the postage. Generally, recruiters will not share your résumé with any employer or give your name to anyone else without obtaining your specific permission to do so. The recruiter will call first, talk to you about a particular position, and then ask your permission to share your résumé with that employer.

Recruiters are professionals. They recognize that in order to assist job seekers and professionals in their career development, they will need to assure the professional of strict confidentiality. What this means is that the recruiter will hold all of your information confidential at all times. It is, in fact, safe to submit your résumé to a search firm and not worry that the search firm will let it leak out that you are job searching. Recruiters will call you every time they wish to present you to an employer in order to gain your permission. Only after they have gained your permission will they submit your name or résumé to the identified employer. The wonderful aspect of working with search firms is that you can manage your career and your job search in confidence and privacy. Also, keep in mind that recruiters know about your industry, and they know about job openings that you may never hear about on your own. Pick a handful of trusty recruiters you will allow to follow you throughout your career. They can also be good confidants, sounding boards, and advisors, whether or not you are contemplating a job change.

Recruiters and search firms work for the employer or hiring entity. The employer pays them a fee for locating the right individual for the job opening. This is important to remember in that when you interact with executive recruiters, you are essentially interacting with an agent or representative of the employer. Recruiters are more loyal to employers than they are to job candidates, because they work for the employer. This should not present a problem, but should cause you to develop your relationship with the recruiter with the same integrity and professionalism that you would with the employer.

Recruiters are paid fees in one of two ways—retainer fees or contingency fees. This is an important distinction and will affect your process with both the employer and the recruiter. Some employers prefer working with contingency firms and some with retained firms. Both are respected by employers and are useful in your job search, but the two types of firms will not be handling the same positions with the same employers simultaneously. The "retained" recruiter entered an exclusive contract with an employer to fill a particular position. The retained recruiter is then likely to advertise a position, and share the specifics of the position, location, and employer openly. The retained firm feels a great obligation to fulfill the contract by finding the best person for the job. The contingency recruiter, on the other hand, usually does not have an exclusive relationship with the employer and is only paid a fee if the job search is successful.

Often, if the employer uses contingency firms, there will be more than one contingency firm competing to fill a certain position. As a job hunter, if you are sent to an interview by a contingency firm, you may find that you are competing with a larger number of applicants for a position. Generally, retained firms only send in three to five candidates for a position.

Recruiters will be paid fees equal to about 25 to 35 percent of the resulting salary of the successful candidate plus expenses. This does not come out of the job candidate's salary. This is paid to the recruiter through a separate relationship between the employer and the search firm. These may seem like large fees to you, but keep in mind that recruiters incur a great many expenses when searching for successful job candidates.

They spend enormous amounts of money on computer systems, long-distance calls, mail-outs, travel, and interviews. Recruiters work very hard for these fees. Employers recognize the value of using recruiters and are more than willing to pay recruiters the fees. All you have to do is contact the recruiter to get the process moving.

Some search firms work exclusively in healthcare, and others may work in several fields at once. Some of the larger generalist firms will have one or more search consultants who specialize in healthcare. It is important for you, as a job hunter, to assess the recruiters' knowledge of your field. If you use industry buzzwords in describing your skills, experience, or career aspirations, you may or may not be talking in a language the recruiter fully understands. It is wise to explore fully with the recruiter his or her understanding of your field and area of specialization.

Recruiters, like many professionals, move to new firms during their careers. Often you will find that recruiters will work at several firms during their careers. It is much more effective to address your letters to a person rather than "To Whom It May Concern," so it is smart for job hunters to have accurate and up-to-date information about who is who and where, because this can change frequently. Search firms also move their offices, sometimes to another suite, street, or state. If you have a list of recruiters that is over 1 year old, you will certainly waste some postage mailing your résumés and cover letters. Many of your mail-outs will be returned to you stamped "nondeliverable" unless you obtain an up-to-date list.

Some recruiters specialize in managed care executive positions, healthcare financial positions, or health administration positions. Others may specialize in finding doctors, nurses, or physical therapists. Generally, an employer does not engage a recruiter's assistance in filling a position unless it is hard to fill. Sometimes employers will engage search firms to save them the valuable time of advertising or combing through dozens of résumés. Contingency recruiters tend to work with more midlevel management and professional positions, but this is not always the case.

Retained firms generally work with the higher-level clinical or administrative positions. One thing you will be assured of is that if a recruiter is working on a position, it means that the employer is willing to pay a fee. That usually means that the position is a valued position and one worth closer inspection on your part.

WORKING WITH A PHYSICIAN RECRUITER: A CHECKLIST

Try to get as much information as possible in the first-call contact:

- Kind of practice (single specialty group, multispecialty group, health maintenance organization, etc.)
- Salary (guaranteed salary, equal share, productivity based, fee for service)
- Number of associated physicians and their length of service
- Call schedule
- Prepare answers to potential questions about
  - Your strengths
  - Your weaknesses
  - Your goals
  - Benefits (to you) of your residency training program

NEGOTIATING A CONTRACT WITH AN EMPLOYER

Negotiating an employment contract is often an adversarial process with each party trying to get the most while giving up the least. Enter such negotiations with priorities in mind (make a priority list). Consider the following:

- Reimbursement Plan
  - Fee for service
  - Equal share—net income of the practice (total income less expenses) is divided equally among the group
  - Salary guarantee—salary is set and independent of practice income
  - Productivity based—income is based on an individual physician's contribution to overall practice income (in capitated/managed care, the amount of money saved by limiting costs)
  - Benefits
  - Health, dental, vision care for self and family
    - High deductible or low deductible?
    - Health savings account (HSA) or health reimbursement arrangement (HRA)? Traditional coverage, insured or self-funded?
  - Disability insurance
  - Retirement program (nonprofits: 403b plan; for-profits: 401k plan)
  - Malpractice insurance
  - Hospital dues
  - Professional membership dues
  - Subscriptions and professional books
  - Continuing medical education (CME) tuition
  - Travel to professional meetings
  - Vacation
  - Moving expenses
- Work Restrictions
  - Restrictive covenants and noncompete clauses that restrict a physician from working in the same geographic region after leaving an employer
  - Hours—length of the work week?
  - Moonlighting—permissibility? Employer wants a percentage of moonlighting income?
  - Working with competing groups or arrangements in your off time
  - Volunteer service (team physician, local mission, etc.)

Working with search firms can be rewarding or frustrating. It depends on market need for your specialty and the credentials and demands of other candidates vying for the same position. In healthcare manpower shortage areas, you will find lots of opportunities, but your spouse may have a problem with the living conditions, opportunities for cultural enrichment, or lack of reputable schools for your children.

Plan your work and work your plan. Have patience. Keep smiling. Keep that CV current. Persistence will pay off with the right position, acceptable pay, and rewarding work—whatever you desire.

3 An Introduction to the Group Practice Environment

The group practice environment is unique and distinct from solo practice in many ways. Three distinct differences are the organizational powers, properties, and characteristics, which are defined through organizational bylaws, contractual agreements, policies, and procedures.

The legal structure of group practice in this day and age of managed care and increased litigious behavior can be set up as a regular corporation, an S-corporation, or a professional limited liability corporation (PLLC). Many of the established practices of yesteryear have actually restructured themselves as PLLCs, not only for liability purposes, but also for the tax incentives still present under Internal Revenue Service (IRS) regulations. Many tax experts, however, state that these incentives may be short lived.

The management structure of the group practice has changed throughout the country. There are still a fair amount of self-managed group practices, but many practices have either hired a professional management firm to handle day-to-day business operations or have outright sold their interest in the practice for cash and stock to physician practice management (PPM) firms. This trend is also seeing some attrition and backfire as physicians experience the PPM style of practice management and decision making and decide for themselves that this may not be the panacea they initially identified.

In a group practice, the physician or owner is also the producer of the majority of the revenue. Difficulty arises when the interests of the members of the group are misaligned. Even more difficult is the group practice where some of the physicians are owners and others are nonowner employees of the corporation. This type of group practice requires some strategic planning and vision, just like any other business, to survive. An additional problem that compounds the difficulty of steerage of the group practice is that oftentimes physicians, being the creative and intellectual persons that they are, often have difficulty with leadership and communication. Sometimes communication and leadership require even the gentlest form of confrontation, and through their entire professional training, they are taught that confrontation among peers is taboo. The lack of communication and leadership can often lead to a breakdown of the entire group, because no one speaks up, and problems are allowed to fester until it is too late and the relationship among the parties breaks down.

In my own experience in practice management, I have seen this happen for a number of reasons. In one instance, two established subspecialist physicians brought in a third physician who had been in academic medicine. The third physician, who had no patients, was assessed one-third of all practice expenditures against what he brought into the practice as a full and equal partner. He sat in his consultation office most days and read journals until a patient arrived.

As nephrologists, the three physicians thought it would be nice to purchase an automated multichannel blood processor and other equipment for ambulatory blood pressure monitoring tests. (This was in the 1980s.) The new doctor now had even more contributory responsibility. However, doctor number three was too shy to self-market to primary care physicians for referrals and did not do much to develop his own following. The receptionist tried diligently to add new patients to his schedule, but often, referring physicians wanted consultations and management by the established physicians.

So, doctor number three signed up on every managed care plan that came through the door. He signed up as an internist wherever possible and also as a specialist where he could. This caused quite a stir among the other two physicians for several reasons: (1) He deteriorated the pricing integrity of the practice and trashed any margins with the ultra-low fee schedules that the managed care plans paid; (2) he attracted an adverse selection of expensive-to-manage patients with end-stage renal disease, diabetes, malignant hypertension, and other metabolic diseases, as well as kidney transfer candidates, while the practice was at risk for primary care referral expenses; and (3) he consumed more than his fair share of the staff time for referral processing and telephone calls with all the new patients.

Shortly after the first year, he was asked to leave and take his newfound managed care patients with him. He went on his own, and his nurse followed. He ended up establishing a solo practice that has since remained a solo practice. In addition, of the two original and remaining established physicians, differences of opinion and division of responsibility issues resurfaced and led to a further dissolution of their partnership, and now each is on his or her own. The moral of this story is that group practices require communication and alignment of strategy before becoming a group, and that meaningful communication be exchanged routinely in order to survive.

When physicians form a group practice together, there must be recognition that self-interest must often, but not always, be subjugated to the needs of the group. As a physician entertaining any thoughts for employment with a group practice, my advice is to look for these best practices:

1. A written strategic plan for the group
2. Mandatory meetings between staff and management on a weekly basis with a written agenda
3. Expectation that each physician will spearhead tasks of personnel, finance/purchasing, managed care contracting, and so forth
4. Rotation of each task among the physicians quarterly or semiannually so that all group physicians develop these management skills
5. Examination of policies and procedures manuals and visiting for a day or two to see if the policies and procedures are generally adhered to or if they are simply paper policies

6. Internal standards of care and practice similarity if liability risk is to be shared
7. Provision by the group practice of an environment that allows for competition and retention of a stable patient base
8. If risk contracts are entertained, some methodology for dealing with the potential financial and participatory negative impact of one member's utilization standards if different from the rest of the group members (What if the aberrant one is you?)

If you have made the decision to accept an employment offer from a group practice, several areas of the contract require thorough examination. The physician employment contract will no doubt be connected by reference to other documents you will need to peruse. Among others, these include the policies and procedures manual, any quality and utilization management documents, bylaws or operating agreements of a PLLC, and malpractice policies that either do or do not place the group at risk for an individual's performance.

The acceptance of an employment contract begins the individual physician's mainstream into the group's corporate culture, organizational form, and characteristics. In a group, a standardized contract promotes group unity and commitment. Any deviation or special deal may undermine the team spirit of the group and may not be received well if the commitment and unity are already there and a newcomer starts changing things. Therefore, it might be wise to know what a good contract looks like and commit to take what is offered if it is acceptable rather than demonstrate your prowess in contract analysis and revision. Demonstrate your prowess by asking good questions if something is written ambiguously. Obtain written clarifications, and keep the provided clarifications in a file in the event that the relationship goes bad. Chances are the contract will require some form of dispute resolution, such as arbitration or mediation, and those clarifications may come in handy if they are available.

Keep in mind that any changes to a contract should require a board decision that is formally documented in the corporation's minutes. The amendment or exception would have to be signed by an authorized officer. This is where the bylaws come into play. The corporate minutes should have your amendment attached as an exhibit. Any change to a standardized contract may have a ripple effect that requires others to be informed about your change. For example, the Centers for Medicare and Medicaid Services (CMS) may wish to review the change if it has to do with risk incentives where earnings are 25 percent or more at risk. Independent practice associations (IPAs) and physician health organizations (PHOs) may require review dependent upon managed care participation contract requirements, and even certain managed care agreements have payer stipulations where changes to employment contracts for a group member cause them to be the subject of review prior to allowing participatory status with their health maintenance organization (HMO) or preferred provider organization (PPO). There may also be Stark II ramifications depending on what the change is based on if the change can be associated with referrals, patient volume incentives or other similar concerns. Therefore, a written legal opinion from a health law attorney should be sought and included in the attachment to the corporate minutes, demonstrating that the change passes all regulatory requirements imposed upon the healthcare industry and physicians in their private business dealings.

Suffice it to say that you will be observed carefully in how you respond and react to a group employment contract, both verbally and behaviorally. Inferences will be made as to your willingness and commitment to group culture, policies, and procedures in the group practice setting.

SETTING YOUR EXPECTATIONS

You may wish to list and review your expectations of joining a group practice in writing before signing an employment contract with anyone. This is important to a new physician and a physician and shareholder prospect. For communication to be objective, such a checklist should provide a foundation for good exchange, eliminate misunderstanding, serve as an outline for ongoing communication, and act as a priority list to be able to get your needs met in your employment agreement. Some of the questions you may wish to obtain answers for include

1. Why is the practice expanding?
2. Is there any negative impact from the decision to expand on existing owners, associates, or partners? (The answer should be "yes," because an individual physician's generated revenue will shift temporarily downward as the new physician takes a representative share from each existing physician.) Also, staff (a medical assistant, a nurse, and possibly a personal secretary) may need to be increased, thereby increasing each physician's proportionate share for expenses while not having the expense offset from increased revenue for some time.
3. What will the anticipated positive impact be on owners and associates?
4. What measures will be taken to minimize problems and increase satisfaction?
5. Are all parties of the existing group in agreement that another physician is required to continue the growth and development of the group? If there was dissent, what were the reasons?
6. Will the existing office location accommodate the growth, or is a move anticipated? If a move is anticipated, to what location? Have plans already been initiated to secure the location? (This may impact where you decide to live.)
7. What will it take to obtain staff appointments at each hospital? Are there any contractual or political considerations regarding which hospitals to apply to for privileges?
8. How is the weekend call covered? Is it shared with outside groups?
9. How is the practice marketed to gain market share within the community?
10. What is the goal for the new physician in volume? (For primary care, it may be an average of 40 patients per day, and for a surgeon, an average of three surgeries and 20 patients per day.)
11. Will you have meaningful participation in governance of the practice? If not in the beginning, when?

12. Will you have an opportunity to pursue marketing to the public through speaking, writing, and special promotional activities? (Do you like that sort of thing? Are you good at it? What if it is required and you hate that sort of activity?)
13. May you examine and review the following?
    a. Fee schedules
    b. Billing policies and procedures
    c. Credit and collection terms
    d. Discounting policies
    e. Referral policies and procedures
    f. Vacation policies
    g. Continuing medical education reimbursement and scheduling policies
    h. Call rotation and trade policies and procedures
    i. Risk management protocols
    j. Utilization management and quality assurance guidelines
    k. Formulary compliance guidelines and medical records/transcription practices
    l. Staff evaluation protocols
    m. Medical staff governance (bylaws/operating agreements)
    n. Policies regarding access to financial data
    o. Personnel résumés and experience
    p. Medicare fraud and abuse compliance policies
    q. Impaired physician policies
    r. Type of electronic medical records system they are using
14. What are the buy/sell arrangements, exit strategies, and requirements?
15. May you review the partnership agreements?
16. May you see the previous financial performance reports?
17. What are the existing and projected major issues anticipated by the group over the next 3- to 5-year period? Are there written strategic plans?
18. What are the projected major capital expenditures over the next few years?
19. May you see the minutes of the board of directors, departmental, and department chairmen meetings over the preceding year?
20. What are the income expectations over a 3-year period and the basis for such assumptions?
21. What are the average work hours per day and year?
22. Are there board certification requirements? Are there continuing medical education (CME) credit hour requirements?
23. What are the goals of the practice over the next 3 to 5 years?

Although there are many other considerations when joining a group practice, these questions will get you headed in the right direction. By no means are they complete and inclusive. Their structure is open ended, allowing for even more questions based on the answers you will receive and the information you will read in the requested documents. Be prepared to sign a nondisclosure or confidentiality document before gaining access to the information you will request. Make sure that you can share the information with professional counsel, including accountants, attorneys, and consultants you may wish to use.

4 Medicare and Medicaid Antikickback Concerns, Fraud and Abuse Concerns

More than $1 trillion is spent each year on healthcare costs in the United States. Despite the enormous sum of money spent in this area, many Americans continue to be discontented with existing or missing healthcare services. One possible explanation for the disparity between what Americans expect from healthcare and what they get is that a considerable portion of the money the U.S. government pays out is lost to healthcare fraud. In 1992, the Government Accounting Office estimated that losses from fraud and abuse account for about 10 percent of total healthcare spending. That translates to roughly $100 billion each year that winds up in the pockets of fraud perpetrators. Physicians, as traditional patient advocates, are in a unique position to support patients in obtaining and keeping the healthcare services they need by helping to combat fraud. Fraud is generally considered an act of deception or misrepresentation designed to obtain something of value held by another. Fraud may be measured in a particular case by determining whether the scheme demonstrated a departure from fundamental honesty, moral uprightness, fair play, or candid dealings in the general life of the community. Healthcare fraud mainly deals with false claims, kickbacks, and other schemes to divert money from the government. Fraud is intentional. When physicians submit Medicare claims for services never performed, they are committing fraud. When podiatrists misrepresent compensable services they performed that are truly not compensable, they are also committing fraud. When providers deliver services but bill for others that pay better than those performed, or bill for unnecessary services, they are also practicing fraud. Abuse, which is often difficult to distinguish from fraud, may occur when health professionals use methods or practices for which there may be a medical purpose but the use of which appears extravagant, improper, unnecessarily costly, or at odds with customary medical practice.

PROBLEMS WITH FRAUD CONTROL

Healthcare fraud is designed to be invisible. No one knows it has occurred unless someone goes looking for it and they know what to look for. Moreover, there do not appear to be any suffering victims the way there are with crimes like assault, burglary, or murder. It is difficult to allocate resources to fraud investigations when violent crimes besiege American cities. Fraud perpetrators know this and capitalize on the opportunity to pass off fraudulent claims among the hundreds of millions of claims processed each year.

Defrauders pride themselves on being one step ahead of law enforcement and fraud investigators and therefore regularly change the type of fraud they practice. Cracking fraud schemes takes time and skill on the part of investigators and law enforcement. Once a fraud control approach proves successful, it is generally used again and again. Agencies keep pursuing the types of fraud they have learned to recognize; criminal prosecutors keep pursuing the types of fraud cases they have learned will be winners. Oftentimes, however, this approach results in nabbing the novice fraud artist while sophisticated types of fraud continue to propagate. With no one minding the store, innovative defrauders benefit as investigators are kept busy with small-dollar-yield fraud cases. Insurance companies experience the same type of frustrating circularity. The fraud unit staff at insurance companies often find it difficult to convince their employers that they need additional resources to help uncover new types of fraud. In addition, they may be competing for funds that financial advisors suggest should be allocated for investments or activities that yield a greater profit than fraud control. Some companies deny the presence of fraud altogether. Certainly an organization's fraud record appears stellar if no one is looking for fraud in the first place.

Another problem develops if a new type of fraud is uncovered. The amount of staff-power needed to pursue the investigation often taxes the unit beyond its capacity. Overburdened fraud control staff, often out of necessity, are then forced to resume traditional, familiar approaches that tend to focus on the commonplace fraud practices they know well. Again, clever defrauders are serendipitously placed out of reach of the system designed to catch them.

Finally, an alarming problem with fraud control stems from some people's belief that defrauding the government or private healthcare payers is acceptable—an "entitlement" to get back money that they perceive will otherwise go to insurance company executives or government employees. A 1993 Insurance Research Council survey showed that 41 percent of mid-Atlantic state residents thought it was all right to pad insurance claims to make up for past premiums. Fraud results in higher insurance premiums for all Americans. Moreover, those individuals most in need of healthcare are the ones who suffer the most when the cost of fraudulent acts results in service cutbacks.

LAWS GOVERNING HEALTHCARE FRAUD

There are a number of state and federal laws and regulations with accompanying penalties, fines, and sanctions that may be enforced against healthcare providers who engage in fraud. State laws generally mirror the federal laws and carry their own consequences. Defrauders may be subjected to the penalty of mandatory exclusion from Medicare and Medicaid, which also results in notification of state licensing officials. They may be charged civil monetary penalties, be subjected to peer review sanctions, and have reimbursement payments suspended.

Federal, civil, and criminal actions arise from several federal statutes: the False Claims Act, the False Statements Accountability Act, mail and wire fraud statutes, conspiracy and money laundering statutes, the Medicare/Medicaid Anti-Kickback Act, the Ethics in Patient Referrals Act, and the qui tam provisions.

If a health professional submits a false or fraudulent claim to the U.S. government, such as billing for services not rendered, or makes a false statement, which includes concealing material facts as well as providing fictitious or fraudulent representations, he or she has committed a crime that carries a 5-year prison sentence as well as fines. The United States can also pursue a false claims civil action against the defrauder and recover $5,000 to $10,000 per false claim plus three times the amount of damages that the government sustained because of the fraudulent act.

Mail and wire fraud statutes prohibit the use of mail or wire to carry on schemes to defraud. Therefore, a health professional who uses the U.S. Postal Service to mail false claims to Medicare or Medicaid may be prosecuted for mail fraud. Violators are subject to fines, imprisonment, or both.

A healthcare fraud perpetrator who works with another person to effect a scheme may be guilty of conspiracy, which is punishable by fines, imprisonment, or both. If a health professional obtains money from a fraudulent activity, then uses that money to continue the unlawful activity, he or she may be prosecuted for money laundering and subject to fines up to $500,000 or twice the property involved in the transaction, whichever is greater, imprisonment for up to 20 years, or both.

The Medicare/Medicaid Anti-Kickback Act makes it a felony to make false statements or representations in connection with claims submitted for reimbursement by Medicare or Medicaid. The act also forbids the knowing and willful solicitation or receipt of any remuneration including any kickback, bribe, or rebate directly or indirectly, overtly or covertly, in cash or in-kind in return for referrals for services charged to Medicare or Medicaid. Under the act, it is unlawful for clinical laboratories to offer financial incentives to physicians in exchange for referrals for services payable by Medicare or Medicaid. Durable medical equipment (DME) suppliers, physical therapy, and other supportive therapy agencies also may not offer physicians any remuneration for Medicare or Medicaid referrals. Violators are subject to a $25,000 fine, imprisonment for up to 5 years, or both. The only safety net for providers is to check whether a certain activity is mentioned in the Safe Harbor regulations and therefore not a violation of the act. Hospitals that violate the antikickback statute may also lose their tax-exempt status.

Because Congress believed that having a financial interest in a clinical laboratory could affect a physician's decision to order tests, it passed the Ethics in Patient Referrals Act. The law, which took effect January 1, 1992, is familiarly called Stark I, named for its primary sponsor, Rep. Pete Stark (D-CA). Stark I bans referrals by physicians to an entity with which they or immediate family members have a financial relationship. Stark II, which became effective January 1, 1995, expanded the ban to include 10 other categories of health services in addition to clinical laboratories. These additional services include physical therapy; occupational therapy; radiology; radiation therapy; DME; parenteral and enteral nutrients, equipment, and supplies; prosthetics; home health; outpatient prescription drugs; and inpatient and outpatient hospital services. There are exceptions to the self-referral ban that physicians need to evaluate; otherwise, violators are subject to civil penalties and exclusion from participation in Medicare and Medicaid.

WHAT DO YOU DO WHEN YOU LEARN THAT A COLLEAGUE OR EMPLOYER IS CORRUPT?

Approximately one of every three dollars recovered through false claims cases relates to healthcare fraud. The False Claims Act imposes civil liability on any person or entity who submits a false or fraudulent claim for payment to the U.S. government. The False Claims Act also prohibits making a false record or statement to get a false or fraudulent claim paid by the government; conspiring to have a false or fraudulent claim paid by the government; withholding property of the government with the intent to defraud the government or to willfully conceal it from the government; making or delivering a receipt for the government's property that is false or fraudulent; buying property belonging to the government from someone who is not authorized to sell the property; or making a false statement to avoid or deceive an obligation to pay money or property to the government.

CAUSING THE SUBMISSION OF A FALSE CLAIM

It is also improper to cause someone else to submit a false claim. For example, if a subcontractor provides false information to a contractor, who in turn bills the government based on that false information, the subcontractor is liable for causing the submission of a false claim.

DAMAGES UNDER THE FALSE CLAIMS ACT

Damages under the False Claims Act are severe. A person who violates the act must repay three times the amount of damages suffered by the government plus a mandatory civil penalty of at least $5,000 and no more than $10,000 per claim.

This means that, for example, a person who submits 50 false claims for $50 each is liable for between $257,500 [($2,500 × 3) + (50 × $5,000)] and $507,500 [($2,500 × 3) + (50 × $10,000)] in damages under the False Claims Act.

The stiff penalties have made the False Claims Act one of the government's favorite tools to combat fraud and abuse in government-funded programs.

QUI TAM (WHISTLEBLOWER) PROVISIONS OF THE FALSE CLAIMS ACT

The False Claims Act allows an individual who knows about a person or entity who is submitting false claims to bring a suit, on behalf of the government, and to share in the damages recovered as a result of the suit. The person who brings the case is called a qui tam relater, or whistleblower.

In the past, hundreds of qui tam suits have been filed. These suits have resulted in over $1 billion in recoveries for the U.S. Department of the Treasury. The relaters who filed these suits have received more than $100 million for their efforts.

Whether it is a mighty corporate Goliath being accused of fraud or the local hospital shelling out millions to settle false billing charges, many healthcare providers are looking increasingly like a lineup for "Medicine's Most Wanted." The focus is now on "whistleblowers" who file claims as the relater to the federal government in the form of a qui tam. (Qui tam comes from a longer Latin phrase translated as "he who brings an action for the king as well as for himself.")

These individuals, who often risk their livelihood and reputation to expose wrongdoing, are empowered by a 135-year-old federal law known as the False Claims Act. The legislation—amended in 1986 to expand protections for many whistleblowers—now provides legal recourse against retaliation as well as the powerful incentive of a qui tam settlement, a cut of which goes to the whistleblower.

Armed with such protection, healthcare workers ranging from doctors to billing clerks are blowing the lid off a myriad of fraud and abuse cases, with staggering results. Since 1987, the number of qui tam cases filed annually has risen from 33 to 530. During that time, the U.S. Department of Justice has recovered $1.8 billion in healthcare fraud settlements. The U.S. Justice Department has recovered billions in healthcare fraud and abuse settlements, with millions stemming from false claims in Medicare and other federal programs. Prosecutors secured more than $625 million stemming from false claims in Medicare and other federal programs. A qui tam action can also be brought where a health maintenance organization has deprived its subscribers of services that should be covered by the Medicare system.

Disturbed by what they view as overly aggressive enforcement, hospitals and other institutions have gone on the offensive, sponsoring a bill to weaken the False Claims Act. The Department of Justice headed off a legislative coup by issuing new guidelines to avoid possible abuses. They acknowledged that the tone of some of the demand letters sent to hospitals was excessive. Despite this, the act is by far their most important civil tool to address healthcare fraud and abuse.

Court rulings, however, hold that independent contractors cannot sue for retaliation under the qui tam statute. And the False Claims Act applies strictly to programs reimbursed by federal funds, thus leaving many medical researchers out of the safety net. In the world of research, scientific misconduct rarely involves clear-cut billing deceit, precluding qui tam protections.

In these cases, reporting fraud or abuse can be a lonely struggle. The main resource for research whistleblowers—the Office of Research Integrity (ORI), an arm of the Public Health Service established in 1992 to investigate charges of scientific misconduct—lacks the power to stop employers from retaliating against those who speak out. The ORI has made a conscientious effort to vindicate scientists who challenge wrongdoing according to its director of the Government Accountability Project, but in terms of stopping reprisals, it has not made a noticeable difference.

A survey of 68 whistleblowers by the Research Triangle Institute in October 1995 reported that 69 percent of them experienced some form of retribution, ranging from job loss to delays in processing grant applications. A month later, the Commission on Research Integrity, created by Congress to help eliminate fraud in science, issued a report detailing the "destructive and painful retaliation" experienced by some 30 whistleblowers.

The hard reality is that, outside of qui tam lawsuits, there are effectively very few protections for whistleblowers. Doctors who refuse to participate in an unethical or illegal activity, or report that activity to the authorities, often are fired. And they have difficulty getting employment again in the medical arena.

Even the False Claims Act has its limits. A story comes to mind of Dr. J. Hilton Brooks, 46, who was an internist practicing at Pineville Community Hospital in Kentucky in 1992; he filed a qui tam suit after learning the hospital was billing for histories and physicals that were never performed. (He first tried to stop the false billing internally, to no avail.) After a two-and-a-half-year investigation and legal battle, the hospital and two doctors agreed to pay more than $3 million in legal fees and fines. By then, Dr. Brooks had been forced to relocate his practice to another town to escape a campaign of harassment and intimidation.

After reporting the fraud, Dr. Brooks found that his colleagues grew hostile, berating him or refusing to work with him. Then, the hospital threatened to strip him of his privileges. Finally, the threats became personal—a black rose delivered to his office, late-night calls at home, even death threats. At one point, the physician felt compelled to ask for police protection. Ultimately, he was vindicated and in some respects lucky: He continues to practice and walked away nearly $600,000 richer. But the experience left him a shaken and disillusioned man.

"A doctor who discovers inappropriate activities has got to make a decision—whether to jeopardize his family and financial security, or to protect his patients," Dr. Brooks said. "It's a terrible decision to have to make."

Although critics agree, they say the law is most unfair to medical institutions. Because the new penalties are so harsh—triple damages and $5,000 to $10,000 for each false claim—most defendants negotiate a settlement rather than risk going to court. If you lose, you are talking about potential bankruptcy.

Whistleblowers, on the other hand, stand to gain 15 to 30 percent of the recovery, plus attorneys' fees. Critics contend that the lucrative award creates the wrong incentive, often referring to qui tam money as "30 pieces of silver." Even though the whistleblower should receive some modest reward, paying whistleblowers millions of dollars takes this out of the realm of "doing the right thing." It is more like a lottery ticket. File a suit, and win the lottery.

But plaintiffs' attorneys argue chances are better that the act will merely protect whistleblowers by offering them legal recourse. Assuming they can prove retaliation in court, they are entitled to reinstatement and may be eligible for double back pay and other financial awards.

Former federal prosecutor and attorney Steve Simms of Baltimore, Maryland, says that "all the amended act did was assure whistleblowers that if they venture the qui tam route, it's less likely they're going to be retaliated against, and if they carry out the qui tam filing and there's a recovery, they'll be compensated for it."

To say the odds are stacked against whistleblowers seems an understatement. When a qui tam action is filed, it remains under seal, sometimes for years, while the Department of Justice investigates the case and decides whether to join it. Four out of five times it does not, for a variety of reasons. The whistleblower and his or her lawyer must then decide whether to prosecute the case on their own, an expensive and risky proposition. Few of the more than 1,000 qui tam cases the Department of Justice has declined to join have been settled in the prosecution's favor.

Almost all of the cases the department takes on end successfully, due in no small part to the upfront work by the whistleblower and his or her attorney. "For the Department of Justice to accept a False Claims action, the evidence has to be crystal clear and the case has to be served up on a platter, with garnish," said Simms. Even then, the whistleblower must be ready for a long, grueling ordeal.

Although lucrative financial incentives cannot be discounted as a factor in the growth of qui tam actions, there is no evidence to suggest they have created a rash of frivolous lawsuits or breaches of medical ethics. Particularly in the case of doctors, the opposite tends to be true: The likelihood of hitting the jackpot is so small, and the risk of ruining one's career so great, that principles rather than profits are the primary motivation. "We find that whistleblowers are people with a strong ethical center," said Simms. "Invariably they start talking about their parents: 'My father always taught me that right is right and wrong is wrong, and you have to stand up for what's right.'"

With physicians, there also seems to be a backlash against the constraints of managed care. "There are a lot of docs who are terribly troubled about being asked to compromise patient care, even to breach their fiduciary duty to patients," said Simms. "What they see is they're being punished for doing the right thing. Qui tam suits offer them a respectable way to do the right thing."

Many doctors are taking that risk and are coming forward now. These are people who feel very strongly that they entered an honorable profession and are sometimes willing to throw their entire career aside to keep it that way.

The advice to potential whistleblowers is to document what is going on. If you are going to file a claim, you need good notes with lots of detail. If you are aware of any person, corporation, or entity that you think may be violating the federal False Claims Act, you should contact an attorney who can assist you in evaluating your potential claim.

Be careful not to discuss the matter with anyone other than an attorney. A potential relater faces two major obstacles to recovery, public disclosure, and the "first to file" rule:

Public Disclosure—If the allegations are somehow disclosed before a relater files suit, he or she could be precluded from any recovery.

First to File—Only the first relater to file a claim has the ability to share in the recovery. A subsequent relater is precluded, even if he or she had equal or superior knowledge than the first relater.

A qui tam action must be filed in a federal district court. A copy of the complaint, along with a written disclosure statement of pertinent information in the relater's possession, must be served upon the Attorney General and the local U.S. attorney in the district court where the lawsuit is initiated. The complaint must be filed under seal, which means that all information must be kept confidential. The seal period will last for at least 60 days. During this period, the federal government investigates the allegations. After the government concludes its investigation, it then decides whether or not to join the relater's lawsuit.

Any employee who is discharged, demoted, suspended, threatened, or harassed by his or her employer for filing, investigating, or initiating a valid qui tam lawsuit is entitled to relief to make the employee whole. As the whistleblower, you are entitled to reinstatement of seniority status, double the amount of back pay owed you, including all interest owed, plus any special damages that may have occurred. You may also receive litigation costs and attorneys' fees.

Of course, whistleblowing remains a gamble. A lucky few are well rewarded for their efforts; others end up losing their careers. Despite the risks, almost all say they never felt they had a choice. There is an ethical and legal duty to report what you witness regardless of the impact it would have professionally. If you cannot expose unethical behavior, you should not be in medicine.

Some of the cases filed in past years are highlighted as follows:

SmithKline Beecham: SmithKline Beecham Clinical Laboratories, Inc., paid the government more than $325 million to settle allegations that its clinical laboratory division defrauded Medicare, Medicaid, and other federally funded health insurance programs. This historic settlement was the result of a joint effort between the government and private citizens, or "whistleblowers," including Robert J. Merena, a former employee of SmithKline's National Billing System. The SmithKline settlement is the largest whistleblower-assisted recovery in the history of the United States.

Merena, a resident of Berks County, Pennsylvania, was the first of three private citizens whose "whistleblower" claims led to the SmithKline settlement. Merena filed his suit "under seal" on November 12, 1993, in the U.S. district court for the eastern district of Pennsylvania. For 9 years, Merena worked for SmithKline's National Billing System, which was responsible for approximately three fourths of SmithKline's clinical laboratory billings nationwide. In the course of his job, Merena became aware of a number of questionable billing practices at SmithKline. Unable to resolve his concerns internally within SmithKline, Merena retained attorney counsel from a firm that concentrates its practice on "whistleblower," or "qui tam," suits and healthcare-related matters. During the 3 years after he filed his suit, Merena actively assisted the government's investigation and spent hundreds of hours working with the government task force assembled in Philadelphia that investigated the allegations against SmithKline.

National Health Laboratories (NHL): This case, which was settled in December 1992, is perhaps the most notorious qui tam case to date. NHL agreed to pay over $100 million as a result of a variety of schemes it employed to overcharge the government for clinical laboratory testing services it provided to Medicare and Medicaid beneficiaries. The relater in that case, Jack Dowden, earned in excess of $15 million for the information he provided.

Blue Cross/Blue Shield of Michigan: The government hired Blue Cross/Blue Shield (BC/BS) of Michigan to administer a portion of the Medicare program. The government agreed to pay BC/BS of Michigan based on its costs of handling the Medicare claims. BC/BS of Michigan was obligated to charge to the Medicare program only those costs expended administrating the program and to see to it that its books and records were accurate. Based on information provided by a qui tam relater, the government uncovered that BC/BS of Michigan had improperly charged unrelated costs to the Medicare program and submitted false documentation to support those improper charges. BC/BS of Michigan paid the government $27.6 million as a result of these practices. The relater, Darcy Flynn, earned $5.5 million for her information.

Rugby Laboratories: As a result of information provided by a qui tam relater, the government learned that Rugby Laboratories systematically overcharged the Department of Veterans Affairs for generic prescription drugs. As a result, Rugby paid the government $7.5 million, and the relater, Eileen Doran, earned $1.05 million.

Medline Industries: In April 1996, Medline Industries agreed to pay the government $6.4 million to settle a qui tam suit alleging that Medline sold the Department of Veterans Affairs cheaper, foreign supplies and equipment even though it said that the supplies and equipment were domestically manufactured. The relater in the case, Mr. Rybacki, earned $1 million for his information.

Advanced Care Associates: In June 1996, Advanced Care Associates, Inc., agreed to pay the government $4.03 million to settle a qui tam case alleging that it falsified documents related to lymph-edema pumps and sleeves provided to Medicare beneficiaries. Without the falsified documents, the government would not have paid for the pumps and sleeves. The relater, Mr. Piacentile, earned over $600,000.

Life Centers Limited: Life Centers Limited, along with its owner, Howard Wurtzel, MD, paid $500,000 to settle allegations of false Medicare and Medicaid claims. The relater, Linda Brandimarte, was a former office administrator for the company. In that position, Brandimarte became aware that Life Centers systematically presented fraudulent claims for payment to the Medicare and Medicaid programs. According to Brandimarte, Wurtzel and Life Centers regularly billed Medicaid and Medicare for psychotherapy services that were either never performed or not covered by Medicaid. There was also an allegation that the defendants misdiagnosed Medicare and Medicaid beneficiaries as having mental illnesses so that they could bill for services that would otherwise not be covered. Pursuant to the provisions of the False Claims Act, the whistleblower could receive 25 percent of the government recovery.

Blue Cross/Blue Shield of Florida: In August 1994, Blue Cross/Blue Shield of Florida agreed to pay $10 million to the government after a qui tam relater alleged that BC/BS of Florida had mishandled Medicare claims and overcharged the government for services it provided to the Medicare system.

Allied Clinical Laboratories: In March 1995, Allied Clinical Laboratories agreed to pay the government $4.9 million to settle a qui tam case alleging that it had billed the Medicare system for clinical laboratory testing that was not medically necessary. The relaters, Ramona Wagner and Jeannie Deter, were former billing clerks for Allied. They earned over $800,000 for their information and assistance.

RESOURCES

Always check with experienced counsel. When I have Medicare fraud and abuse questions, one attorney I tap for advice from time to time as a sounding board is Gabriel Imperato, Esq., of the firm Broad and Cassel in Fort Lauderdale, Florida. You may reach him directly at (954) 764-7060. He or any of his capable health law section associates can assist you. The reason I prefer Gabe is that his background includes having served as an attorney for the Office of the Inspector General in the Medicare and Medicaid Fraud and Abuse division.

Gabe's most memorable advice to me was, "If it smells bad, it probably is." Sign-on bonuses "smell" like fraud and abuse problems brewing to me.

The author would like to acknowledge the kind editorial review for accuracy by Ellen E. Stewart, Esq., a partner of the law firm Berenbaum, Weinshienk & Eason, PC (4800 Republic Plaza, 370 Seventeenth Street, Denver, Colorado 80202; phone: (303) 592-8310; fax: (303) 629-7610; e-mail: estewart@bw-legal.com).

5 Antitrust Concerns for Physicians

In the wake of increased competition for shrinking patient care revenue, antitrust laws pertaining to restraint of trade or unfair competition have become more important to individual physicians and group practice organizations, their administrators, and the physicians they employ because of noticeable increased litigation in this area of law. Many of the antitrust lawsuits now pending pertaining to healthcare are the result of actions filed by individual physicians, groups, and related healthcare organizations against hospitals for denial or revocation of medical staff privileges. In some instances, individual physicians who had been named as coconspirators in these suits were not serving in a hospital committee member capacity. These antitrust actions and the potential for an increase in subversive acts among physicians—primarily precipitated by competition participation in integrated groups may be little more than "club commiserate" with little or no risk sharing. These days, it is a requirement that physicians and the groups they belong to become highly educated regarding these antitrust laws to reduce their risk of violation.

Group practice organizations should consider including a clause in their physician employment contracts protecting against a physician's involvement in subversive acts that could precipitate antitrust action against the group or individual physicians. The clause should stipulate that such involvement could result in termination for cause in accordance with established written policies and procedures. This sounds harsh, but it is necessary.

Underlying our country's economic philosophy is faith in the value of competition. Implicit in this faith is the idea that competition provides the best allocation of our economic resources—producing the highest-quality products and services at the lowest prices. To preserve free and open competition, Congress enacted the antitrust laws. Essentially, antitrust laws are there to protect the spirit of competition—not the competitors themselves.

ANTITRUST LAWS IN GENERAL

The basic federal antitrust statutes are the

- Sherman Act
- Clayton Act
- Federal Trade Commission Act
- Robinson-Patman Act

The Sherman Act prohibits contracts, combinations, and conspiracies in restraint of trade. It also condemns monopolization, and attempts and conspiracies to monopolize.

The Clayton Act prohibits various kinds of business conduct that have a tendency to lessen competition or monopolize trade. Among the practices made illegal by this statute are exclusive arrangements, acquisitions, and mergers that lessen competition to monopolize trade. Among these practices are exclusive, or "sweetheart," deals, acquisitions, and mergers that lessen competition and interlocking directorates.

The Federal Trade Commission (FTC) Act bans unfair methods of competition and unfair or deceptive acts and practices.

The Robinson-Patman Act prohibits price discrimination where the effect is to lessen competition. In addition, most states have enacted statutes similar to the Sherman and FTC Acts.

The U.S. Supreme Court has said that not every contract in restraint of trade constitutes a violation, but only those that unreasonably restrain trade are unlawful. A court will look at all the facts and circumstances surrounding the conduct in question to determine if there has been unreasonable restraint of trade and a violation of the law.

Certain conduct, however, is conclusively presumed to be unreasonable and is therefore unlawful per se. This is referred to as per se illegal. This includes certain practices that clearly restrain competition and have no other redeeming benefits— examples include agreements to establish prices (naked price fixing), agreements to refuse to deal with third parties (boycotts), and agreements to allocate markets or limit production. Other conduct is evaluated by rule of reason analysis, a situation that applies to many activities in healthcare business dealings.

ANTITRUST ENFORCEMENT

The Sherman Act is enforced by the U.S. Department of Justice and by private suits for treble damages by persons or firms alleging injury by antitrust violations. Government suits may be either civil or criminal in nature. In the civil suit, the government seeks an injunction to prohibit the offender from violating the law in the future. Criminal actions seek to impose fines or imprisonment.

The FTC Act is enforced by the Federal Trade Commission. The FTC issues cease-and-desist orders when a practice is found to violate the law. The violation of an FTC order may result in a penalty of up to $10,000 per day. An association judged in violation of antitrust laws can be dissolved by court order. Does this remind you of the landmark case against a big software developer?

In recent years, with the increase in physician and hospital integration activities, there has been a marked increase in antitrust proceedings undertaken by federal and state governments and by private parties. A violation of the Sherman Act is now a felony, punishable by jail sentences of up to 3 years. Formerly, such violations were a misdemeanor, subject to maximum sentences of 1 year. In addition, the fine for Sherman Act violations has been increased to a maximum of $1 million for corporations and up to $100,000 for individuals. Formerly, the maximum fine for corporations and individuals was $50,000. The Antitrust Improvements Act of 1976 gave new authority to state attorney generals to file treble damages suits on behalf of citizens of a state who had allegedly been injured by an antitrust violation.

Antitrust lawsuits brought by governments or private parties can be extremely disruptive to an organization—and expensive to defend. Even if the entity is eventually found free of liability, the cost of winning can be high. As a result, you should avoid organizational involvement in conduct that may give even the appearance of impropriety.

CONSPIRACY IN RESTRAINT OF TRADE

As noted above, Section 1 of the Sherman Act prohibits contracts, combinations, and conspiracies in restraint of trade. Simply defined, a conspiracy is an unlawful agreement. The "agreement" is very broadly defined: It can be oral or written, formal or informal, or express or implied (e.g., a "gentlemen's agreement") to hold the line on prices or fees.

Conspiracies are usually "proven" on the basis of circumstantial evidence—a course of business conduct from which a jury may infer that a conspiracy existed. Considered separately, the circumstances may be entirely innocent and lawful. When viewed in the aggregate, however, the circumstances may amount to conspiracy.

A typical set of circumstances from which a jury might infer the existence of a conspiracy include a period of price or fee instability in the industry or profession; a meeting of competitors at which prices or fees were discussed; and increased prices or fees by those participating in the discussion. Eliminate the price or fee discussion, and it is impossible to establish that a conspiracy existed. That is why it is so important to avoid discussion of prices or fees at any meetings of your independent practice association (IPA) or physician hospital organization (PHO), or even the doctors' lounge.

It is essential that physicians individually and as part of a group practice organization recognize their responsibility for taking preventive steps in addressing antitrust. Physicians must identify and educate medical staff regarding

- The definition of their state's "state-action doctrine" for peer review
- Governmental immunity to peer-review activities
- State board of medical examiners' list for "good faith" peer review standards, if available
- Development and implementation of written, in-house policies and procedures that govern medical staff peer-review activities that include both internal and external organizational activities and noncompliance

Antitrust laws and their increasing application to group practice activities are complex and difficult to defend. Therefore, groups should develop written governing policies and procedures pertaining to antitrust. It is also essential that the input of a lawyer knowledgeable and experienced in antitrust law be sought in the development of policies and procedures. Governing policies can help prevent and minimize the possibility of the organization, or individually employed physician, unknowingly entering into the gray or red zone of healthcare antitrust laws.

Additionally, all policies and procedures should be submitted to the group's liability carrier for review and written verification of coverage thereunder, prior to implementation. The treble damages clause in antitrust law makes it potentially one of the most economically damaging evolving legal issues facing groups today. For more about antitrust activity in healthcare, contact your local office of the Department of Justice or the Federal Trade Commission and ask for Statements of Antitrust Enforcement Policy in Healthcare, or contact your local health law attorney.

6 Medicare Physician Incentive Plan Requirements

Legislators have passed numerous laws to regulate physician incentives. They have chased the changes in the healthcare system. When it was thought that physicians in a fee-for-service environment were benefiting by referring patients inappropriately, the federal government and some state governments passed laws to ensure that physicians were not improperly influenced by financial considerations. The laws first prohibited a physician from receiving anything of value in exchange for the referrals, and then they prohibited referral to entities in which the referring physician had an ownership interest or from which he or she received compensation.

After these laws were passed, managed care became increasingly prevalent. Managed care is a market response to overutilization by individual physicians' excessive referrals. The growth in managed care focused attention on the possibility that plans may not provide enough care. There is a counterweight to scrimping on care—the plans' need to provide quality care in a competitive market and the professionalism of their participating physicians. Plans, however, may seek to neutralize that countervailing influence by implementing physician incentive plans (PIPs) that align physician incentives with their own. This may be done through capitation, withholding some compensation and paying it only if certain financial targets are met or, conversely, by paying lower compensation and paying a bonus to those who meet financial targets.

The Center for Medicare and Medicaid Services (CMS) now regulates these PIPs. The most comprehensive regulation is the CMS's rules concerning PIPs that affect referrals by physicians in plans that serve Medicare or Medicaid beneficiaries.

Under CMS, federal law prohibits such a plan from giving a financial incentive to a physician to limit any individual patient's access to medically necessary services. PIPs are lawful only if the financial incentives are applied more broadly. Even then, a PIP is permitted only if certain conditions are met. Most generally, the plan must describe the PIP to CMS and the state Medicaid agencies.

The rules are more complicated when the physician is put at "substantial financial risk." This term is defined in regulations issued by CMS on March 27, 1996. It has since been reiterated as recently as 2005. I expect changes to again be made under healthcare reform.

Under the rules, a PIP would put the physician at substantial financial risk for referrals if his or her compensation could be increased 33 percent or more by bonuses, decreased 25 percent or more by withholds, or changed 25 percent or more by a combination of withholds and bonuses. If the physician is capitated, substantial financial risk would occur if the capitation risk for the cost of referral services was 25 percent or more of the compensation or if the capitation arrangement was not clearly explained in the contract.

The plan must also provide adequate stop-loss protection for physicians who are at substantial financial risk. The regulations define the amount of coverage that must be provided. The plan must pay for the stop-loss coverage, but it may require physicians to bear some of the risk (up to 10 percent of the cost of referral services that exceed 25 percent of potential payments). If the PIP puts the physician at substantial financial risk, the plan must conduct annual surveys of its enrollees—and former enrollees—to determine the extent of their satisfaction with the plan. The plan also must provide information about its PIPs to Medicare or Medicaid beneficiaries requesting it, including the results of the satisfaction surveys.

Discussion of what compensation arrangements should be permitted will continue for a long time. By its PIP rules, the government is trying to strike just the right balance between letting plans impose incentives on their physicians, which will help the plans meet their goals, and preventing plans from making their physicians inappropriately reluctant to make referrals. It is always good to have the government struggle to resolve the unresolvable.

Following are the frequently asked questions and answers provided by CMS for further information on this subject.

PHYSICIAN INCENTIVE PLAN REGULATION QUESTIONS AND ANSWERS

Following is a section recently provided by the CMS that addresses most of the frequently asked questions about the PIP requirements. These questions and answers are verbatim from the CMS text. Please consider the following disclaimer: "The following is merely supplied for informational purposes to inform the reader that such documentation exists. As a paralegal, it is unethical or illegal for me to offer specific legal advice. Therefore, please seek qualified advice and interpretations from a skilled, licensed attorney, with a specialty in health law."

SUBSTANTIAL FINANCIAL RISK

Definition:

In specific terms, substantial financial risk is set at greater than 25 percent of potential payments for covered services, regardless of the frequency of assessment (i.e., collection) or distribution of payments. The term "potential payments" means simply the maximum anticipated total payments that the physician or physician group could receive if the use or cost of referral services were significantly low. The cost of referrals, then, must not exceed that 25 percent level, or else the financial arrangement is considered to put the physician or group at substantial financial risk.

For example, a doctor will contract with a managed care organization (MCO) and that MCO holds back a certain amount of the doctor's pay (e.g., $6 per member per month). The MCO will give the doctor the $6 per member per month only if the cost of referral services falls below a targeted level. Those $6 are considered to be "at risk" for referral services. The amount equals the difference between the maximum potential referral payments and the minimum potential referral payments (but does not include bonus payments unrelated to referral services). It is put into the numerator of the risk equation. The denominator of the risk equation equals the maximum potential payments that the doctor could receive for direct or referral services, or administration. Therefore, if the same doctor receives $24 per member per month for the primary care services he/she provides, and is subject to the $6 withhold, the risk equation is as follows:

Risk level: 6/24 = 25 percent net substantial financial risk.

In addition to the stop-loss insurance, the MCO must provide a survey of patient satisfaction that includes information from current enrollees and disenrollees. Note: If a physician group's patient panel is more than 25,000 patients, then that physician group is not considered to be at substantial financial risk, its arrangements do not trigger the need for a beneficiary survey, and the group is not required by the regulation to have stop-loss protection. For the purpose of making this determination, the patients of the group can be pooled across MCOs and across Medicare, Medicaid, and commercial enrollees if specific criteria are met. See Question 5 in this document's section on stop-loss protection.

SUBSTANTIAL FINANCIAL RISK QUESTIONS AND ANSWERS

Question 1:

For purposes of calculating substantial financial risk, are ancillary services considered referral services?

Answer: If the physician group performs the ancillary services, then the services are not referral services. If the physician group refers patients to other providers (including independent contractors to the group) to perform the ancillary services, then the services are referral services. In contrast, services provided within the physician group are not considered referral services.

Question 2:

Why is the threshold for substantial financial risk set at 25 percent? This level seems too high.

Answer: The following factors are among those that determined the 25 percent threshold:

Information available to CMS at the time the regulation was developed indicated that the average withhold used by plans was between 10 and 20 percent. As indicated in the proposed rule, we determined that an outlier approach was preferred and that we wanted to consider anything that exceeded the average as substantial risk:

- Actuarial data supported this value; and
- Physicians typically give up to 25 percent discounts to preferred customers.

Question 3:

Did CMS consider using a 20 percent risk threshold?

Answer: Yes. We considered a range of percentage thresholds. We also received comments in favor of both higher and lower thresholds. The information available to us indicates that the 25 percent threshold provides adequate protection to beneficiaries. We estimate that between one-third and one-half of all physician compensation arrangements will exceed this threshold. We will continue to monitor this issue.

Question 4:

How does the regulation affect provider groups that are licensed in a state and are allowed to accept full risk?

Answer: The regulation does not prohibit groups from accepting full risk for all health services. It requires appropriate parties to ensure that adequate stop-loss is in place and to conduct beneficiary surveys.

Question 5:

a. If a physician is paid straight capitation (i.e., uses no withholds or bonuses), and that capitation covers services that the physician does not provide, would the physician be at substantial financial risk?

b. What if the MCO has a performance history of 3 or 5 years and can show that its physicians have not lost more than 25 percent of the capitated amount?

Answer: Yes, this situation would be one of substantial financial risk, because the risk is not limited. If a capitation has no limit on the referral risk, it essentially equals 100 percent risk (with potentially greater risk).

Regarding the use of past history as a means of predicting future behavior, such experience is no guarantee of future referral behavior or the future healthcare needs and costs of the current enrollees served.

Question 6:

Does the determination of risk apply only to Medicare and Medicaid covered benefits, or if the MCO provides additional benefits at its own expense, should these be included in the determination?

Answer: All payments related to referral services furnished to enrolled Medicare or Medicaid beneficiaries are to be included in the risk determination, even if those services are not Medicare or Medicaid covered services. This regulation's requirements apply to contracts serving persons covered under a Medicare risk or cost contract, Medicaid HMO contract, or certain Medicaid Health Insuring Organizations (HIOs). These regulations do not apply to incentive arrangements applicable to Medicare enrollees who are covered by the MCO through an employer group (e.g., working aged and their dependents), those who are not enrolled in a Medicare risk or cost contract, and those Medicaid beneficiaries enrolled in Prepaid Health Plans or HIOs that are not subject to section 1903(m) of the Social Security Act.

Question 7:

Will CMS include quality bonuses in the denominator of the equation for substantial financial risk?

Answer: No. The regulation currently does not include quality bonuses as a factor in the substantial financial risk calculation. Although CMS supports the concept of quality bonus payments, limited information exists on their effectiveness as an incentive to provide quality healthcare. CMS acknowledges that some MCOs believe that the current regulation may create a disincentive for them to adopt quality-based bonuses. However, we are willing to revisit this issue in the future after more information is available on the use of such bonuses and the extent to which they are used effectively. To assist CMS in considering this matter, MCOs and their subcontractors are asked to voluntarily submit information about the use of quality bonuses in addition to the required disclosure information.

HYPOTHETICAL SITUATIONS

Question 8:

Would a physician be at substantial financial risk if his/her MCO's annual payments to him/her for services and administration total $100,000 and the organization withholds 25 percent (or $25,000) to cover deficits in the referral or inpatient hospital pool? Assume the MCO does not hold the physician liable for referral costs that exceed the withhold.

Answer: No. The physician is not at substantial financial risk because she/he was not at risk for more than 25 percent of payments.

Question 9:

Please clarify how substantial financial risk is determined when various risk arrangements are used. For example, say an MCO pays its doctors $100 per member per month and puts $24 at risk through a withhold, then the same doctors are part of a physician-hospital risk pool where they can get $50 if utilization goals are met. Is the risk seen as 24/100, 50/50, 74/150, or something else?

Answer: The risk is 74/150 and therefore the doctors are at substantial financial risk. That number is arrived at by adding the amount at risk for referral services (here, the amounts of the withhold and hospital pool or [24 + 50]) then dividing by the amount of maximum potential payments (150).

Question 10:

If a contractor capitates a physician group comprised of physicians (e.g., psychiatrists) and nonphysicians (e.g., other mental health providers), would the calculation to determine substantial financial risk assumed by the group change if the group is comprised exclusively of physicians?

Answer: No. As long as physicians are part of the group and the contracted services include physician services, the calculation of the amount of risk transferred to the physicians remains the same.

Question 11:

Would a physician be at substantial financial risk in the following example? An MCO's annual payments to this physician total $100,000 and the MCO imposes a 20 percent withhold ($20,000) for referrals. In addition, the MCO holds the physician liable for up to $5,000 of any referral costs not covered by the withhold. The physician's referrals total $35,000, exceeding the withhold by $15,000; however, the MCO does not hold its physicians liable for amounts over 25 percent of payments (or $25,000).

Answer: No, the physician is not at substantial financial risk because the risk is limited to $25,000. However, if the MCO held the physician liable for all amounts over the withhold (instead of limiting liability to $5,000 for referral costs not included in the 20 percent withhold), then the physician would have been at substantial financial risk. This is because, having accrued referral costs of $35,000, she/he would have exceeded the 25 percent risk threshold by $10,000.

Question 12:

Is a physician at substantial financial risk if his/her payments from the MCO total $75,000, she/he does not exceed utilization targets for referral and inpatient hospital services, but she/he is eligible for a $25,000 bonus (33 percent of $75,000)?

Answer: No, because this physician's bonus did not exceed the limit of 33 percent of potential payments, not counting the bonus itself (in other words, 25 percent of the potential payments if you included the bonus as part of the potential payments). However, any incentive arrangement other than a bonus alone must be no greater than 25 percent of potential payments or else it will be considered as substantial financial risk.

Question 13:

What if an MCO has the following arrangement: A physician is not permitted to keep any savings from the referral account. Then if referrals cost less than $100,000, the physician must return the remainder of the referral account to the MCO. If referral costs are more than $100,000, she/he may be liable for up to 25 percent of the capitation for his/her own services. The contract clearly states the following: If referrals exceed $125,000, the physician will receive no less than $75,000. If referrals are less than $100,000, the physician will receive no more than $100,000. Is this physician at substantial financial risk?

Answer: No. The difference between the highest possible payments ($100,000) and the lowest possible payments ($75,000) is no more than 25 percent of the maximum payments (here, the difference is $25,000); therefore, the physician is not at substantial financial risk.

STOP-LOSS PROTECTION

Definition:

Organizations whose contracts or subcontracts place physicians or physician groups at substantial financial risk must ensure that those providers have either aggregate or per-patient stop-loss protection. The aggregate stop-loss protection requires coverage of at least 90 percent of the costs of referral services that exceed 25 percent of potential payments. The per-patient stop-loss protection requires coverage of 90 percent of the costs of referral services that exceed specified per-patient limits.

QUESTIONS AND ANSWERS

Question 1:

What does stop-loss protection mean?

Answer: Stop-loss is a type of insurance coverage designed to limit the amount of financial loss experienced by a healthcare provider. An MCO or physician group normally buys this insurance so that, if the liabilities of the MCO or group exceed what is expected based on prior experience, the insurer will "stop" further losses by paying the liabilities which exceed either a total dollar (aggregate) amount, or a per-patient amount.

Question 2:

Is the MCO required to provide stop-loss protection to physicians or physician groups at substantial financial risk?

Answer: The final rule held the MCO accountable for stop-loss insurance by requiring it to either provide the stop-loss itself or reimburse physician groups for the cost of stop-loss purchased by them to cover costs attributable to the MCO's enrollees. CMS originally planned to require MCOs to provide proof that they paid for the insurance. Based on industry comments and our understanding of industry practices, we have concluded that we do not need to mandate how the payment for stop-loss insurance is arranged. The MCO merely needs to provide assurance to either CMS or the State Medicaid Agency that the proper stop-loss protection is in place.

Question 3:

Does stop-loss protection apply only to referral services?

Answer: Generally, stop-loss protection applies to the costs of all services furnished by a physician or physician group. For the purposes of this regulation, however, stop-loss coverage must cover at least 90 percent of the costs of referral services above the substantial financial risk threshold. The physician or physician group is liable for no more than 10 percent of the remaining referral costs above the threshold.

Question 4:

If an MCO or physician group chooses to obtain per-patient stop-loss protection for the purposes of this regulation, what are the appropriate per-patient stop-loss deductibles, or attachment points, that are required?

Answer: See the following answers.

Question 5:

Why do stop-loss limits increase as panel size increases? Are the plans providing more protection as panel size increases?

Answer: As patient panel size increases, stop-loss protection under the per-patient stop-loss requirement decreases. That is because with increasing panel size, payments to a physician or physician group increase and the element of risk decreases with the increased payments; thus a physician group with a panel size of 15,000 patients has more income with which to sustain a financial loss and, therefore, requires less stop-loss insurance than would a group with income generated only due to 5,000 patients.

Question 6:

Does aggregate stop-loss take panel size into account?

Answer: Yes. To the extent that aggregate stop-loss limits require coverage of 90 percent of the costs of referral services that exceed 25 percent of potential payments, those limits reflect payments based on panel size.

Question 7:

Under what circumstances is pooling permissible for purposes of determining the appropriate stop-loss limit?

Answer: The Medicare, Medicaid, and commercial enrollees of one or more MCOs served by a physician group may be pooled as long as certain criteria are met. The pooling of patients calculation will be relevant to one of two scenarios. The calculation may show that the physician group serves more than 25,000 patients and, therefore, is able to spread referral risk over a wide enough patient base so that stop-loss protection is not needed. Or the calculation will show that the physician group serves 25,000 or fewer patients, in which case stop-loss is required if the incentive arrangements put the group at substantial financial risk. If per-patient (as opposed to aggregate) protection is obtained, it must be for the single combined or separate professional and institutional limits shown above. In this case, the group's pooled patient panel size would determine how much stop-loss to acquire. Pooling of patients across MCOs and/or patient categories (e.g., Medicaid, Medicare, commercial) is allowed only if the following five criteria are met:

1. Referral risk must have been transferred in each of the physician incentive arrangements applicable to the pooled enrollees.
2. The incentive arrangements related to the compensation for those enrollees must be comparable with respect to the nature and extent of the risk borne.
3. The payments for all pooled enrollees must be held in a common risk pool.
4. The distribution of payments from the risk pool must not be calculated separately by patient category or by MCO, and
5. No provider contracts can require that risk be segmented by MCO or by patient category.

Question 8:

If the capitation rate or fee-for-service schedule is different between three lines of business due to the expected differences in healthcare needs and resultant costs for the Medicare, Medicaid, and commercial populations, does this mean these patients cannot be pooled?

Answer: No, but specific criteria must be met in order to pool patients across product lines and/or across MCOs. See Question 7 above.

DISCLOSURE

Question 1:

If an MCO agrees to provide stop-loss and to conduct surveys, must it still disclose the information to CMS as required by the regulation?

Answer: Yes. Pursuant to the regulation, MCOs must still disclose the information. This information serves many purposes. It will be used to monitor compliance, evaluate the impact of the regulation, and to ensure the delivery of high quality healthcare. In enacting this legislation, Congress clearly intended MCOs to disclose at least some information about the nature of physician incentive compensation arrangements and the extent to which physicians are being placed at substantial risk by the arrangements.

Question 2:

It seems that the information disclosed pursuant to the regulation is proprietary and should be protected under the Freedom of Information Act (FOIA). What information is proprietary?

Answer: For information submitted to CMS, a precise determination of what is proprietary information cannot be made until we have reviewed specific FOIA requests. At that time, the FOIA office will request that the plan involved specify what it feels is proprietary and the office will then determine what is proprietary. An MCO may, if it so desires, designate the information as proprietary at the time of submission. Requests will be evaluated on a case-by-case basis, balancing the needs of the party to protect proprietary information against the public interest in disclosing information that will serve the goals of the regulation. After several cases have been reviewed, we will publish general guidance in manual publications describing what is proprietary information. For MCOs disclosing to State Medicaid Agencies, individual states' rules regarding the protection of proprietary information will apply.

CMS will also publish aggregate information that summarizes the more sensitive details of incentive plans. At a minimum, basic information will be available to the public. Such information will include items such as whether or not an incentive plan covers referral services, what type of incentive arrangements (e.g., withhold or capitation) are used by an MCO or its subcontractors, whether adequate stop-loss protection is in place, and the summary results of any surveys required by the regulation.

Question 3:

Will disclosure to beneficiaries of financial incentives information be required at the time of their enrollment? Also, will MCOs be allowed broad discretion to decide how the information is presented?

Answer: MCOs will be required to publish in the evidence of coverage (EOC) notices, or such other notice as approved by the applicable CMS Regional Office or the State Medicaid Agency, that beneficiaries can request summary information on the MCO's physician incentive plans. These EOC notices are available at enrollment; therefore, the information will be available to patients upon enrollment. The nature of the disclosure to beneficiaries will be general, as opposed to providing physician-specific financial incentives information. Materials must convey information about the types of incentives used in contracts affecting physicians in the MCO's network. MCOs will not be required to disclose for each beneficiary requesting it the details of the particular incentive arrangement under which that beneficiary's physician operates. MCOs will be allowed some discretion in crafting language to convey the required information to beneficiaries. A separate document of recommended language for beneficiary materials is available from CMS or your State Medicaid Agency.

Question 4:

Will subcontractors to the MCO be allowed to attest that they have no physician incentive plan or no physician incentive plan related to the use of referral services for Medicare or Medicaid enrollees? If so, will MCOs be able to rely upon these attestations without need for a further audit of the subcontractor's compensation arrangements (assuming the MCO has no reason to believe the attestation may be false)?

Answer: Yes. Reporting entities will be allowed to make such attestations and MCOs will not be required to conduct validation audits unless they have reason to believe the attestation or other information submitted by a subcontractor is false.

Question 5:

Will CMS facilitate the survey requirement by using such items as a standard survey questionnaire, detailed instructions on survey design, and/or a comparative report card?

Answer: The final rule did not specify that the plans must conduct a specific survey for this regulation because most plans already administer surveys that meet the requirements of this regulation. In late spring of 1997 the Office of Managed Care (OMC) began conducting a nationwide consumer satisfaction survey of Medicare beneficiaries in MCOs. It has continued to do so and has expanded the access to the data on its Web site. All Medicare contracting plans that meet the criteria set for inclusion (e.g., have had a Medicare contract for at least 1 year) are expected to be required to participate. The primary purpose of the survey is to provide information to consumers that enables them to make plan-to-plan comparisons and ultimately make more informed choices. This survey will be administered by a third-party contractor to CMS. This contractor will use the Consumer Assessments of Health Plans Study (or CAHPS® survey), under development by the Agency for Healthcare Policy and Research (AHCPR). The contractor will survey a random sample of Medicare beneficiaries in each participating MCO. The CAHPS survey, which has modules for use with Medicare, Medicaid, and commercial enrolled populations, addresses the basic requirements of the regulation: it includes questions regarding access, quality, and satisfaction.

By participating in the CAHPS survey, a Medicare MCO will be able to meet the survey requirement related to enrollees without having to conduct its own survey. MCOs and states should note, however, that neither the current Medicare nor the Medicaid CAHPS surveys contain modules for disenrolled members. The CAHPS disenrollee modules will be available for both Medicaid and Medicare in 1998. In the meantime, in order to facilitate MCOs' compliance with the requirement for a survey of disenrollees, CMS will supply standardized disenrollment surveys and sampling specifications for MCOs to self-administer in 1997. These additional tools will be available in the spring of 1997. A separate document providing guidance in development of a survey is available from CMS or your State Medicaid Agency.

With regard to the Medicaid program, the CAHPS survey includes a Medicaid version that can be separately administered to Medicaid enrollees. This instrument will yield data that meet the requirements of the regulation. Although CMS will not require that the CAHPS survey be administered for Medicaid MCOs, states will have the option to make such a requirement.

Question 6:

Will the surveys that are required as part of the disclosure requirement include questions about referral problems?

Answer: Yes. The surveys should include questions that deal with referral problems.

Question 7:

What are the specifications on release of the beneficiary surveys?

Answer: The surveys are required of all MCOs whose contracts or subcontracts place physicians or physician groups at substantial financial risk. They are required to be conducted within 1 year of an MCO's initial disclosure to CMS or a State Medicaid Agency. They will be required annually thereafter. Summary survey results must be submitted to regulators and to any beneficiary who requests the information of an MCO.

Question 8:

For purposes of the disclosure requirement, who does the term "beneficiaries" include?

Answer: The term refers to persons receiving Medicare and/or Medicaid benefits. It includes potential enrollees, current enrollees, and disenrollees of MCOs contracting with the Medicare or Medicaid programs.

Question 9:

Regarding disclosure to enrollees—how does this regulation fit in with CMS's policy of fully informing beneficiaries?

Answer: In the preamble, we encouraged MCOs to disclose to beneficiaries. We considered the possibility of requiring the disclosure rather than only making the information available upon request by beneficiaries. We are not sure, however, that the level of interest in this information on the part of beneficiaries, and its value to them, warrants such a requirement. In the coming year, we will be providing all Medicare beneficiaries with comparable information about the services and quality of care provided by their managed care organizations. In addition, we support and encourage interaction between consumer advocacy groups and MCOs as a means of disseminating information to beneficiaries.

Question 10:

Does the disclosure requirement apply to all MCOs or just those putting doctors at substantial financial risk?

Answer: It applies to all MCOs. However, if an MCO has a subcontract with a physician group and the group's contract with its physician members does not place those members at substantial financial risk, then the MCO does not need to disclose any details on the incentive arrangements between the group and its members. Financial arrangements between physicians or groups and any other entities (e.g., PHOs [physician hospital organization], the MCO) must be disclosed, regardless of whether or not the physician or group is at substantial financial risk.

Question 11:

a. What about Pools of Doctors (PODs) (i.e., groups of independent physicians who are aggregated into a single risk pool by an MCO or PHO), which aren't actually private corporations like a physician group or an IPA? Would they need to report if the POD includes PCPs only sharing risk for their own services?

b. What about if the POD includes PCPs and specialists sharing risk for their services as a POD?

c. Finally, would PODs need to report if comprised of PCPs, specialists, or hospital and ancillary services?

Answer: In all three instances, some reporting would need to occur, but the extent of the disclosure would vary. In the first two examples, the MCO would simply report that the POD was not at risk for services it did not provide. In the third example, disclosure would need to detail the types of risk arrangements used (e.g., capitation, withhold, bonus), the percentage of total potential income at risk for referrals, and if that percentage exceeded 25 percent, information about stop-loss protection.

MISCELLANEOUS

Question 1:

Why was Congress concerned about physician incentive plans?

Answer: As we indicated in the March 27, 1996, final rule (page 13,434), Congress was concerned with ensuring that under-use of necessary services does not occur. We believe the final rule implements the federal law to ensure adequate protection of Medicare and Medicaid beneficiaries so that they have access to all necessary and appropriate care.

Question 2:

What was the purpose of a comment period with the March 27, 1996, final rule?

Answer: This rule applies to Medicare HMOs and competitive medical plans and Medicaid HMOs and those Health Insuring Organizations subject to section 1903(m) of the Social Security Act. However, the provisions of this rule may also affect entities that would not have been affected at the time we published the proposed rules (December 14, 1992). This is because of the physician self-referral rules in section 1877 of the Social Security Act, as amended by the Omnibus Budget Reconciliation Act of 1993. Section 1877 provides that a physician (or an immediate family member of the physician) who has a financial relationship with certain entities may not make a referral for designated health services to that entity for Medicare or Medicaid beneficiaries. Various exceptions to this referral prohibition exist. Under certain circumstances, a physician can use compliance with the physician incentive regulations in order to be excepted from the referral ban. Thus, entities not directly affected by the physician incentive rule may now be affected by it due to the physician self-referral ban. The additional entities potentially affected include preferred provider organizations, MCOs that do not contract with Medicare or Medicaid and are not Federally Qualified, Prepaid Health Plans that contract under Medicaid, and some Medicaid managed care programs authorized under sections 1915(b) or 1115 of the Social Security Act. As a result, we issued the March 27, 1996, rule as a final rule, but permitted a period for public comment to accommodate new entities potentially affected by the rule. Based on the public comments we received, we will be issuing a revised final rule in the near future.

Question 3:

Do the physician incentive plan final rules apply to both Medicaid Federally Qualified HMOs and State-Plan Defined HMOs?

Answer: The rules apply to Medicaid prepaid organizations subject to section 1903(m) of the Social Security Act, including both Federally Qualified HMOs and State-Plan Defined HMOs, as well as certain Health Insuring Organizations (HIOs). Those HIOs not subject to 1903(m) (namely, HIOs that began operating prior to January 1, 1986, and California county–sponsored HIOs eligible for exemption from 1903[m] due to section 4734 of the Omnibus Budget Reconciliation Act of 1990) are not subject to the physician incentive rules.

Question 4:

Where in the laws or regulations is information available on the physician self-referral ban?

Answer: Section 13562 of the Omnibus Budget Reconciliation Act of 1993 (OBRA '93) amended section 1877 of the Social Security Act to incorporate the physician incentive plan rules as part of the physician self-referral ban. Under the provisions, compliance with the physician incentive plan rules will be necessary to meet the exemption for personal services arrangements if a personal services compensation arrangement involves compensation that varies based on the volume or value of referrals. To qualify for this exemption, an organization or person must also meet several other conditions. See Section 1877(e)(3). We are developing regulations to implement the physician self-referral ban provisions.

Question 5:

Do the physician incentive plan rules apply to Medicaid prepaid health plans (PHPs), particularly behavioral health PHPs?

Answer: While the physician incentive plan rules, for purposes of Medicaid prepaid contracts, apply only to Medicaid organizations subject to section 1903(m) of the Social Security Act (and PHPs are not subject to section 1903[m]), the physician self-referral ban requirements incorporate physician incentive plan rules as indicated above. The physician self-referral ban, as it applies to the referral for "designated health services," applies to PHPs, including behavioral health PHPs, if physician compensation varies based on the volume or value of referrals. Therefore, physicians in a PHP will need to comply with the physician incentive plan rules if they wish to receive the personal services exception from the physician self-referral ban regulation once that regulation goes into effect.

Question 6:

How do the physician self-referral ban rules apply to states' Medicaid managed care programs under section 1115 waivers?

Answer: CMS has granted several states the authority for their Medicaid managed care contracts to not be subject to some of the provisions in section 1903(m) of the Social Security Act. CMS could choose to use this waiver authority to exempt Medicaid MCO or HIO contracts in a State from the physician incentive plan rules. However, given the quality concerns at the heart of this regulation, it is unlikely that CMS would choose to waive this particular requirement for states operating 1115 programs.

Question 7:

What is CMS doing in the area of quality measures?

Answer: CMS is working with the National Committee on Quality Assurance to refine the Health Plan Employer Data and Information Set (HEDIS) 2.5. We are also working with the American Public Welfare Association (APWA) to implement the HEDIS 3.0 measures, which were released in June 1996. We expect these measures to be implemented in June 1997. Finally, CMS is collaborating with other agencies (Department of Defense, AHCPR) and private sector purchasers to develop and use other quality measures (for example, the Foundation for Accountability).

Question 8:

When will CMS begin monitoring MCO compliance with the physician incentive plan rules?

Answer: The effective date of the physician incentive plan rules is January 1, 1997. The specific compliance date for each MCO depends on when the contract first becomes effective, renews, or has its anniversary date during the 1997 calendar year. We will expect MCOs to make good faith efforts at coming into compliance by their own particular compliance dates.

Question 9:

How is a withhold different from capitation?

Answer: Capitation means a set dollar payment per patient per unit of time (usually per month) that an MCO pays a physician or physician group to cover a specified set of services and administrative costs without regard to the actual number of services provided. The services covered may include the physician's own services, referral services, or all medical services. A withhold is the percentage of payments or set dollar amounts that an MCO holds back from a physician or physician group's capitation or fee-for-service payments. This amount may or may not be returned to the physician/ group, depending on specific predetermined factors.

Question 10:

Do the regulations prohibit situations in which the utilization management procedure provides incentives for the use of outpatient services, as appropriate?

Answer: No. As long as the incentives are for the furnishing of outpatient care, as appropriate, there is no such prohibition on these arrangements.

GLOSSARY

Bonus means a payment a physician or entity receives beyond any salary, fee-for-service payments, capitation, or returned withhold. Bonuses and other compensation that are not based on referral levels (such as bonuses based solely on quality of care, patient satisfaction, or physician participation on a committee) are not considered in the calculation of substantial financial risk.

Capitation means a set dollar payment per patient per unit of time (usually per month) that is paid to cover a specified set of services and administrative costs without regard to the actual number of services provided. The services covered may include a physician's own services, referral services, or all medical services.

Intermediate entities are entities that contract between an MCO or one of its subcontractors and a physician or physician group, other than physician groups themselves. An IPA is considered an intermediate entity if it contracts with one or more physician groups in addition to contracting with individual physicians.

Panel size means the number of patients served by a physician or physician group. If the panel is greater than 25,000 patients, then the physician group is not considered to be at substantial financial risk because the risk is spread over the large number of patients. Stop-loss and beneficiary surveys would not be required.

Physician group means a partnership, association, corporation, individual practice association (IPA), or other group that distributes income from the practice among members. An IPA is a physician group only if it is composed of individual physicians and has no subcontracts with other physician groups.

Physician incentive plan means any compensation arrangement at any contracting level between an MCO and a physician or physician group that may directly or indirectly have the effect of reducing or limiting services furnished to Medicare or Medicaid enrollees in the MCO. MCOs must report on physician incentive plans between the MCO and individual physicians and groups and also between groups or intermediate contracting entities (e.g., certain IPAs, PHOs) and individual physicians and groups. The MCO only needs to report the details on physician incentive plans between groups and individual physicians if those physicians are placed at substantial financial risk by the group's incentive arrangement.

Potential payments means the maximum anticipated total payments (based on the most recent year's utilization and experience and any current or anticipated factors that may affect payment amounts) that could be received if use or costs of referral services were low enough. These payments include amounts paid for services furnished or referred by the physician/group, plus amounts paid for administrative costs. The only payments not included in potential payments are bonuses or other compensation not based on referrals (e.g., bonuses based on patient satisfaction or other quality of care factors).

Referral service(s) means any specialty, inpatient, outpatient, or laboratory services that are ordered or arranged, but not furnished directly. Situations may arise where services not normally considered referral services will need to be considered referral services for purposes of determining if a physician/group is at substantial financial risk. For instance, an MCO may require a physician/group to authorize "retroactive" referrals for emergency care received outside the MCO's network. Insofar as the physician/group can experience an increase in bonus (if emergency referrals are low) or a reduction in capitation/increase in withhold (if emergency referrals are high), then these emergency services are considered referral services and need to be included in the calculation of substantial financial risk. Also, if a physician group contracts with an individual physician or another group to provide services that the initial group cannot provide itself, any services referred to the contracted physician/group should be considered referral services.

Substantial financial risk means an incentive arrangement that places the physician or physician group at risk for amounts beyond the risk threshold, if the risk is based on the use or costs of referral services. The risk threshold is 25 percent.

Withhold means a percentage of payments or set dollar amounts that are deducted from the service fee, capitation, or salary payment, and that may or may not be returned, depending on specific predetermined factors.

WHERE TO FIND MORE INFORMATION

To research updates on this, please visit Justia.com and search for

42 C.F.R. § 422.208 Physician incentive plans: requirements and limitations.
Title 42—Public Health
Title 42: Public Health: PART 422—MEDICARE ADVANTAGE PROGRAM
Subpart E—Relationships with Providers

HEALTHCARE REFORM AND PHYSICIAN INCENTIVES

Naturally, in the midst of healthcare reform in the United States, one has to wonder how all these regulations will hold up in the face of PPACA and the new Accountable Care Organizations.

In addition to Medicare Advantage payment cuts and potential reductions in fee-for-service payment updates, PPACA includes various provisions intended to facilitate ongoing Medicare cost containment, notably creation of the Independent Payment Advisory Board and the Center for Medicare and Medicaid Innovation. In addition to CMI's broad scope, PPACA requires specific pilot projects, including (in Section 3022) demonstration of accountable care organizations (ACOs).

I have summarized Section 3022 below. (This is taken from my Web site, www.mariatodd.com/ppaca.)

SECTION 3022. MEDICARE SHARED SAVINGS PROGRAM

- Amends the Social Security Act by adding a new section on a Shared Savings Program that promotes accountability for a patient population and coordinates items and services under Medicare Parts A and B, and encourages investment in infrastructure and redesigned care processes for high-quality and efficient service delivery. Under such a program,
  - Groups of providers of services and suppliers meeting criteria specified by the Secretary may work together to manage and coordinate care for Medicare fee-for-service beneficiaries through an accountable care organization (ACO).
  - ACOs that meet quality performance standards established by the Secretary are eligible to receive payments for shared savings.
- The following groups of providers of services and suppliers that have established a mechanism for shared governance are eligible to participate as ACOs under the program under this section:
  - ACO professionals in group practice arrangements
  - Networks of individual practices of ACO professionals
  - Partnerships or joint venture arrangements between hospitals and ACO professionals
  - Hospitals employing ACO professionals
- The Secretary shall determine appropriate measures to assess the quality of care furnished by the ACO and may incorporate reporting requirements and incentive payments related to the physician quality reporting initiative (PQRI), including such requirements and such payments related to electronic prescribing, electronic health records, and other similar initiatives.
- Payments shall continue to be made to providers of services and suppliers participating in an ACO under the original Medicare fee-for-service program under parts A and B in the same manner as they would otherwise be made except that a participating ACO is eligible to receive payment for shared savings if
  - The ACO meets quality performance standards established by the Secretary.
  - The ACO meets the savings requirements.
- Defines "ACO professional" as a physician or a practitioner.
- No later than January 1, 2012, the Secretary must establish a shared savings program.

CONCLUSION

I hope that this chapter has not confused you but instead has enlightened you to the fact that your salary may be based upon revenues of the practice, not so much in the compensation formula, but instead on the practice's ability to have the cash to pay you. If the practice is engaged in capitated contracts and accountable care organizations, you may wish to review the books or have your accountant do so, as well as have access to a few contracts. Done incorrectly, they may not have the means to pay their bills without the necessary reinsurance. In my career, I have seen many physicians lose their practices, their homes, and their assets with bad third-party reimbursement contracts and participation agreements.

7 Corporate Practice of Medicine

A company such as Sears generally cannot employ a doctor and open a doctor's office in one of its stores. The reason for this prohibition is something called the Corporate Practice of Medicine Doctrine. Basically, the doctrine provides that only people with medical licenses, and not companies, may practice medicine.

However, if Sears cannot employ doctors, why can a hospital? Some would argue that hospitals are different because some are nonprofit and all are licensed. Nevertheless, in most states, there is no definitive rule allowing or prohibiting hospitals from employing physicians. But that situation is changing.

For example,

Illinois

An Illinois state court refused to enforce a hospital's employment contract with a physician, finding that a hospital may not contract directly to employ physicians to provide medical services. In *Berlin vs. Sarah Bush Lincoln Health Center*, the Illinois health center sued to enforce a restrictive covenant contained in a physician's employment agreement with the center. The physician had entered into a 5-year employment agreement with the health center that stated the doctor could not affiliate with any competitor within a 50-mile radius of the center during the term of the agreement and for 2 years after.

The physician later resigned from the health center to take a position with a competitor 1 mile from the center. The center sued to enforce the restrictive covenant. The physician argued that the agreement was unenforceable because it violated the Illinois prohibition on the corporate practice of medicine.

In addition to the restrictive covenant, the physician's employment agreement provided that he was required to devote his full working time and attention to the practice of medicine on behalf of the health center. This also stipulated that the health center would set professional fees and that the health center had exclusive billing rights to all fees collected for the physician's professional services.

The physician was paid a salary for his professional services and received fringe benefits comparable to those received by full-time management employees of the health center. The employment agreement also contained a provision providing that all patient medical records belonged to the health center.

The court refused to enforce the restrictive covenant contained in the physician's employment agreement, because it found that the health center "was practicing medicine in a real sense" based on the characteristics of the physician's relationship with the center and that such a relationship was at odds with the long-standing legislative restrictions on the corporate practice of medicine in Illinois.

The court asserted that only licensed physicians could practice medicine. Therefore, the center, as a corporate entity, could not meet the requirements of the state's Medical Practice Act.

Under the act, the right and privilege to practice medicine could be obtained only by individuals and corporations under limited circumstances, none of which applied to the center. Thus, the court found that it would be against public policy to enforce the restrictive covenant and limit the physician's medical activities.

Tennessee

The Tennessee legislature enacted legislation specifically permitting hospitals and hospital-affiliated entities to employ physicians, a practice that was previously prohibited by the state's corporate practice of medicine doctrine.

The Tennessee Hospital Association's legislative initiative to repeal that state's corporate practice of medicine doctrine culminated with the passage of relatively new legislation that became effective June 12, 1995. Prior to passage of the legislation, Tennessee hospitals were banned from hiring physicians. Generally, the law repealed the prohibition against the corporate practice of medicine and outlined certain provisions for employment relationships between hospitals and physicians that include

The independent medical judgment of physicians may not be restricted in any employment agreement.

Only reasonable limitations may be placed on the geographic and time provisions in restrictive covenants.

If a restrictive covenant is part of the purchase of a physician's practice, the physician must have the right to repurchase the practice.

Employed physicians must have the same rights and protections with regard to medical staff privileges as nonemployed physicians.

The legislation also provided that the prohibition against physician employment would continue for such hospital-based physicians as anesthesiologists, pathologists, radiologists, and emergency physicians. It also specifies that service contracts with such physicians must contain protections relating to notice of termination and the termination of staff privileges.

The legislation also allows physicians to recover attorney's fees and other expenses associated with the cost of litigation, arbitration, or a peer-review action if there is a dispute with an employer over compliance with the requirements of the new law. However, this requirement can be waived by contract.

Always check with counsel about any limitations or relaxations in the corporate practice of medicine doctrine in the state that you intend to render services and bill for them.

WALK-IN RETAIL CLINICS AND MEDICAL MARIJUANA CLINICS

In *Megatrends*, the classic book by John Naisbitt, the author mentioned retail clinics and employer on-site clinics. Many dismissed him and his ideas. The practice of medicine has undergone many changes. Once medicine was practiced at a doctor's home, or at patients' homes, and now we have walk-in clinics at the grocery store, the pharmacy, and the mini-mall, and they are staffed with physicians and physician "extenders."

As many consumers of healthcare have no insurance, they also may not have a regular relationship with a physician. For a simple, one-time fee, one can now pick up a quart of milk, a dozen eggs, bread, and a tetanus shot at Wal-Mart, Super Target, or a host of other sites that are part of the retail clinic movement.

This market response is an innovative alternative to the other alternative primary care settings for those without an established doctor–patient relationship, namely, the emergency department of the local hospital. The walk-in clinic is often in a compact space of a mall, superstore, drugstore, supermarket, and even train stations and airports. Often staffed by a physician, most are more often staffed by a nurse practitioner or physician's assistant who is licensed by the state to practice without the direct supervision of an on-site physician.

These clinics offer quick diagnoses and treatments of low-level medical conditions, such as cold and flu symptoms, sore throats and minor infections, rashes and allergies, minor injuries, and preventive services such as flu shots, glucose and cholesterol checks, and blood pressure checks.

For a traveler like me who often moves quickly from city to city as a speaker, these clinics have been a major convenience for me and my colleagues. Although I may not be able to land an appointment with a local physician or find my way to his or her office from a downtown hotel, often I can find one nearby who can tell me what I have and what to take for it. These professionals also have prescriptive authority in many cases and can order medications if needed.

These lower-cost, quick alternatives are much less expensive than the emergency room and offer almost immediate access in comparison to many inner-city hospital emergency departments that may have waiting times calculated in hours, not minutes. Health insurers seem to favor these establishments, too. Most are covered on any health plan and only the routine copay is charged, instead of any emergency department disincentive copayment.

As for corporate America, investors are raising capital to open or expand operations, and major national chains such as Wal-Mart, Target, and Walgreens have introduced walk-in clinics in a number of states. CVS, one of the largest drugstore chains, acquired the Minute Clinic chain of some 83 walk-in clinics, many of which were already located in CVS stores. With fees ranging from $30 to $100 or more depending on the service, these clinics appeal to many uninsured individuals as well as to those who have insurance but want quick and simple care.

Some major healthcare systems have taken notice of this trend and are establishing their own satellite walk-in clinics in retail locations as a way not only to keep ahead of the competition but also to capture referrals to their hospitals and physicians. One of my clients in rural Illinois who owns a walk-in clinic at the local discount general mercantile, similar in business model to a Wal-Mart but much smaller, sees that clinic as a way to further the mission of outreach to the community and employs physicians as employees of the hospital to staff the clinic. Patients treated for a minor problem at a walk-in clinic can then be referred to a system-affiliated primary care physician and potentially begin a long-term relationship with the physician and the system.

As for the corporate practice of medicine, however, anyone considering opening walk-in clinics must be fully aware of the legal and regulatory requirements for the delivery of healthcare services. Remember, I am not an attorney, so you really need good legal advice here. My purpose here is to make you aware that you need good counsel. Here is how it has been explained to me: Many states still have a strict prohibition on the corporate practice of most professions, including medicine. As a physician who may not have access to the right kind of health law expert, the reader must remember to ask about his or her counsel's knowledge of this, as some health law attorneys representing healthcare providers sometimes miss this important issue, even though the proscription is closely akin to that against the corporate practice of law. In many cases, the prohibition is not limited to physicians and osteopaths. It is a prohibition on the corporate practice of professions and, therefore, would include dentistry, podiatry, chiropractic, and so forth.

When I ask many lawyers about this, even health law "specialists," the response is often a guffaw accompanied by the dismissal that while it is still in effect, they know of no prosecutorial action of recent times. My attitude is that I would not want to be "the chosen one" to test it. Here is why:

> The prohibition on the corporate practice of medicine is an old one, and its origins can be found in both statutory and common law. The state's power historically has included licensure and regulation of all learned professions such as the law, medicine, architecture, engineering, and so on. Medical services dealing with public health is one of the fundamental areas of public safety and has long been viewed as appropriate to oversight and regulation by the state. Even though I am not a fan of more government, I will give them this much.
> The prohibition against the corporate practice of medicine seeks to assure that medical decisions are made by licensed medical professionals and to prevent interference in lay persons (corporate types like accountants, venture capitalists, and efficiency experts) in medical judgments or the provision of medical care.

The ban on the corporate practice of medicine is not found in one place but consists of three separate prohibitions. In some cases, it could include the operation of an unlicensed medical facility, unauthorized practice of medicine, and illegal fee splitting—which also touches on referral patterns and the antikickback and anti-self-referral acts in many states.

Let us suppose for the purpose of an example that Jones (not a physician) incorporates the Jones EZ Care clinic, a business corporation, in which he is the sole shareholder. Jones leases business space in a mini-mall, purchases diagnostic and imaging equipment, hires technicians, hires physicians and radiologists, and proceeds to market the operation to the public in the community.

Jones begins receiving referrals of patients, who come to the clinic for radiology and other rapid testing services. The required tests are performed on his equipment; the clinic's salaried doctors and radiologists read the films and produce written reports, and those results are forwarded to the referring physician. The clinic bills the patient's insurance carrier for both the use of the machines (technical) and the radiologist's reading fee (professional). This arrangement may sound perfectly reasonable from a business standpoint. The clinic may, however, be illegally engaged in the corporate practice of medicine, depending on the state in which this is happening. In states where there is such a prohibition, a nonphysician may not employ a physician to provide care to patients.

In our example, Jones has employed radiologists to practice medicine by reading films and rendering medical reports on those films. Jones is not a professional corporation (which can only be owned by professionals, such as physicians) but a business corporation. It is not licensed by the state regulatory or authoritative body as a diagnostic and treatment center, hospital, or other facility authorized to provide radiology services.

Therefore, Jones is illegally operating an unlicensed facility providing medical care in violation of state law. The clinic may also be acting in violation of some business corporation laws, which in some states require that a business corporation may not have as one of its purposes the establishment or maintenance of a hospital or facility providing health-related services. This is true in New York and many other states.

Jones and his clinic corporation are engaged in the unauthorized practice of medicine. In hiring doctors and providing medical services (i.e., radiology testing, diagnostics, and medical care), they are holding themselves out as being able to practice medicine and provide medical care to patients. They are ingratiating themselves into the physician–patient relationship, even though Jones is not a physician, and the clinic is not a properly licensed entity.

A radiologist who reads a patient's x-ray film has a physician–patient relationship with that patient as surely as does the physician who is the primary medical provider and who referred the patient for testing. A radiologist examines a patient's film, makes observations, and draws conclusions upon which treatment decisions will be made. In this case, the patient's x-ray reading should be done by a physician in private practice or by a physician in a licensed facility (such as a hospital) that is authorized to provide testing and reading services. That is clearly not happening in our example.

The key is in exclusivity, the preservation of a direct physician–patient relationship and continuity of care from the referring physician to another physician (the radiologist) or a licensed entity (e.g., a hospital). Jones, or the walk-in corporation, should not have come between the patient and the physician.

The courts in many cases have held that a physician–patient relationship is created "when the professional services of a physician are rendered to and accepted by another person for the purposes of medical or surgical treatment." Jones and the clinic could be engaged in the business of practicing medicine without a license.

The radiologists hired by Jones may be guilty of fee splitting in violation of some state and federal laws. With few exceptions, physicians rendering medical services must do so either as private practitioners, in a partnership or professional corporation with other physicians, or as an employee of a licensed facility.

When a physician renders medical services, that physician is expected to bill and collect for those services and is generally prohibited from sharing fees with nonphysicians. Here, the radiologists are performing a medical service and improperly sharing the proceeds with Jones by accepting compensation from his clinic in return for allowing his clinic to keep the proceeds of the billings for their services. The only recognized exception is in cases where a physician uses an outside agency to perform billing and collection services; the physician may pay for these services on a percentage basis provided the percentage is reasonable.

In many instances, a violation of this kind is a felony and is further subject to injunctive relief. What this means is that the courts may impose an injunction as an equitable remedy in the form of a court order, whereby a party is required to do, or to refrain from doing, certain acts. The party that fails to adhere to the injunction faces civil or criminal penalties and may have to pay damages or accept sanctions for failing to follow the court's order. In some cases, breaches of injunctions are considered serious criminal offenses that merit arrest and possible prison sentences. In addition, there may be fines in the thousands of dollars per violation and possible forfeiture of any moneys earned by the unlicensed facility. In many states where this prohibition has not been set aside, fee splitting constitutes unprofessional behavior and may be punishable by revocation, suspension, or annulment of the physician's license to practice medicine and up to, in some cases, a $10,000 fine for each violation.

So, in essence, the attorney general may be authorized to seek injunctive relief against repeated fraudulent or illegal acts and may be further authorized to bring an action to dissolve a corporation inter alia for exceeding its legal authority or conducting or transacting its business in a persistently fraudulent or illegal manner. If Medicare, Medicaid, or insurance is involved, there may also be penalties under federal laws as well as some states' anti-self-referral laws.

Simply put, this century-old prohibition means that a general business corporation (as opposed to a hospital corporation or a professional corporation) may not employ licensed professionals (such as doctors, nurses, physician assistants, etc.) to provide medical services. In these states, a walk-in clinic must be owned and operated either by a licensed facility, such as a hospital or a diagnostic and treatment center, or by a properly licensed professional or group of licensed professionals practicing in a professional corporation or partnership.

Although a general business corporation is prohibited from owning and operating a walk-in clinic or hiring licensed professionals, it can provide nonclinical business management support services (such as computers, clerical and billing services, book- and record-keeping, and the like). Once again, the fees paid by the walk-in clinic for these services must be based on the value of the services and not on a percentage of the walk-in clinic's revenues.

Walk-in clinics are usually so small that privacy becomes an issue. The federal Health Insurance Portability and Accountability Act (HIPAA) regulations, as well as state laws, protect the confidentiality of a patient's medical information. The operator of a walk-in clinic must take steps to ensure that discussions with a patient being treated are not overheard by other patients or passersby and that medical records are properly secured.

Managed care plans and other health insurers approached about admitting a walk-in clinic to their network of approved providers will likely perform extensive due diligence reviews to determine that the clinic is owned and operated by properly licensed professionals. Clinics that are illegally structured can be denied payment for services provided. If that happened and your salary was tied to revenue, that would pose a significant problem.

Walk-in clinics can be profitable and successful and can fill a growing consumer demand, but like any other medical service, they must comply with a wide variety of legal and regulatory requirements and restrictions before and after they open for business and hire physicians as employees.

For more information on the corporate practice of medicine, an excellent white paper is available online (www.nhpco.org/files/public/palliativecare/corporate-pract ice-of-medicine-50-state-summary.pdf).

8 Contract Law Basics

Employment agreements follow the basic elements of contract law. The contract is essential to free enterprise in our economic system. Each party in the contract is legally obligated to observe the terms of the agreement and the rights of others created and protected by those contracts. A contract is a binding agreement. In the Uniform Commercial Code (UCC), a contract is defined as a total legal obligation that results from the parties' agreement as affected by [the Code] and any other applicable rules of law. By one definition, a contract is a promise or set of promises, the breach of which the law gives a remedy or the performance of which the law in some way recognizes as a duty. Contracts arise out of agreements; hence, a contract is often defined as an agreement creating an obligation.

The essential elements of a contract include the following:

1. An agreement between competent parties based upon genuine assent (often referred to as a "meeting of the minds" of the parties
2. Support by consideration (money) and made for a lawful objective in the form required by the law

The parties to a contract include the promisor, or obligor, and the promisee, or the obligee. A party to a contract may be an individual, a partnership, a corporation, or a government. A party to a contract may be an agent acting on behalf of another person. There may be one or more persons on each side of the contract. In some cases, there may be three-sided contracts, such as a managed care agreement between provider, payer, and patient, or in the case of an employment arrangement, that of hospital, established practice, and new physician. Along with the original parties to the contract, other persons may have rights or duties with respect to it.

A contract arises when an agreement is reached. The offeror makes an offer, and the offerree accepts. If either is lacking, there is no contract. Each contract includes specific information including but not limited to

1. The date
2. The name and address of each party
3. The promise or consideration of the seller
4. The promise or consideration of the buyer
5. The signatures of the two parties

Working arrangements between two parties are sometimes not regarded as "contracts," because it is not the intention of the parties to enter into a binding agreement that could be interpreted as nonperformance if the two parties are not satisfied with the outcome.

When a working arrangement is part of a clearly contractual relationship, the transaction remains a binding agreement, because the purpose of a working arrangement is merely to provide flexibility to a contract. Are all parties to the contract clearly identified by name? Before a physician enters into a contract with an employer or contractor in the case of an independent contractor relationship, the physician needs to assure predictability of patients, a place to work, certain policies and procedures, and compensation. The provider needs to obtain the following information:

- Who owns the entity, and what type of management/administration does it have?
- Is the contracting entity the actual employer? The party identified in the contract will be the entity legally responsible for the compensation of the physician being contracted and any other promises or financial undertakings. The physician must review the financial stability and the management expertise of the legal organization identified in the contract.
- Who are the other physicians under the contract with the entity? What are their credentials?
- What is the entity's volume of active patients? How is the entity marketing to new patients?
- What obligations would be imposed upon you as an employee? Are you able and willing to comply with them?
- Must you accept all patients referred to you?

INCORPORATION OF EXHIBITS AND ATTACHMENTS

Many contracts contemplate future events or benefits. In the course of negotiation or discussion leading up to a contract, one party may show the other party various charts, tables, and statistical projections to show the actual dollar value of the particular transaction to the other party. It is a question of intent as to what extent such matter is merely illustrative and to what extent it is part of the contract. This is why it is necessary to have all exhibits and attachments incorporated into the contract so that, in the event of default, there can be a proven breach of contract, and liability can be imposed accordingly.

Sometimes the contract will expressly refer to and incorporate into the contract the terms and conditions of other writings or statements. In this case, it is necessary to have the wording "a copy of which is attached hereto and made a part of this contract." Specified services: A detailed list of the duties required is necessary. This should include things like hospital visits, surgery, surgical assists, night and weekend call, to name a few.

STANDARDS OF CARE

Physicians must avoid provisions of any agreement that require them to provide services under a different standard of care than otherwise required by state law. Many times, contracts require providers to provide care "of the highest quality." In a malpractice context, if a physician agrees to provide care "of the highest quality," a higher standard of care than required by state law will be imposed upon the provider.

EXCLUSION OF OTHER STATEMENTS

The opposite of incorporation, the contract may declare that there is nothing outside of the contract. This means that in the offeror's eyes, there was never anything offered, or promised, and that any prior agreement was merely a preliminary step that is finally canceled out, or erased, and the contract in its final form is stated in writing.

CONTRACT OF RECORD

A contract of record arises when one acknowledges before a proper court the obligation to pay a certain sum unless a specified thing is not done. Some of these obligations may be known as recognizance. When an agreement is made with an administrative agency, such as the Federal Trade Commission (FTC), that the entity will cease and desist engaging in a particular business practice that the FTC has found unlawful, the business is bound by its agreement and cannot disregard it afterward.

EXPRESS OR IMPLIED CONTRACTS

Simple contracts may be classified in terms of the way they are created as express or implied contracts. An express contract is one where the parties have made oral or written declarations of their intentions and the terms of the agreement. An implied contract is one where the evidence of the agreement is shown by acts and the conduct of the parties. An example of an implied contract would be where one party orders a meal in a restaurant, eats the meal, and then honors the bill for the meal and pays it. In terms of effect, there is no difference between an implied contract and an express contract. The difference relates solely to the manner of proving the existence of a contract.

QUASI-CONTRACTS

Under certain circumstances, the law imposes an obligation to pay for a benefit received as though a contract had actually been made. This will be done in a few situations in order to attain an equitable or just result. When a physician delivers services with the expectation to be paid for such services, it may be implied that the entity receiving the services would be unjustly enriched if the services delivered their expected outcome and the physician did not receive payment for the services as expected. In order to distinguish this from a true contract, which is based on the agreement of both parties, the obligation is called a quasi-contract. It is to be distinguished from an implied contract by circumstances such that a reasonable person would expect to be paid for delivering such services, like a good Samaritan circumstance. Although the objective of the quasi-contract is to do justice, one must not jump to conclusions that a quasi-contract will arise every time there is an injustice.

For example, no quasi-contractual agreement arises when an employed physician merely confers upon the employer a benefit to which the payer was already entitled.

A quasi-contractual obligation would not exist if performance of a contract proves more difficult or more expensive than had been expected. It would also not entitle a party to extra compensation when there was no misrepresentation as to the conditions that would be encountered or the events that would occur, particularly when the party complaining is experienced with the particular type of contract and the problems likely to be encountered.

Another case where a quasi-contract would not exist is in the event of disappointed expectations. If a physician wrongly concludes that there is a binding contract and proceeds to make a purchase of a home, for instance, on that assumption, there may be no right to recover for the loss sustained when the other party refuses thereafter to enter into a binding contract. Still a third example where there is no quasi-contract is in the case of contracts involving third parties. When a physician has a binding contract with a third party, only that person is required to pay for performance made under the contract. Even though the performance is conferred as a benefit upon the defendant, the physician might not be able to prevail against a defendant for quasi-contract when the third party fails to make payment under the contract. To borrow from billing examples, a physician who does not accept assignment of insurance benefits from a patient but bills the insurance company as a courtesy, in private indemnity insurance circumstances, cannot sue the insurance company if the insurance company fails to pay.

One of the most important sections of contract law that you must understand is the agreement. An agreement is formed when an offer is accepted. There are different types of agreements. Offers are conditional promises upon an act, a forbearance, or a return promise that is given in exchange for the promise or its performance.

To constitute an offer, there must be an intention of the managed care payer, or case manager, to create a legal obligation, or he or she must appear to intend to do so. It is not necessary to expressly state that a contract is being made. When there is neither intention nor the appearance of intention to make a binding agreement, there is no contract. It makes no difference whether the provider takes any action on the apparent offer.

DEFINITENESS

An offer, and the resulting contract, must be definite and certain. If an offer is indefinite or vague, or if an essential provision is lacking, no contract arises from an attempt to accept it. The problem arises because the court cannot ascertain the intentions of both parties.

An offer and the resulting contract that by themselves may appear "too indefinite" may be made definite by referencing another writing (or exhibit or attachment) such as a fee schedule, table of inclusions in case rate contracts or capitation inclusion listings, utilization management program details, quality assurance program details, formularies, sanction policies, and the like. An agreement may also be made definite by reference to the prior dealings of the parties and to trade practices. This might include "rollover" or "evergreen" contract terms and conditions.

Although an offer must be definite and certain, not all of its terms need to be expressed. Some omitted terms may be implied by law. Terms may also be implied by conduct. There may also be an agreement that consists of two or more parts and calls for corresponding performances by each part of the parties involved. This type of agreement is called divisible.

The purchaser agrees to purchase different articles at different prices at the same time. When the contract contains a number of provisions or performances to be rendered, the question arises as to whether the parties intended merely a group of separate, divisible contracts or whether it was to be a packaged deal so that complete performance by each party is essential to delivery. Think of this as rendering care, seeing patients in-hospital, being on time, and following policies and procedures. This would be a packaged deal and indivisible.

There may be three common situations for this to occur: If the term of an agreement that is too vague is not important, it may be ignored sometimes. If the balance of the agreement is definite, there can be a binding contract. The law has come to recognize certain situations where business necessity makes it desirable to have some form of a contract, yet the situation makes it impossible to make the terms and conditions definite in advance.

OTHER TYPES OF CONTRACTS

In your professional career, you will be asked to consider many creative contracting opportunities with suppliers, managed care payers, independent practice associations (IPAs), physician hospital organization (PHOs), and other arrangements. You may also encounter mortgages, leases, and other contractual arrangements that may be confusing. The following are some other types of contract concepts with which you should familiarize yourself. A cursory familiarization now may prove beneficial later when you need to use this book as a reference for some of these other arrangements.

Cost-plus contracts are valid against the contention that the amount to be paid is not definite when the contract is made. Futures contracts, or output contracts, are valid against the contention that the contract was not binding and was illusory because there was no obligation on the part of the buyer to purchase any quantity from the seller. A contract to supply medical goods as necessary is likewise binding against the objection that it is too indefinite and does not state a price. An entity may desire to be assured that the services of a given person, ordinarily a specialist or professional, will be available when needed. It is thus becoming valid to make a contract with the professional to supply services thought required by the professional, although this is indefinite and would appear to give the professional the choice of doing nothing. Under such contracts, the duty to act in good faith supplies the protection found in most contracts in the usual rules as to certainty and definiteness.

Contracts with no specific time limits are valid. The law meets the objection that there is a lack of definiteness by interpreting the contract as being subject to termination at the election of either party. An agreement is not too indefinite to enforce, because it does not state the exact price to be paid but states that the price shall be in prevailing market terms, or the "usual, reasonable, and customary" marketplace allowance. A contract may contain preemptive rights when the employer gives the employed physician first right of refusal or privilege to engage in a certain activity such as purchase of stock or equity in the practice.

TERMINATION OF AN OFFER

An offer gives the provider power to bind the payer by contract. This power does not last forever, though, and the law specifies that under certain conditions the power ends or is terminated. Offers may be terminated in a number of ways: counteroffer, revocation of the offer by the offerree, lapse of time, death or disability of either party, illegality, and rejection.

DURESS ISSUES

Economic pressures on a contracting party may be so great that they will be held to constitute duress. Economic duress occurs when the victim will be threatened with irreparable loss for which adequate recovery could not be obtained by suing the wrongdoer. Usually, a threat of economic loss or the pressure caused by economic conditions does not constitute duress that makes a contract voidable. The fact that a payer drove a hard bargain also does not give rise to the defense of economic duress.

Mistake, fraud, undue influence, and duress may make the agreement voidable or, in some instances, void. If this happens, the following remedies are available: recision, liquidated damages, or reformation.

INTERPRETATION OF CONTRACTS

The terms of managed care contracts and agreements should be clearly stated, and all important terms should be defined and included as recitals. If they are not, the parties may construe different meanings. The author of the offer always retains the privilege to interpret the offer. When such differences cannot be resolved satisfactorily by the parties and the issues are brought forth to an arbitrator or court, certain principles of construction and interpretation are applied. A contract is to be enforced according to its terms. It is the binding intention of the parties that must prevail. No particular form of words is required, and manifesting the particular intent of the parties is sufficient. A word will not be given its literal meaning when it is clear that the parties did not intend such a meaning. For example, "and" may be substituted for "or" and "may" for "shall" when the parties' intentions are clear.

Must the provider abide by unspecified "operational policies?" Who establishes these policies? Where can they be obtained in writing?

Employment agreements may require physicians to participate in utilization reviews, peer reviews, and quality assurance activities, and abide by their terms, conditions, and operating policies. Physicians should not blindly agree to participate in such programs. The agreement must specifically reference and incorporate into the agreement the specific utilization review and quality assurance programs so that the programs cannot be changed without notification or approval from the physician by U.S. mail, whether prepaid, certified, return receipt requested, or receipted hand delivery. Providers should make sure that these programs are consistent with the quality of care rendered in their practice and that they do not unduly interfere with the physician's practice of medicine.

Beware of phrases such as the following:

"Provider shall comply with and, subject to provider's rights of appeal, shall be bound by such utilization review program."

When a contract is partly printed or typewritten and the written part conflicts with the typewritten part, the written part prevails over the typewritten part. If there is an ambiguity, more often than not, it is interpreted more strictly against the drafting party. Thus, printed forms of a contract, such as insurance policies, which are supplied by one party to the transaction, are interpreted against the supplier and in favor of the other party when two interpretations are reasonably possible. If the contract is clear and unambiguous, it will be enforced to its terms even though this benefits the party who drafted the contract. The rule that an ambiguous contract is interpreted against the drafter is not applied when the other party knew what the drafter intended.

The statement, "I hereby read, understood, and agreed to the aforementioned terms and conditions of this Agreement," usually precedes the signature. Therefore, if you do not ask, your silence may indeed infer such understanding.

ASSIGNMENTS

The parties to a contract have both rights and duties. This is so in employment agreements as well. An assignment of rights is a transfer of rights. The party making the assignment is the assignor, and the party to whom the assignment is made is the assignee. An assignee may generally sue directly on the contract, rather than sue in the name of the assignor. An assignment may take any form, written or spoken, to show that intention to transfer or assign will be given the effect of an assignment.

In employment agreements, there should be mutuality as to the ability or privilege to assign the benefits of performance under a contract, provided that both parties agree to obtain the written consent of the other party before doing so. This is especially important when contemplating the future sale of a business or additions such as mergers or new providers coming under the same corporation as the assignor.

Here, neither party should be able to assign the rights and benefits under a contract without the prior express written consent of the other.

DELEGATION OF DUTIES

In certain instances in employment agreements, it may be necessary to sign on a contract that requires duties that you cannot personally perform. The service may be laboratory testing or radiologic services that you may not be able to render personally for whatever reason: no equipment, restrictive covenants on leases, services that you normally outsource, cross-coverage, and so forth.

This situation may be more frequently seen with IPA and PHO single signature contracts, management services organization (MSO) contracts, and the like. A point of law of concern under the concept of assignment is the delegation of duties. This happens when duties to perform under a contract by a party to a contract are delegated to a third person who is to perform them. Under certain circumstances, a contracting party may obtain someone else to do the work. When the performance is standardized and nonpersonal so that it is not material who performs, the law will permit the delegation of performance of the contract. In such cases, however, the contracting party remains liable for the default, if any, of the person doing the work just as though the contracting party had performed the duty or attempted to perform the job. One who is entitled to receive performance under the contract may agree to release the person who is bound to perform and to permit another person to render the required performance. When this occurs, it is not merely a question of assignment of liability under the contract but is really one of abandoning the old contract and substituting in its place a new contract. This change of contracts is called a novation.

DISCHARGE OF CONTRACTS

When two parties enter into a binding agreement, a contract may be discharged by performance, mutual consent, the impossibility of performance, operation of law, or material breach. A contract is usually discharged by the performance of the terms of the agreement. In most cases, both parties perform their duties and promises, and the contract ceases to exist and is thereby discharged.

If performance of the contract on or within the exact time specified is vital, it is said that "time is of the essence." Time is of the essence when the contract relates to property that is perishable or that is rapidly fluctuating in value. An express statement in the contract that time is of the essence is not controlling. When it is obvious that time is not important, such a statement will be set aside by the courts. Time may be essential, for example, when a contract for discharge planning, or startup of outpatient therapy, is required within 24 hours of the initiation to dispatch services by imposing a time limitation on performance. This may be more commonplace on outpatient ancillary and behavioral health agreements. When the time for performance is not indicated, it will be assumed that the performance called for in the contract will be rendered within a reasonable amount of time.

A contract may be discharged by the operation of one or more of its clauses, such as bankruptcy terms, mutual consent and notification to the other, material breach without remedy, waiver of responsibility by one party to another, substitution, novation, accord and satisfaction, release, temporary impossibility due to weather or weather clauses, impossibility due to materials not being available anymore, death or disability, change of law, economic or commercial frustration, or discharge by operation of law such as alteration, destruction of the contract, merger, bankruptcy, statute of limitations, contractual limitations, renunciation, or incapacitation.

For the sake of relevance, we will examine a few of these that are more germane to employment contracts.

A discharge by agreement may be terminated by the operation of one of its provisions or by a subsequent agreement. Often we see this in the "rollover" clause, where the contract automatically renews with the mutual consent of both parties. When a contract provides for a continuing performance but is nonspecific as to how long the contract is good for, it is terminable by either party with the same consequences as though it had expressly authorized termination upon notice.

A contract is discharged by waiver when one party fails to demand performance by the other party or to object when the other party fails to demand performance according to contract terms.

The parties may also decide that their contract is not the one that they want. They may mutually consent to replace it with another contract. If they do, the original contract is said to be discharged by substitution.

Impossibility of performance refers to external or extrinsic conditions as contracted with the obligors' personal inability to perform them. Thus, the fact that a debtor does not have money to pay and cannot pay a debt does not present a case of impossibility. The fact that it will prove more costly to provide a service than originally contemplated or that the obligor has voluntarily gone out of business does not constitute impossibility, which excuses performance. No distinction is made in this connection between acts of nature, people, or governments.

A contract is discharged if the law changes materially in the state, city, or county in which the contract is to be performed. This may come into play in states where there may be a change in the prohibition of the corporate practice of medicine. Many states are actively removing this prohibition or are contemplating it at this time.

BANKRUPTCY

In the event of bankruptcy, most debtors either voluntarily enter into federal court of bankruptcy or are compelled to do so by their creditors. In bankruptcy court, a trustee takes the assets that a creditor has and distributes them as far as they will go. Once the trustee distributes the assets as far as they will go, the court grants the creditor a discharge in bankruptcy if it concludes that the debtor has acted honestly and has not attempted to defraud its creditors.

Even though all creditors have not been paid in full, the discharge in bankruptcy is a bar to subsequent enforcement of ordinary contract claims against the debtor. The cause of action or contract claim is not destroyed, but a bankruptcy discharge bars a proceeding to enforce it. As the obligation is not extinguished, the debtor may waive the defense of discharge in bankruptcy by promising to pay the debt later. Such a waiver is governed by state law. In a few states, the waiver must be written.

What are the employed physician's obligations if the employer goes bankrupt? Is there a provision of the contract requiring notification of the initiation of any filing for protection under bankruptcy laws? If the practice declares bankruptcy, you must still provide for continuity of care. Will you be able to bill for services directly to insurance or third parties or patients directly as a result? Will you be able to keep all the monies collected or will you be required to pay a marketing fee to the bankrupt practice for connecting you with the patient in the first place? Will you have a place to practice and see patients?

Here is a tip: Ask for notification of any initiation of petition for bankruptcy protection by U.S. mail, certified, return receipt requested, within 72 hours of the submission of the appeal for protection under bankruptcy.

BREACH OF CONTRACT

There is a breach of contract whenever one of the parties fails to perform the contract. A contract is discharged by breach if, when the breaching party breaks the contract, the other party accepts the breach.

A breach does not result in the discharge of a contract if the term broken is not sufficiently important. When there is a failure to perform under a contract, the agreement is not terminated, but the defaulting party may be liable for liquidated damages.

There are several remedies for breach of contract, one or more of which may be available to the injured party. The injured party may bring action for damages, rescind the contract, bring suit to obtain specific performance, or commence a proceeding to obtain relief from an administrative agency of the government.

In a claim for damages, the injured party is under duty to mitigate the damages if reasonably possible. In other words, the injured party is required to take measures to generally stop any performance under the contract in order to avoid running up a larger bill. Here, recovery is limited to direct loss and not consequential loss. If there is nothing that the injured party can do to reduce damages, there is, by definition, no duty to mitigate damages.

LIQUIDATED DAMAGES

The parties may stipulate in their contract that a certain amount shall be paid in case of a default. Such an amount will be enforced if the amount is not excessive, and if the contract is of such a nature that it would be difficult to establish the actual damages. When a liquidated damages clause is held valid, the injured party cannot collect more than the amount specified by the clause. If the liquidated damages clause calls for payment of a sum that is clearly unreasonably large and unrelated to the possible actual damages that may be sustained, the clause will be held void as penalty.

Liquidated damages clauses require a sum of money to be paid by one party to the other party if he or she breaches a term in the agreement. Sometimes a managed care entity will attempt to add in a liquidated damages clause, causing the provider to pay for patients retained posttermination at some negotiated rate per member.

In a court challenge with Humana and a Florida physician, Humana filed action against the physician for failure to pay $700 per patient that remained with the physician posttermination of the agreement. The courts found that the physician was not held responsible for this sum of money as the patients were not the property of the insurance company, the clause interfered with the patient–physician relationship, it was against public policy, and the patients had the right to see whomever they chose as a provider of healthcare services. Similar situations could arise in an instance where an employed physician leaves the employer's practice and strikes out on his or her own.

9 A Checklist for Managed Care Agreements as They Apply to the Employed Physician

Now that we have examined the basic concepts in contract law, let us apply them to some of the most popular terms of the employment agreements seen in various group and other practice settings.

1. Does anyone or any organization, other than physicians, control determinations of quality of care?
2. Does the physician indemnify the employer entity against liability? If so, does the physician's professional liability policy cover such contract liability? Will the employer care indemnify the physician in case of liability on the behalf of the other physicians in the group? "Hold harmless" agreements require a physician to reimburse a contracted entity for any costs, expenses, and liabilities incurred by the entity because of action by the physician. These provisions jeopardize the coverage of a physician's professional liability insurance coverage. These provisions are known as liabilities assumed by contract. If a physician agrees to this type of arrangement, the physician often does so without the benefit of reimbursement from the physician's professional liability policy and must often pay for these expenses himself or herself. Limited liability corporations are often created to mitigate such exposures. Check with your attorney to clarify the options and interpretations in your state.
3. Does the contract permit unilateral changes in terms and conditions of the contract without prior notice to or the prior consent of the employed physician?
4. If the contract states that the physician will be bound by articles of incorporation, bylaws, or other documents of the employer, has the physician perused such documents? Is there a contractual provision for the physician to be advised of modifications to such documents? Is the physician bound by such modifications? Does the contract make reference to peer review or a utilization review program? Has the physician obtained and perused the program documents? Are the procedures of these programs subject to unilateral change without prior notice to the physician and without the prior consent of the physician?

SAMPLE WORDING

"The employer shall provide to the provider any changes in any operating policy not less than [X] days of implementation of said changes." Allow them to make changes, but reserve the right to notification 30 days in excess of the "bailout" time provided in the "Termination Without Cause" clause prior to your responsibility to the change, and request that notification be provided by U.S. mail, postage prepaid, certified, return receipt requested, or by receipted hand delivery.

Are there any limitations on referrals? Are they realistic? Are there expectations that you must refer patients to a certain provider? This would be in conflict with Medicare and Medicaid and various state rules, regulations, and statutes. What physicians, hospitals, pharmacies, and ancillary services are available to your patients? Are you satisfied with the quality of the panel of referral specialists, ancillaries, and hospitals? How are out-of-network services handled for managed care agreements? Can you live with them? Are there negative financial sanctions for out-of-network referrals?

5. Is the employer corporation subject to statutory licensing requirements? Has it complied?
6. How are disputes resolved? Is arbitration or mediation allowed? Mandated? If so, refer to the chapter on alternative dispute resolution for further information. The grievance procedure should be spelled out specifically. Each step of the process should be outlined so that the physician may be aware of the remedies available before giving up the grievance and making a business decision as to whether to go forth with the contract or "opt out."
7. What obligation does the physician have if his or her patients are seen by physicians covering for the employed physician? Does the contract require the physician to be available on a 24-hour basis? Does the contract require a "contracted" physician to arrange for another "contracted" physician to cover during absences and vacations? Must the physician guarantee or warranty performance or indemnify the employer for any professional liability issues arising from the treatment of patients by the covering physician?
8. Does the contract obligate the physician to perform any services after the contract is terminated? Even without a contractual provision, providers have an ethical, continuing duty not to abandon their patients. State Medical Practice Acts typically require the continued care and treatment of patients who are under the physician's care.
9. What is the term and termination policy? How much time is required to give notice of termination without cause? Does this window of time match all prenotification for unilateral changes to the contract, with an additional window of time to make business decisions relative to those unilateral changes?
10. What is the renewal system? Is the renewal of the contract covered under an "evergreen" or "rollover" clause? If so, what is the time frame to request renegotiation of terms prior to automatic renewal of the contract? Are there provisions for increases in the negotiated compensation and terms that keep reimbursement current with market conditions with these automatic renewal clauses?

11. What are the definitions of material breach of the contract? Are there remedies available and a limited time frame to implement remedies by either party in the event of a material breach?

12. Did you check the Boiler Plate Clauses, such as Entire Agreement and Assignment clauses?

   Entire Agreement clauses mean that any verbal representations or other marketing materials do not become part of the agreement. Therefore, promises made in recruiting that are not specifically mentioned as an addendum or attachment in the agreement and incorporated into the agreement as referenced do not become part of the agreement. This also implies that the signer has read and understands all materials referenced in the contract before signing. Such documents as the provider relations manuals, utilization management and quality assurance policies, bylaws, and so forth, are part of this consideration.

   Are assignment clauses mutually beneficial? A physician should ensure that the contract is not assignable to a third party without prior written consent. Otherwise, that employer may assign the contract to another organization with less financial or management resources or an entirely different patient base.

13. Are you aware of any assumed or created liabilities? Liability issues may arise by signing a managed care agreement.
   a. *Ostensible agency liability*: Realize that you may be held accountable for the actions of those providers to whom you refer patients.
   b. *Respondeat-superior liability*: Realize that you may be held accountable for utilization management decisions if you deny care or discontinue care because the managed care payer states will not pay for more care, visits, and so forth. The provider ultimately carries the decision-making responsibility on clinical issues.
   c. *Vicarious liability*: Realize that in an independent practice association (IPA) or a physician hospital organization (PHO), due diligence is required for credentialing and recredentialing members.

14. Have you checked the language of the text? Let action verbs be your cue. The words am, is, are, was, were, be, being, been, do, does, did, have, had, has, shall, will, should, would, could, may, might, must, and can suggest a state of being. The state of the text may imply that the policy is unspecified or indefinite at the time of signing. Seek to clarify.

15. Did you clarify unspecified terms? Sample wording you will see from time to time includes adequate, reasonable, material, sufficient, appropriate, and so forth. Always ask for clarification.

16. Have you ensured that policies and procedures are defined? "Provider shall be bound by and abide by all policies and procedures as set forth in the Manual." Ask for disclosure on all policies and procedures you must be bound by and attach them as exhibits to the contract. Then, add the language into the contract.

17. What are the continuing medical education (CME) expense budgets, time off for CME, and vacation and sick time benefits? Have everything spelled out.

18. Are moving benefits spelled out specifically? Ensure that maximum benefit, what is considered reasonable moving expenses (i.e., daycare, kennels, meals while possessions are in transit or being set up, cancellation fees for early termination of any leases or other contracts that incur penalties for early termination, etc.), is defined.

As always, it is wise to seek out competent health law attorneys to evaluate a contract before signing a managed care agreement. This chapter is provided to make you more able to do some prenegotiation and review before incurring charges for such evaluation. It will also make the attorney read-over more meaningful to you.

10 Alternative Dispute Resolution (ADR)

The movement toward alternative dispute resolution (ADR) in the United States began after World War I and reached its first milestone with the passage of the first modern arbitration statute in New York in the mid-1920s. Since then, the movement has grown steadily, achieving explosive growth since 1980.

Today, ADR methods have achieved broad acceptance by America's business, labor-management, and legal communities. The annual ADR caseload processed by the American Arbitration Association (AAA) alone has surpassed 60,000 cases—a figure equivalent to one-fourth of the cases now handled each year in the federal courts. In fact, our courts have recognized the value of ADR. Today, in many state and federal jurisdictions around the country, there are mandatory and voluntary court-sponsored ADR programs to divert cases that might be settled without litigation.

The American Arbitration Association, a public-service, nonprofit organization, has been the leading advocate of alternative dispute resolution since 1926. ADR is a term that refers to a variety of techniques for resolving disputes without litigation. In keeping with its mission, the AAA is in the forefront of efforts to create alternative systems that respond to the needs of parties involved in disputes.

Two of the better-known methods of ADR are mediation (in which the parties to a dispute reach a voluntary settlement with the help of a skilled facilitator) and arbitration (in which the parties choose a disinterested neutral to whom to present their case for a legally binding ruling). Many specialized rules and procedures have been developed in cooperation with interested organizations and industries to facilitate these dispute-resolution processes.

GLOSSARY OF DISPUTE RESOLUTION TERMS

It is important for anyone in healthcare administration or otherwise entering into a contract either with an employer or a managed care organization to understand this process and its language in order to best benefit from its availability. Therefore, a cursory glossary of the most commonly used ADR terminology follows.

Arbitration is submission of a dispute to one or more impartial persons for a final and binding decision.

Awards are the decisions of arbitrators. Awards are made in writing and are enforceable in court under state and federal statutes. Enforcement actions, when necessary, are brought by the parties to the arbitration.

Case administrators are the AAA staff persons assigned to administer cases. The case administrator is responsible for the general management of a particular case, including panel selection, scheduling and exchange of information among the parties, and all the other administrative details involved in moving cases through the system.

Caucuses are meetings in which a mediator talks with the parties individually to discuss the issues.

Claimants are what we call the filing parties, also known as plaintiffs.

Counterclaims are counterdemands made by a respondent in his or her favor against a claimant. They are not mere answers or denials of a claimant's allegations.

Demands for arbitration are unilateral filings of claims in arbitration based on a contractual or statutory right (also the form used).

Discovery or fact-finding is a process by which parties present the arguments and evidence to a neutral person who then issues a nonbinding report on the findings, usually recommending a basis for settlement.

Hearing is a proceeding in which evidence is taken for the purpose of determining the facts of a dispute and reaching a decision based on evidence.

Mediation is a process in which a neutral assists the parties in reaching their own settlement but does not have the authority to make a binding decision.

Mediation-arbitration (med-arb) employs a neutral selected to serve as both mediator and arbitrator in a dispute. It combines the voluntary techniques of persuasion, as in mediation, with an arbitrator's authority to issue a final and binding decision when necessary.

Mini-trial is a confidential, nonbinding exchange of information intended to facilitate settlement. The goal of mini-trial is to encourage prompt, cost-effective resolution of complex litigation. Mini-trial seeks to narrow the areas of controversy, dispose of collateral issues, and encourage a fair and equitable settlement.

Negotiation is a process in which disputants communicate their differences to one another and, with this knowledge, try to resolve them.

Parties are the disputants.

Respondents are responding parties, also known as defendants.

Submission is filing of a dispute to a dispute resolution process after it arises.

ADVANTAGES OF ALTERNATIVE DISPUTE RESOLUTION

Most people do not want to become involved in lawsuits. Litigation can entail lengthy delays, high costs, unwanted publicity, and ill will. Appeals might be filed, causing further delay, after a decision has been rendered. Arbitration, on the other hand, is usually faster and less expensive, and it is also conclusive.

Based on nearly 70 years of experience, the AAA processes each case so that it moves smoothly from initiation to resolution. If problems arise, a case administrator will assist the participants. Each dispute is handled with confidentiality and integrity. Professionalism is the key to the AAA's services, which explains why so many parties bring cases to the AAA. The following are additional advantages of ADR:

SPEED

Despite the best efforts of our court systems to improve the processing times of civil disputes, the burdens of criminal cases, tight budgets, and other factors still create delays when bringing a case to court in many jurisdictions. This delay can sometimes last years. Appeals extend the time required to reach a final result still further.

In ADR, there is no "docket"—no line in which to wait for your day in court. The only elements governing speed are the eagerness of the parties to end the dispute and the complexity of the cases to be resolved. Most mediations processed by the AAA are completed in a few weeks; most arbitrations are decided within a few months of filing. The AAA offers expedited services for disputes where the parties agree that speed is of the essence or where the claims are not large or complex.

CHOICE AND EXPERTISE OF IMPARTIAL NEUTRALS

Parties who resolve their disputes through ADR enjoy the assistance of neutrals who are already expert in the subject matter of their disputes. The AAA's panel consists of expert and knowledgeable neutrals from many professions and industries.

For example, parties to a construction industry dispute might select an architect, a contractor, or a lawyer with a lifelong practice in construction law to serve as their mediator or arbitrator. The "subject-matter expertise" of the neutral reduces the time typically required to attempt to educate a judge or jury about the technical elements of a dispute, and it raises the confidence level of the parties involved that the result of the process will be well informed. The association maintains a panel of more than 20,000 individuals with expertise in a broad array of businesses, technology, insurance, labor relations, and many other fields.

INFORMALITY AND FLEXIBILITY

ADR is conducted in a manner that is more businesslike than litigation. Each party tells its side of the story to the arbitrator in an atmosphere that is less formal than a court proceeding.

For example, where a court must apply complex rules of evidence, and the decision of the trial judge can be overturned if he or she admitted evidence that should have been excluded, arbitrators have a duty under law to admit any evidence that might be relevant. Arbitrators will, of course, discount questionable testimony and evidence, such as obvious hearsay, but the relaxed rules of evidence allow each side to present their case in a more informal manner. The parties better understand the process and feel confident that they had the opportunity to present their whole story.

Because the parties control the process, they enjoy tremendous flexibility. Hearings might take place at the site of the dispute or during evening hours. Testimony might be taken by telephone.

PRIVACY

Arbitration, mediation, and other forms of ADR are not open to public scrutiny like disputes settled in court. The hearings and awards are kept private and confidential, which helps to preserve positive working relationships.

ECONOMY

Time saved is money saved. ADR processes are designed to be faster, more streamlined, and more informal than litigation. Many of the costly procedures associated with formal court processes, such as filing appeals and motions, can be eliminated.

FINALITY

AAA arbitration awards are final, binding, and legally enforceable, subject only to limited review by the courts. The court does not second-guess the arbitrator's decision as to the facts or the law. Of course, parties may also agree in advance that awards will be advisory only.

WHO ARE THE NEUTRALS?

More than 20,000 individuals in diverse fields and professions are listed on the AAA's national roster of arbitrators and mediators. These neutrals represent a broad spectrum of expertise. Many are nominated to the roster by leaders in their industry or profession. Others are invited directly by the AAA.

Participation by business executives and professionals as arbitrators is vital to the system. Because of their specialized knowledge and experience, the parties are not required to spend time educating the arbitrator about relevant industry practices and customs. In labor-management relations, impartial experts arbitrate disputes arising out of the application and interpretation of collective bargaining agreements.

Biographies of neutrals describing their occupations, qualifications, and availability are maintained in the AAA's computerized network for submission to the parties.

WHO USES ALTERNATIVE DISPUTE RESOLUTION?

Virtually every sort of dispute that can be litigated can be mediated or arbitrated. The AAA's caseload includes disputes involving business, insurance, labor relations, the environment, public policy, family, securities, technology, employment, international trade, and many other areas.

Business controversies arise from millions of commercial contracts containing clauses that provide for arbitration of disputes. Even if a clause has not been included in a contract, parties can agree to use an ADR method administered by the AAA.

Labor-management disputes can also be resolved using the association's procedures. Labor contracts usually contain provisions calling for the arbitration of grievances that cannot be settled. The disputes arbitrated involve issues in such areas as discipline, discharge, demotion, promotion, productivity, pensions, and seniority.

Insurance claims are also administered by the AAA under its arbitration and mediation rules. Claims arising out of automobile accidents involving uninsured or underinsured motorists can be filed under the AAA's accident claims rules. Uninsured-motorist coverage protects motorists against financial loss from personal injuries inflicted by uninsured drivers. No-fault insurance claims can be arbitrated in those states (New York, New Jersey, Minnesota, Hawaii, and Oregon) that have no-fault legislation providing for arbitration of unresolved disputes regarding personal injuries.

Securities arbitration is an area of steady case growth. Disputes arising out of contracts between stockbrokers and customers are generally handled under the association's securities arbitration rules. An important feature of these rules is the requirement that the majority of arbitrators on a roster be people who are not affiliated with the securities industries.

Trade associations and professional societies in many specialized fields use the AAA's services to resolve disputes. Procedures and rules are developed to meet their needs. Rosters of neutrals familiar with the field and the technical questions involved are recruited and trained.

In a sometimes overly litigious society, it makes sense to recognize the potential for disputes in every relationship, to develop a strategy to avoid disputes by anticipating how they might arise, and to plan for the most effective methods to resolve conflicts once they occur. A simple one-sentence ADR clause in your agreements can ensure that your disputes will stay out of court.

In the healthcare industry, another prominent organization in ADR is the American Health Lawyers Association (AHLA) in Washington, DC. Their caseload for health law matters is beginning to outnumber those of the AAA. The AHLA charges 25 percent less for their administrative fees and has experts in the field of healthcare business and law.

HIGH-LEVEL COMPARISON AND CONTRAST: ARBITRATION AND MEDIATION

This section will serve you well not only in employment contract matters, but also when you are evaluating purchase agreements, managed care agreements, and leases that state that the dispute resolution will be handled by one of these forums instead of litigation.

Arbitration is submission of a dispute to one or more impartial persons for a final and binding decision. The arbitrators may be attorneys or businesspeople with expertise in a particular field. The parties control the range of issues to be resolved by arbitration, the scope of the relief to be awarded, and many of the procedural aspects of the process. Arbitration is less formal than a court trial. The hearing is private. The courts review few awards because the parties have agreed to be bound by the decision of their arbitrator. In some cases, it is prearranged that the award will only be advisory.

Mediation is best defined as a meeting between disputants, their representatives, and a mediator to discuss settlement. The mediator's role is to help the disputants explore issues, needs, and settlement options. The mediator may offer suggestions and point out issues that the disputants may have overlooked, but resolution of the dispute rests with the disputants. A mediation conference can be scheduled very quickly and requires a relatively small amount of preparation time. The conference usually begins with a joint discussion of the case followed by the mediator working with the disputants both together and separately, if appropriate, to resolve the case. Many cases are resolved within a few hours. Perhaps most important, mediation works. Statistics show that 85 percent of commercial matters and 95 percent of personal injury matters end in written settlement agreements.

What do these techniques have in common? Control. Think of dispute resolution as a continuum with maximum control at one end and minimum control at the other. An example of maximum control might be thought of as any relationship in which disputes never arise (not a very common occurrence). Minimum control would be a solution that is imposed upon the parties to a dispute by the public courts. ADR consists of every alternative in between.

Varying degrees of party control over the outcome marks the ADR band within the continuum. In negotiation, the parties achieve an agreeable outcome without the need for the involvement of any neutral party. In dispute avoidance strategies, like partnering, a neutral is involved to help parties anticipate likely sources of future disputes in order to prevent them. In mediation, a neutral party is again involved, this time after a dispute has arisen. The mediator is called in to help facilitate the parties' own settlement process. In arbitration, the neutral provides the parties with a binding ruling after hearing each side argue its case.

Although the degree of control over the outcome varies from one method to another, in all methods, the parties control the process. They will agree to the procedures and to the individuals who will assist in the dispute-resolution process. The parties can agree to fashion a process or combination of processes especially well suited to the dispute between them.

ARBITRATION AND THE LAW

Many of the cases that the AAA handles stem from the inclusion of an arbitration clause in a contract between the parties. Rules applicable to specific types of disputes are available from the AAA free of charge.

Arbitration awards are legally binding and enforceable in most jurisdictions. The Federal Arbitration Act provides for enforcement of arbitration agreements and awards in interstate-commerce and international contracts.

Arbitration is less formal than litigation, and mediation is less formal than arbitration. Unlike an arbitrator, a mediator does not have the power to render a binding decision. A mediator does not hold evidentiary hearings as would an arbitrator but instead conducts informal joint and separate meetings with the parties to understand the issues, facts, and positions of the parties. The separate meetings are known as caucuses. In contrast, arbitrators hear testimony and receive evidence in a joint hearing on which they render a final and binding decision known as an award. In joint sessions, or caucuses with each side, a mediator tries to obtain a candid discussion of the issues and priorities of each party. Gaining certain knowledge or facts from these meetings, a mediator can selectively use the information derived from each side to

- Reduce the hostility between the parties and help them to engage in a meaningful dialogue on the issues at hand.
- Open discussions into areas not previously considered or inadequately developed.
- Communicate positions or proposals in understandable or more palatable terms.
- Probe and uncover additional facts and the real interests of parties.
- Help each party better understand the other parties' views and evaluations of a particular issue, without violating confidences.
- Narrow the issues and each party's positions and deflate extreme demands.
- Gauge the receptiveness for a proposal or suggestion.
- Explore alternatives and search for solutions.
- Identify what is important and what is expendable.
- Prevent regression or the raising of surprise issues.
- Structure a settlement to resolve current problems and address the future needs of the parties.

PRACTICALITIES OF ARBITRATION AND MEDIATION

Looking for more flexibility than arbitration? Let's look at mediation. The benefits of successfully mediating a dispute to settlement vary, depending on the needs and interests of the parties. The most common advantages include the following:

- Parties are directly engaged in the negotiation of the settlement. The mediator, as a neutral third party, can view the dispute objectively and can assist the parties in exploring alternatives that they might not have considered on their own.
- As mediation can be scheduled at an early stage in the dispute, a settlement can be reached much more quickly than in litigation. Parties generally save money through reduced legal costs and less staff time.
- Parties enhance the likelihood of continuing their business relationship.
- Creative solutions or accommodations to special needs of the parties can become a part of the settlement.

In the interest of swift and low-cost dispute resolution, arbitrations pending under the rules of the AAA can be submitted to mediation under the applicable mediation rules at no additional administrative fee.

Mediations can originate in different ways. First, mediation can occur when a dispute initially arises and before a lawsuit is ever filed. Second, mediation can occur as an adjunct procedure to pending litigation. That is, as soon as the parties file a lawsuit, they can use mediation in an effort to resolve the dispute at the inception of litigation or at any time thereafter but prior to a trial being held. Third, mediation can occur during or immediately after a trial but before a decision is announced by a judge or jury. Fourth, mediation can occur after a judgment has been rendered in litigation. There might be a disagreement over the meaning or manner of carrying out a judgment, or concern about the possibility of lengthy court appeals. The parties can seek the assistance of a mediator to help them resolve these problems.

FOCUS ON MEDIATION

TYPES OF DISPUTES RESOLVED BY MEDIATION

Any type of civil dispute can be resolved by mediation. The kinds of conflicts brought to AAA mediations have been as varied as the types of industries and business specialties using the process. Just about any type of dispute that parties want resolved quickly and inexpensively can be submitted to mediation.

MEDIATION NEUTRALS

Mediators are carefully selected attorneys, retired judges, and experts in various professional and business fields. Each candidate may have been trained by the AAA, the American Medical Association (AMA), or one of its affiliate chapters, or taken a college or university program in mediation skills and been closely evaluated to determine the level of skills attained. Often, highly respected and experienced individuals are selected to be mediators. The mediators on the panel are chosen to serve on a particular case based on their expertise in the area of the dispute.

SCHEDULING A MEDIATION

Once parties have agreed to submit their dispute to mediation and have executed the appropriate forms, mediation can be conducted on the first mutually available date. Of course, the parties may agree to have their mediation set for an earlier or later date depending on the circumstances of their case.

STAGES OF MEDIATION

Below, I briefly describe the stages of mediation. They are not really that complex. Each stage requires an open mind and a commitment to settle the difference between the disputants.

The Agreement to Mediate

As mediation is a voluntary process, the parties must agree in writing that their dispute will be conducted under the applicable mediation rules of the AAA, the AHLA, or some other rule-setting organization. This may be accomplished in a number of ways.

Request for Mediation

The parties can provide for the resolution of future disputes by including a mediation clause in their contract. A typical mediation clause reads as follows:

> If a dispute arises out of or relates to this contract or the breach thereof and if the dispute cannot be settled through negotiation, the parties agree first to try in good faith to settle the dispute by mediation administered by the [name of the organization] under

its commercial mediation rules before resorting to arbitration, litigation, or some other dispute-resolution procedure.

The clause may also provide for the qualifications of the mediator, the method of payment, the locale of meetings, and any other item of concern to the parties. When a party files a request for mediation, the requesting party must forward a copy of the mediation clause contained in the contract under which the dispute arose.

Where the parties did not provide in advance for mediation, they may submit an existing dispute to mediation by the filing of a submission form that has been duly executed by the parties or their authorized representatives.

An Alternative Submission Process

Any party may request that the mediation organization invite other parties to join in a submission to mediation. This request may be made by a letter or a telephone call. Upon receipt of the names, telephone numbers, and addresses of the parties to be contacted and a brief description of the dispute, the mediation organization will write to the other parties to explain the program, enclosing a submission form and a copy of the rules. Within 10 days of sending that letter, a representative will telephone the other parties to further explain the program and answer questions. Although several telephone calls might be necessary to gain a submission, this has proved to be a most effective way of obtaining an agreement. Frequently, once the letter has been sent and the mediator or mediation organization has made telephone contact, the parties engage in discussion, which then leads to a settlement. If the other parties do not agree to submit the matter to dispute resolution, there will be no charge to the filing party, except that if the case settles after AAA involvement but prior to submission to dispute resolution, the filing party will be charged a filing fee.

The document initiating mediation, whether in the form of a request for mediation or a submission, is filed with the mediator or mediation organization and should include a brief description of the nature of the dispute, together with the appropriate administrative fee. The parties are also free to conduct the mediation through correspondence in lieu of an oral presentation, provided that all of the necessary information is included. Upon receipt of a properly filed request or submission form, the mediation organization assigns the case to a case administrator. It is the function of the administrator to appoint a mediator, to make the necessary arrangements for the scheduling of a meeting between the mediator and the parties, and to be generally at the disposal of both the parties and the mediator, offering whatever assistance is required in accordance with the applicable rules.

Selection of the Mediator

Upon receipt of the request for mediation or the submission to dispute resolution, the administrator will appoint a qualified mediator to serve on the case. The parties will be provided with a biographical sketch of the mediator. The parties are instructed to review the sketch closely and advise the case administrator of any objections they may have to the appointment. Because it is essential that the parties have complete confidence in the mediator's ability to be fair and impartial, the case administrator will replace any mediator not acceptable to the parties.

Preparation for the Mediation Session

1. Define and analyze the issues involved in the dispute.
2. Recognize the parameters of the given situation.
3. Identify your needs and interests in settling the dispute.
4. Prioritize the issues in light of your needs. Determine courses of action, positions, and trade-offs and explore a variety of possible solutions—an initial proposal (ideal "wants" high enough to allow room to negotiate), a fallback proposal (acceptable alternative proposal), and a bottom-line proposal (a final option that you absolutely must have).
5. Seek to make your proposals reasonable and legitimate and be willing to accommodate needs of the other party.
6. Ascertain the strengths and weaknesses of your case.
7. Prepare facts, documents, and sound reasoning to support your claims.
8. Anticipate the other party's needs, demands, strengths and weaknesses, positions, and version of facts.
9. Focus on the interests, not the position, of each party.
10. Develop your strategies and tactics through discussion of issues, presentation of proposals, and testing of the other party's positions.

THE MEDIATION CONFERENCE

The parties should come to the mediation conference prepared with all of the evidence and documentation they feel will be necessary to discuss their respective cases. Parties are, of course, entitled to representation by counsel.

At the outset, mediators describe the procedures and ground rules covering each party's opportunity to talk, order of presentation, decorum, discussion of unresolved issues, use of caucuses, and confidentiality of proceedings.

After these preliminaries, each party describes his or her respective view of the dispute. The initiating party discusses his or her understanding of the issues, the facts surrounding the dispute, what he or she wants, and why. The other party then responds and makes similar presentations to the mediator. In this initial session, the mediator gathers as many facts as possible and clarifies discrepancies. The mediator tries to understand each party's perceptions, interests, and positions on the issues.

When joint discussions have reached a stage where no further progress is being made, the mediator often meets with each party in caucuses. While holding separate sessions with each party, the mediator may shuttle back and forth between parties and bring them back to joint sessions at appropriate intervals. During each caucus, the mediator attempts to clarify each party's version of the facts, priorities, and positions; loosen rigid stances; explore alternative solutions; and seek possible trade-offs. The mediator probes, tests, and challenges the validity of each party's positions. The mediator serves not as an advocate but as an "agent of reality." The mediator must make each party think through demands, priorities, and views, and deal with the other party's arguments.

An effective mediator knows that demands and priorities shift as ideas meet opposition, different facts are considered, and underlying circumstances change as parties reappraise and modify positions. In effect, the mediator increases the parties' perceptions of their cases in order to construct a settlement range within which the parties can assess the consequences of continuing or resolving the dispute. By having parties focus on the risks and burdens of litigation, the mediator creates in the minds of the parties the idea that there are alternatives to seek. The parties articulate these possibilities by moving toward trade-offs and acceptable accommodations.

During the final caucuses and joint sessions, the mediator narrows the differences between the parties and obtains agreement on major and minor issues. The mediator reduces a disagreement into a workable solution. At appropriate times, the mediator makes suggestions about a final settlement, stresses the consequences of failure to reach agreement, emphasizes the progress that has been made, and formalizes offers to gain an agreement.

The mediator acts as a facilitator to keep discussions focused and avoid new outbreaks of disagreement. The mediator will often have the parties negotiate the final terms of a settlement in a joint session. The mediator will then verify the specifics of an agreement and make sure that the terms are comprehensive, specific, and clear in the final session.

The Settlement

When the parties reach an agreement, they should reduce the terms to writing and exchange releases. They may also request that the agreement be put in the form of a consent award, for which the case administrator will make the arrangements.

If the mediation fails to reach a settlement on any or all of the issues, the parties may submit to binding arbitration. Such arbitration would be administered under the appropriate arbitration rules, and, in accordance with the rules, the information offered in mediation may not be used in arbitration (or in subsequent litigation).

Administrative Fees

The case-filing fee should be borne equally or as otherwise agreed by the parties. Additionally, the parties are charged a fee based on the number of hours of mediator time. The hourly fee is for the compensation of both the mediator and the case administrator and varies according to region. Check locally for specific availability and rates or call the national offices of either the AAA or the AHLA.

The expenses of the administrative fees and the mediator, if any, are generally borne equally by the parties. The parties may vary this arrangement by agreement. Where the parties have attempted mediation under these rules but have failed to reach a settlement, the AAA will apply the administrative fee of the mediation toward any subsequent AAA arbitration that is filed with the AAA within 90 days of the termination of the mediation. Check with the AHLA for their policies regarding such matters.

Mediation Deposits

Before the commencement of mediation, the parties will each deposit a portion of the fee covering the cost of mediation, as the association will direct, and all appropriate additional sums the mediator or case administrator deems necessary to defray the expenses of the proceeding. When the mediation has terminated, the mediator or the mediation organization will render an accounting and return any unexpended balance to the parties.

Mediation Deposit Refunds

Once the parties agree to mediate, no refund of the administrative fee is usually made.

STAGES OF ARBITRATION

THE AGREEMENT TO ARBITRATE

In this section, we will focus on the method used by the AAA, as it is the most widely recognized in contracts.

The most important step in initiating arbitration is the agreement to arbitrate. This agreement can be one of two kinds: It can take the form of a future-dispute arbitration clause in a contract, or where the parties did not provide in advance for arbitration, it can take the form of a submission of an existing dispute to arbitration. The AAA will, without charge, attempt to get all parties to agree to arbitration of such a dispute.

The parties can provide for the arbitration of future disputes by inserting a standard arbitration clause into their contracts.

STANDARD ARBITRATION CLAUSE

Any controversy or claim arising out of or relating to this contract, or the breach thereof, will be settled by arbitration administered by the AAA under its Commercial Arbitration Rules, and judgment on the award rendered by the arbitrator(s) may be entered in any court having jurisdiction thereof.

Arbitration of existing disputes may be accomplished by the use of the following clause:

> We, the undersigned parties, hereby agree to submit to arbitration administered by the American Arbitration Association under its Commercial Arbitration Rules the following controversy: (cite briefly). We further agree that the above controversy be submitted to (one) (three) arbitrator(s). We further agree that we will faithfully observe this agreement and the rules, that we will abide by and perform any award rendered by the arbitrator(s), and that a judgment of the court having jurisdiction may be entered on the award.

Regardless of how the agreement to arbitrate was reached, filing of a claim with the AAA along with the appropriate filing fee, as provided in the schedule, and serving the defending party are all that are required to set the machinery for arbitration into motion. Upon receiving the initiating papers together with the filing fee, the AAA assigns the case to one of its staff members, whose official title is case administrator, and who, from that point onward, is at the disposal of the parties, expediting administration and assisting both sides in all procedural matters until the award is rendered. Pursuant to the rules, the parties and the AAA may use facsimile transmission, telegrams, or other written forms of electronic communication to give the notices required by the rules.

The AAA will supply these forms free of charge on request, but arbitration may also be initiated through ordinary correspondence, provided that all of the essential information is included.

Special attention is sometimes required to determine in which state and city hearings are to take place. If the place of arbitration has not been designated in the contract or the submission to dispute resolution, or if the parties have not otherwise notified the AAA of their agreement on locale, it will designate the city in accordance with its rules. Among the factors considered are

- Locations of the parties
- Locations of witnesses and documents
- Locations of sites or materials
- Relative costs to the parties
- Places of performance of the contract
- Laws applicable to the contract
- Places of previous court actions, if any
- Locations of the most appropriate panel of arbitrators
- Any other reasonable arguments that might affect the locale determination

Hearings may be held in any geographical area, not just where the AAA maintains regional offices.

Expedited procedures, outlined in sections 53 to 57 of the rules, are applied in any case where no disclosed claim or counterclaim exceeds $50,000, exclusive of interest and arbitration costs. Those procedures provide for direct appointment of the arbitrator, although a list can be obtained at the request of all parties for an additional fee. The procedures also provide for notice of arbitrator appointment and notice of hearing by telephone, and for the award of the arbitrator to be rendered no later than 14 days from the date of the closing of the hearing.

It would be wise to check with your state chapter of the AAA for rules and regulations regarding arbitration and ADR. Several states have existing protocols and regulations regarding ADR. Hawaii and South Carolina are two that I am personally aware of that maintain specific rules in their state code.

ADR is not new but is becoming one of the evolving considerations in the healthcare industry to save time, money, and relationships. In physician employment contracts, it could be an effective mechanism to manage disagreements or if not utilized have a disastrous effect on the group's governance. One area we did not touch upon in this section was the dispute between binding and nonbinding arbitration. This is a personal decision and can sometimes be a deal breaker. Binding arbitration means no further action at law is permitted if you do not care for the decision of the arbiter. Even though arbitration can be seen as beneficial to a group practice and as an alternative to potential litigation, it is by no means an inexpensive or cheap shortcut to all disputes. The input of an experienced attorney or mediator or arbiter should be sought only to explore the language and opportunities for ADR.

TYPICAL DISPUTE RESOLUTION LANGUAGE
IN EMPLOYMENT AGREEMENTS

Employee shall submit a written statement of the matter in controversy together with the Employee's requested remedy to the Managers within thirty (30) days after the controversy arises. The Board shall review the Employee's grievance and shall provide a written response to the Employee either granting or denying such request stating reasons therefore within thirty (30) days of receipt of the Employee's written grievance. Failure of the Board to respond timely to the Employee's written grievance shall constitute denial of the requested relief.

Employee shall demand alternative dispute resolution within five (5) days of the Board's denial of Employee's grievance, or failure to respond timely thereto, which demand shall include the name of the dispute resolution entity, arbiter, or mediator appointed by the Employee, together with a complete statement of the matter in controversy.

Employee and Employer shall each appoint an arbiter to hear the grievance, if arbitration has been so selected. When two arbiters have been appointed, they shall agree on a third arbiter and shall appoint that arbiter by written notice signed by both arbiters with a copy mailed to each party within five (5) days of appointment.

The arbiters shall not only be impartial, but not have any conflict of interest, past or present relationship with the parties or their counsel, whether direct or indirect, whether financial, social, or other kind, without calling attention of the parties or their counsel to such relationship within five (5) days from the date of appointment. The arbiters shall be experienced in matters of employment law in the healthcare industry.

The award of the majority of the arbiters shall be [binding/nonbinding] on the parties thereto [author's note: if binding,] and may be entered thereon in any court having jurisdiction in the State of _____. Both parties shall bear their own respective legal expenses and costs necessarily incurred in the dispute resolution procedures. The cost of the arbiter/mediator and any administrative fees and costs shall be borne equally by both parties.

One last note, mention of venue might be important if you are dealing with a corporate office that is out of state, as in the case of a physician practice management (PPM) or hospital-owned practice. Always try to negotiate the venue of any legal proceedings in your city, your county, and your state.

11 Physician Employment Contracts

Now that we have explored the fundamentals of contracts and dispute resolution, let's take time for you to familiarize yourself with some of the points specific to physician employment contracts. Let's start with a few vignettes to drive home the seriousness of covering details and avoiding vague generalizations in your contract.

A family practice physician was offered a position that involved moving across the United States. She took her contract to a general practitioner attorney for advice, but neither she nor the attorney fully appreciated the problems that arose later on, nor did they attempt to bargain away the problem clauses in the agreement.

Once at the new job, when the physician was asked to perform procedures for which she was neither trained nor qualified, she resigned from employment. However, the group sought to legally enforce provisions of her employment agreement specifying that she would "reimburse" the group $100,000 for her short employment.

A radiologist inexperienced in negotiating an employment contract thought that his many months of talks with an employer were leading to a job. Unfortunately, the employer thought only that the physician was proving difficult to work with. The negotiations soured, and the employer withdrew the offer.

A surgeon was given vague promises of ownership in a private practice; however, these promises turned out to be illusory. It turned out that she was the fourth young physician to leave the group after stays of 2 years or less, as no one was ever actually offered the opportunity to become an owner.

An internist was offered a salary well below that customary for those with his training and skill level but did not know how to back up his claim that he was worth a higher salary.

A plastic surgeon signed an employment contract that included a noncompetition agreement. When that relationship failed, the plastic surgeon discovered that the noncompetition agreement prevented his being able to continue practice in that community. The months of job searching that followed, without an income, were financially devastating.

By signing an employment contract, you are agreeing to be legally bound by its provisions. The employment contract you are offered surely has been carefully crafted by the employer's attorney in a way that fully protects the interests of the employer while giving less attention to your objectives.

Your employment contract may be the most important financial decision you will ever make. Complex in what it says and does not say, the typical contract spells out your pay, determines how you will practice, determines your professional growth, and assigns serious legal risks. Any misunderstandings or possible problems overlooked can cause you extremely painful consequences later.

Receiving your contract is an invitation to bargain. It could be disastrous to sign immediately; you might pay the price later. Before acceptance, you must carefully align the offer with your own objectives and tie it to what is "fair."

The bargaining process is a delicate and time-consuming process, even for the most skilled, involving carefully evaluating terms, redrafting contract language, and negotiating. A consultant may be needed to bring skilled negotiating expertise to the table for you. Employing seasoned negotiators is the best way to avoid the mistakes that the inexperienced make. Because how the contract is negotiated sets the tone for your future employment, you want the negotiations to build a win-win deal, not create discord.

COMPENSATION AND BENEFITS

Salary and performance bonuses: Salaries today vary widely depending on specialty, years of experience, and geographic region. Some compensation levels are rising, others are leveling off, and others are declining.

Compare your salary to industry norms, and determine whether negotiating a higher salary, step increases, and bonuses are possible.

Review whether your compensation is causing you legal risks under inurement, independent contractor, and referral prohibition regulations.

Analyze whether you will get what you think you will (i.e., that disbursements are clearly defined and that there are no ways disbursements can unreasonably be held up).

Benefits: Benefits are a major portion of your total compensation package yet vary widely and often allow room for comparison with industry norms. In negotiations, being able to use comparisons gives you a heads-up position.

Assess the reasonableness of the range of benefits provided, such as health plans, retirement plans, insurance, profit sharing, and relocation expenses.

Review the reasonableness of leave policy for vacation, personal leave, continuing medical education (CME), sick leave, disability, maternity, and other time.

If necessary, help clarify what details about space facilities, supplies, and equipment are available for you and who is responsible for paying for them and upkeep.

Tax consequences: How your compensation package will affect your tax status is important in negotiating your contract. Study the tax consequences of the compensation offering.

OTHER MAJOR CONSIDERATIONS

Scope of duties: The contract should contain a complete job description, so that once you are on the job, you will not find yourself expected to do things you had not counted on. Working relationships, such as to whom you report, who reports to you, and your say in hiring support staff, should be defined.

Performance evaluation: Is a regular and defined personnel evaluation provided? On which benchmarks and performance metrics will you be evaluated?

Ownership opportunities: If there is an opportunity that you might become an owner, vague promises must be crystallized into specific timing, conditions, and methods to be used.

Professional liability insurance coverage: The extent of coverage and who is responsible for premiums are very important. You can work with the prospective employer to make sure that all terms of such insurance are not a cause for any undue burden upon you in terms of costs, indemnification, or liability.

Noncompetition agreement: Frequently, employers ask for a "covenant not to compete" that states you cannot practice medicine for a specific period of time in a geographical area following termination of employment. These terms and conditions have been successfully negotiated away, or made less burdensome. I just went through a rough negotiation with potential business partners that resulted in my backing away from the contractual relationship altogether. It seems that they wanted to own all my intellectual property, including that which was developed prior to my ever meeting them. They wanted to dictate for whom I could and could not consult or speak, censure what I could write and blog, and make it so that I could no longer even comply with the prenegotiated contract to update this book because they wanted to call that consulting and label the contents of the book as competitive. You may have books, articles, guides, manuals, blogs, and the like that you are not ready to give up. Address these at the front end of your contract and avoid misunderstandings and miscommunications.

Outside practice: If outside employment is not permitted, your contract must spell out such prohibitions. Often, you can also draft language to cover under what conditions any allowance for outside practice is to be approved.

Assignability: What happens if the employer is bought out, a frequent happening in today's world of consolidations, acquisitions, and mergers? The contract is likely to provide for assignability, but at whose discretion? These are questions that must be answered adequately to protect your future.

GENERAL CONTRACT TERMS

In addition to compensation and the numerous other key considerations described above, some other important clauses are as follows:

Dispute resolution: Should disputes arise, mediation or arbitration can prove advantageous, but only if the ground rules were specified in advance. The contract must stipulate how to discourage frivolous positions by an opponent should such a dispute arise, attempting to resolve the dispute and save the relationship through arbitration and mediation.

Term: Employment contracts should have both a starting date and an ending date. Contracts often provide for automatic renewal or annual review. You must make sure that all conditions are spelled out.

Termination: Absent an agreement otherwise, employment generally is "at will" (i.e., can be terminated summarily for any reason). It is essential that your contract has proper notification requirements for termination and limits termination to a defined "cause." A memorandum of understandings can provide for early notification of any dissatisfaction and provide for corrective action opportunities that could avoid termination.

Other provisions: You must examine other customary or advisable features of a contract, such as access to financial records upon which compensation is paid, to ensure your interests are well covered.

THE REAL KEY TO SUCCESS

The key is not just to know what to ask for but *how* and *when*. This is where your unique negotiating skills together with expertise from a consultant or attorney knowledgeable in this area can bring you a win-win deal.

12 Where Money Comes from in Order to Pay You

MANAGED CARE PARTICIPATION FOR THE NEWCOMER

Managed care is usually delivered through health plans of various shapes and structures that, on the surface, appear similar. The truth is that they are very different, although most resemble an entity capable of providing care and the insurance component to protect the enrollee from financial exposure for claims arising from incurred covered expenses. This limits the enrollees' choice and access to those providers within the system, other than primary care physicians (PCPs). The systems often limit their ability to self-refer throughout the system of fixed panels of physicians, facilities, and other contracted providers, a methodology known as a "gatekeeper" approach.

The managed care delivery system usually emphasizes preventive care and is often associated with alternative delivery systems such as health maintenance organizations (HMOs), preferred provider organizations (PPOs), exclusive provider organizations (EPOs), independent practice associations (IPAs), physician hospital organizations (PHOs), management services organizations (MSOs), and integrated service delivery systems (ISDNs) utilizing a capitated or discounted fee-for-service reimbursement system. In this chapter, we will study the structure and functional differences of each system.

HEALTH MAINTENANCE ORGANIZATIONS (HMOs)

An HMO is premised, in part, on the idea that aligning incentives between the managed care organization (MCO) and the provider can keep costs down. Studies have shown that HMOs can be successful at reducing costs and preserving measurable quality in many instances.

HMOs are health plans that may be for-profit or nonprofit entities. HMOs may seek qualification on a voluntary basis by Centers for Medicare and Medicaid Services (CMS) in accordance with the HMO Act of 1973, as amended in 1988. The majority of HMO plans classify themselves as for-profit entities. Additionally, HMOs must pass state licensure requirements, which vary by state. The basic regulatory model is that a state insurance department or corporations department reviews rates, policy documents, and compliance with state financial reserve and surplus requirements in the amount necessary to cover all covered expenses up to the minute that they are incurred.

HMO Provider Contracts

Services from certain types of practitioners may be specifically excluded by reference in the plan's evidence of coverage (EOC), or plan handbook. Often, these include chiropractors, optometrists, opticians, podiatrists, and alternative healing arts practitioners such as massage therapists, acupuncturists, nutritionists, Reiki therapists, biofeedback therapists, therapeutic touch specialists, and the list goes on and on. Also, there may be certain treatment modalities that are specifically excluded or nonspecifically excluded as unaccented or experimental standards of practice. Most HMOs contract with an average of over 2,000 physicians, of which about 30 percent are PCPs.

Point-of-Service Products in HMOs

Another product enjoying aggressive growth in the marketplace is the point-of-service (POS) product. Here, we hear references to dual-option and triple-option packages. In a POS product, the member of the plan has a choice of provider at the time when a healthcare service is required. The member can remain within the plan's panel of providers and receive maximum coverage benefits, or choose to go outside the system but pay higher out-of-pocket expenses. Dual choice refers to an HMO-like plan with an additional indemnity plan. Triple choice refers to the addition of a PPO to the dual-choice option.

Many POS programs require the enrollee to select a participating PCP to authorize referrals to any specialist. Also, preadmission certification is often required for admission to nonparticipating hospitals.

Transferring Risk to Providers in the HMO Setting

Many state laws permit the transfer of financial risk from the HMO to contracting providers selected by the HMO. In an HMO setting, the role of the PCP expands to primary care coordinator. There are concerns of ostensible agency theory of liability on the behalf of the PCP, because he or she directs patients to specialty or ancillary providers and facilities from within a restricted list of providers credentialed by another entity. Most HMOs require that the PCP guide the patient through the system and disincentivize the PCP from directing the patient to a provider outside the fixed panel of providers chosen by the HMO. This often places the PCP in a dilemma if he or she feels that the clinical needs of the patient may not be appropriately met by the available panel of providers and that the patient's needs might be better served from outside the panel. In an HMO setting, for covered services, if the physician argues the case as a patient ombudsman, the cost of the time and resources spent to argue the case is a cost risk because that time is uncompensated.

The use of physician extenders provides another exposure to risk. Nurse practitioners and physician's assistants have been used to augment a short supply of PCPs to help provide care. On a state-by-state basis, the physician extenders may provide a lot of care under the direct supervision and protocol of a physician, but the physician will be held accountable for the extenders' actions. Lack of supervision, improper delegation, and lack of due diligence in credentialing may lead to malpractice claims. From a patient satisfaction standpoint, many patients are resistive to care provided by someone who appears to have less training, and they may be quite critical in their evaluation of the care provided. They often cite beliefs that their physician might have picked up on subtle or occlusive symptoms that went undiagnosed or were misdiagnosed.

Another risk in HMO settings is that of utilization management decisions. Often, practitioners are genuinely concerned with keeping within normal utilization patterns. Outliers are often sanctioned financially through withhold mechanisms tied to increased utilization. When the withhold mechanisms do not incentivize corrected behavior, the practitioner may be expelled from the panel. Other times, when utilization is determined to be too low, perhaps causing jeopardy to the health of a patient, the practitioner may also be terminated from a network for a quality issue, usually citing patient endangerment as the cause. Within this monitored and managed utilization system, referrals and testing are controlled; this creates greater exposure to risks. This is because when there is a less than favorable outcome, patients are likely to think that the decision was financially motivated, which could lead to punitive damages if proven. Several cases have been tried in many jurisdictions to establish case law in these matters.

Other instances of risk may come in the number of treatments or days of hospitalization coverage one can access as a coverage limitation. Take, for example, borrowing from the area of physical therapy, a benefit limitation of "20 visits or 2 months of physical therapy treatments per acute condition." In this example, once the patient has reached a maintenance level of care and fails to continue to improve, the limitation may be declared within the first week of treatment if the patient is no longer deemed or documented to continue to be in an acute phase of rehabilitation. Strict monitoring of utilization and documentation might well defend the position of the payer that the care no longer falls under the guidelines of what is "covered." By comparison, unmanaged "indemnity" insurance policies may cite a benefit of physical therapy benefits for as long as the attending physician deems necessary. Thus, the attending physician may continue to prescribe therapy without a limitation of 20 visits or 2 months, and the indemnity carrier must pay. This is why indemnity coverage premiums are so much higher than managed care premiums. By choosing a managed care plan, the buyer is betting against the need for coverage that exceeds the stated benefit limitation.

PREFERRED PROVIDER ORGANIZATIONS (PPOs)

PPOs are networks of providers brought together by some sort of corporation, group, or marketer to contract with providers at a discount for healthcare services.

A PPO is usually not risk bearing and markets itself to insurance companies and self-funded or Employee Retirement Income Security Act (ERISA) qualified plans via an access fee. In this concept, the network is actually rented or leased to the payer or payers.

The panel is often limited in size and may have some utilization review system associated with it. The organization may entertain several accreditations including the National Committee for Quality Assurance (NCQA) or the Utilization Review Accreditation Committee (URAC). The legal sense of the word indemnification means to "make whole again."

In PPOs, the benefit design encourages the covered individual to choose a contracted provider to access the discounted fee-for-service reimbursement system. Typical out-of-pocket expenses, such as coinsurance and deductibles, are less expensive to members when they utilize "in-network" preferred providers. Healthcare providers usually agree to accept payments below their full charges, in accordance to a contractual negotiation that pays the lesser of the provider's actual billed charges or the network's negotiated fee schedule. The provider also usually agrees not to balance bill the patient with the exception of deductibles, coinsurance, and noncovered services. Risk-sharing arrangements such as capitation are not often encountered in PPO plans. Few PPOs in the country engage in risk-sharing with providers. Instead, there are often loopholes in the contracts that put the provider at risk for not receiving payment or defending a denial of payment.

Many times, providers are offered a chance to participate in the network if they are willing to negotiate per diem or case rates at the hospital and ancillary levels and discounted fees for services at the physician level. Per diem and case rates are flat fees for a daily package of services or an episode of care from beginning to end with specific inclusions and exclusions as to what the payment represents. Most PPOs reimburse participating physicians under contract using a maximum allowable fee or fee calculations. Services provided by PPOs vary greatly from plan to plan.

Many PPO plans charge prospective provider applicants a credentialing fee and retain a portion of the net payment as a marketing fee or withhold. When called a withhold with no hope of reclaiming the payment at some later date, the withhold is really a discount. Many providers join PPOs in hopes that they will be sent patients to care for in exchange for negotiating the discount. Providers must remember that the word "send" is a verb, and PPO participation merely makes one accessible to the stream of patients in the system. The essential marketing that takes place is the inclusion of the providers' names in a directory.

THIRD-PARTY ADMINISTRATORS

In most cases, PPOs utilize third-party administrators (TPAs) to process claims. TPAs are organizations outside an insuring organization that handle the administrative duties and sometimes utilization review. TPAs are used by organizations that actually fund the healthcare benefits but find it not cost-effective to administer the plan themselves.

Usually, when a TPA performs the utilization review and management function for a payer, the TPA is accredited through the URAC. In the event that the payer is a self-funded ERISA plan, coverage decisions and utilization management may be outsourced to one of these agencies, but the self-funded plan is still held ostensibly liable for the utilization and payment actions and decisions of the TPA.

Often, the patient is provided a participating provider directory from which he or she chooses a provider of healthcare services. Then, after examination and treatment of the patient, the provider sends a bill for services rendered to the PPO. The

PPO then reprices the claim in accordance with negotiated fees designated in the fee schedule and forwards the bill to the TPA. The TPA verifies the claim, puts it through review for utilization and quality assurance compliance, and if all is in order, submits a payment request to the payer.

As the PPO may rent or lease the network to a myriad of payers, self-insureds, and other sources of funding, the number of fee schedules, repricing schedules, and TPAs multiplies. In essence, one PPO could have this scenario replicated hundreds of times with claims going in hundreds of different directions at the same time. This brokering and marketing leads to a new phenomenon called the silent PPO.

SILENT PPOs

The silent PPO can mean losses of thousands of dollars for providers. These are PPOs that are not really specified in a contract, but the provider is paid at a PPO-discounted fee anyway. Usually, the patient is identified as a policyholder of an indemnity plan because he or she prefers to have no restrictions on choice of provider. When the preverification is performed at the provider's office, it is confirmed that the patient is in an indemnity plan and has 80 percent coverage for the first $5,000 in charges and 100 percent thereafter. The patient is treated and released. The practice sends a bill to the insurance company, billing a full, usual, and customary fee, with no discount. The payer, preferring not to pay full price, calls a broker or TPA who has access to all the lists of providers and discount levels for several legitimate PPOs. The broker searches its rosters and discovers that the physician has a contract with a certain PPO that calls for a 20 percent discount. The broker sends a fax to the payer with that information. The payer then recalculates the physician's bill and discounts the fee 20 percent from the original price, citing that the reason for the lower price is because of a contract with the PPO with which the physician already is contracted.

The billing and collections clerk, upon receiving the Explanation of Benefits (EOB) citing the discount, deducts the discount from the amount owed. Only if the staff members search the patient's intake sheet, view the photocopy of the insurance card, and peruse the list of PPO plan participating groups will they realize that the deduction is cited in error as the patient is not a member of the PPO. Silent PPOs happen when TPAs obtain lists of providers who have PPO contracts in their locality. Anytime the indemnity beneficiary happens to use a physician who is a PPO provider, the TPA tries to claim the discount. Even though the American Medical Association (AMA) has received complaints calling this practice fraudulent, no official investigator has done so. There is nothing illegal about this, because if the provider fights the discount, the payer simply backs down and pays the difference. When the error is not caught, the TPA and the silent PPO split the profit. There is no clause on many contracts that prohibits the broker or TPA from protecting contractual information from being leased out to others.

Although the American Association of Preferred Provider Organizations (www.aappo.org) discourages silent PPOs, its principals believe these are technically legal as long as the physician's contract does not specifically prohibit them. The crux of the issue is informed contracting with the PPOs. A silent PPO will anger providers, and in the long run, these issues, along with all the layering of middlemen within the discount system, are causing the PPOs to lose popularity and transfer the growth rate to physician-driven IPAs, PHOs, and MSOs that choose to rent themselves and own the lists of providers as proprietary. A good number of IPAs and PHOs are now forming MSOs that can obtain a Certificate of Authority in most states to function as TPAs and deal directly with payers without all the discount layers in between.

EXCLUSIVE PROVIDER ORGANIZATIONS (EPOs)

EPOs are similar in purpose and organization to PPOs, but many have the lock-in feature of an HMO. They allow members to go outside the network, but the member must pay the full cost of the services. An EPO is similar to the HMO in that it uses a PCP as a gatekeeper, has a limited provider panel, uses an authorization system, and so forth. The main difference between an EPO and HMO is that EPOs are generally regulated by insurance regulations, if at all, rather than by HMO regulations. EPOs are not allowed in some states because they too closely resemble HMOs.

INDEPENDENT PRACTICE ASSOCIATIONS (IPAs)

The term *IPA* can refer to a variety of newly forming provider entities developing around the country. Many of these entities are being formed for the purposes of managed care contracting and risk management. Physicians are not the only ones forming these groups—all types of similar providers are joining forces to apply some clout in contracting with managed care payers. IPAs may run into antitrust behavior if they are not careful to integrate economically. IPAs may not share fee information among competing groups unless they share risk and function as one business unit for the purpose of contracting collectively.

PHYSICIAN HOSPITAL ORGANIZATIONS (PHOs)

The PHO is a legal entity, which may start out informally, that links hospitals and the attending medical staff. PHOs are also frequently developed for the purpose of contracting with managed care plans. Some PHOs are formed as nonprofits, and others are formed as for-profit entities. The hospital's profit status is often what drives the tax status of the PHO. The nonprofit models do not offer equity but do offer subscription or membership instead. In the event that the nonprofit PHO realizes a profit margin, consensus must be achieved as to how to handle the profit so that all are happy with the outcomes and community benefit is achieved. Memberships and subscriptions are generally not considered as capital and are therefore usually not transferable should a physician retire and sell the practice to someone new.

MANAGEMENT SERVICES ORGANIZATIONS (MSOs)

An MSO is a type of integrated healthcare delivery organization that emphasizes efficient management of a health delivery continuum. Many, but not all, MSOs acquire the tangible assets of practices for a fair market value and provide practice management services under a long-term management services agreement. There are several types of MSOs. Some MSOs are owned jointly by a hospital system and their respective attending medical staffs. Others are owned solely by physicians. Venture capitalists have also taken to the notion that there is money to be made in the managed care market and are sponsoring MSOs. The banking industry has also realized that the price they paid for the learning curve in the evolution of electronic data interchange (EDI) can easily be applied to the managed care market, and they are sponsoring MSO products. Billing services that also incorporate practice management consultation are on the list of "wannabes" in the MSO market.

CONCLUSION

The one thing that rings true about all managed care organizations: If you have seen one IPA, you have seen one IPA. If you have seen one PHO, you have seen one PHO. If you have seen one MSO, you have seen one MSO. The only thing similar in many cases is the alphabetical letters they use to describe themselves. Form follows function in all instances. Not every form will lend itself to every community and every market. The model has to be matched to the market—driven by market need and not the providers' desire to simply build one. Just because the providers build one, doesn't mean the buyers will come.

This chapter was included to give you a brief glimpse of managed care as it relates to being able to afford to pay physicians from contracted revenue proceeds. Together with managed care, Medicare, workers' compensation, and motor vehicle accident insurance proceeds make up the mainstay of physician practice revenues such that they can afford to pay overhead, comply with administrative terms and conditions in the contract, and pay doctors' salaries.

For additional information on managed care, I would be remiss not to refer you to my other book, *The Managed Care Contracting Handbook, 2nd edition.*

13 Employed Physicians in the Hospital-Sponsored Practice

In the early 1990s, with the advent of relaxation of corporate practice doctrines in many states, hospitals began hiring physicians at record rates. It seems as though I remember all of this happening about the time that the first term of the Clinton administration gave rise to accountable health partnerships, purchasing alliances, and a new, more aligned delivery system of healthcare.

In the early 1990s, many large hospital systems rapidly set up training sessions for their administrators and physicians to build management services organizations (MSOs). They then seemed to set the pace for purchasing the hard assets of physicians and hiring them as independent contractors for all hospitals.

I am convinced it was a maneuver to control physician behavior—but I do not think it worked. In fact, at a recent local Healthcare Financial Management Association (HFMA) chapter meeting, I overheard many a conversation that local hospitals were developing strategies to "offload" many of the purchased practices—stating that the theory of control never materialized in reality.

Still, in some communities, it may be a prudent move to hire physicians, either as employees or independent contractors. Especially where there are shortages of physicians and needed specialties, or where the managed care payer or self-funded employer groups in the community wish to purchase health services as a packaged deal.

The typical scenario in which many hospital-sponsored practices operate is as described below.

The physician's full time and effort is often devoted to the performance of his or her duties for an employer pursuant to a contractual agreement. On average, the physician will spend not less than 40 hours per week carrying out his or her duties, which generally include providing professional services and related activities in an office and hospital setting, and being actively involved in corporate, departmental, and medical staff meetings and activities. Often, the physician may be required to work longer than the contractually stated hours, and often without pay because of contractual language and the lack of an employer–employee relationship governed by the laws of the U.S. Department of Labor.

Moonlighting, as it is commonly called, or undertaking any professional obligations of any kind (medical, administrative, executive, or otherwise) for any other entity except the contractor is usually taboo unless permission is obtained in advance.

Together, the physician and the contractor set the physician's work schedule and the sites where the physician will attend to patients in office settings, clinics, or otherwise.

Contracted physicians must usually be available on an on-call basis in accordance with the contractor's standard on-call policies and will arrange coverage for scheduled time off with other physicians employed by the corporation. Often, physician's assistants and nurse practitioners augment physicians' on-call coverage, taking first call in the evenings and only referring those calls that require physician intervention before normal business hours.

Usually, for the period stated by contract, the physician must maintain active and unrestricted membership of the medical staff of, and full clinical and admitting privileges at, the affiliated hospital or hospital system. In the unlikely event that the physician ceases to be a member of the medical staff of the affiliated hospital, or should, for any reason, the physician's clinical or admitting privileges expire without renewal or be suspended or revoked, or the physician loses the license to practice medicine in that state, or the license is suspended, revoked, or canceled, then, effective as of the date the physician ceases to be a member of the medical staff or as of the date of expiration, suspension, revocation, or cancellation of such clinical or admitting privileges or license, the contractor may usually terminate the agreement for cause. These terms are expressed in the contract and may constitute warning that the termination may be done without notice for these specific reasons.

If the physician's clinical and admitting privileges at the affiliated hospital are restricted or made subject to supervision in accordance with the applicable medical staff bylaws, rules, and regulations or comparable rules, regulations, or policies applicable to the practices of physicians, the physician may be terminated for cause or placed on suspension without pay for a stated period of time.

Sometimes the physician may continue to render services only in accordance with restrictions or supervision. If the contractor determines in its sole reasonable discretion that imposition of such restriction or supervision of the physician's privileges unreasonably interferes with the performance of the physician's duties under their agreement, the contractor may often elect to terminate the agreement effective immediately by written notice to the physician.

Physicians in a hospital-affiliated practice are no different than those in private practice in that they must maintain their clinical skills by participating in appropriate continuing medical education (CME) activities and maintain good standing in professional associations. The word "appropriate" may have some bearing on the courses in which the physician may be permitted to enroll at the expense of the contractor.

One important consideration for every contract is that the physician must agree to use his or her best effort to comply with all applicable federal and state statutes, regulations, and compliance policies, and all accreditation standards applicable to the corporation and to the hospital. This is tougher than it sounds, because, by this agreement, the physician contractually assures the other party that he or she is familiar with all these rules, regulations, updates, policies, and procedures. Any failure may be considered a material breach and constitute grounds for termination.

Therefore, it is your responsibility to either obtain copies of these rules, regulations, policies, and procedures or remain ignorant and at risk. The problem is that once you begin digging into these documents, you will never stop, because they keep changing. Therefore, it is of utmost importance that you make sure that the contract stipulates that you will be held to your best effort to comply with these things. The reason for this is that best efforts, if genuine, cannot be litigated.

WHAT TO EXPECT FROM THE CONTRACTOR

In most cases, the contractor or corporation will provide the physician with professional inability insurance coverage through a self-insurance program for professional inability claims or through a licensed carrier. These should cover the physician for any actions that may arise from services rendered by the physician on behalf of the contractor or corporation pursuant to the employment or other contractual relationship. You should obtain a certificate of insurance from the plan in question and retain it for your records. You still may have to provide any tail coverage for actions that may arise from times prior to your contractual effective date.

The contractor or corporation should reserve the right to have itself or its designee bill for professional services rendered by the physician. If so, a written designation is required for these activities by most carriers. Check and see who has the liability for false claims and inappropriate billing activities before you let anyone do your billing. The physician was in the room with the patient. Therefore, only the physician can document what he or she did for the patient and if it was or was not medically necessary in his or her professional opinion. These kinds of things, when done incorrectly, can cost an unwitting physician the privilege to participate in Medicare, Medicaid, or other federal programs and perhaps bring about criminal prosecution for fraud and false claims. You do not want to become involved in any of that. If you do become entangled in such a mess, you will hope you own stock in the company that manufactures H_2 inhibitors.

Usually, any and all fees received in connection with billed services belong to the contractor, or the physician gets paid inadvertently. All monies are usually required to be assigned or endorsed over promptly to the contractor or corporation by the physician.

In most of these settings, the contractor or corporation, or its delegate, has the responsibility for billing or collecting any amounts owed for services provided by the physician rendered under the contract. The contract usually requires the physician to timely provide the contractor or corporation with all necessary, accurate, and complete information and documentation, including but not limited to completion of all medical records to assist the corporation in billing and collecting amounts owed. Sometimes this means taking care of denials and appeals, which adds to dictation duties and telephone activities in order to attempt to solve claims dilemmas.

Sometimes the physician cannot participate in any third-party payment or health delivery plans (such as Medicare, Medicaid, Blue Cross/Blue Shield, health maintenance organizations [HMOs], preferred provider organizations [PPOs], or even independent practice associations [IPAs]) in connection with his or her professional practice without the prior consent of the contractor or corporation. If the physician participates in any third-party payment or health delivery plan, it is usually those designated by the contractor or corporation. Also, the physician is usually required to abide by all applicable requirements and guidelines of each third-party payment or health delivery plan in which he or she participates. Check those third-party contracts for conflicts with established internal policies. Do not assume that because you were directed to sign onto a managed care contract that the contractor knows how to analyze them and revise them to protect you. Remember, if they conflict and you get into trouble for either one, it is your signature on the line.

This will undoubtedly meet with resistance in many cases, but remain steadfast in your assertion that you do not sign anything without reading and understanding it. Once you go into private practice, if ever, and you want to be remiss, you will have to live with your mistakes. In a contractual situation, you could unwittingly find yourself on the street without a job and a derogatory entry in the National Practitioner Data Bank, on file for life, for being terminated from your contract.

The contractor or corporation usually provides the office and clinical space for the physician to provide professional services and also furnishes and maintains all equipment and supplies necessary for the proper rendering of services by the physician. The physician is usually required to promptly notify the contractor or corporation, or its designee, of any perceived deficiency in any equipment or deficit of supplies. Keep written records of any reports and notes as to when they were remedied. It is better to have and not need than to need and not have, especially if the deficiency is a quality issue that comes up in court. A good example of that would be a perceived or suspected malfunction of the autoclave. If there is a postoperative infection later, the attorney will pull service logs and other notes in discovery.

Support staff is usually the responsibility of the contractor or corporation. Make sure that the standard of care is maintained and that you trust those that the corporation has hired for you. Ask if you have any meaningful input into the hiring and firing determinations.

COMPENSATION

The contractor or corporation is required to compensate the physician for the services rendered pursuant to the contract at a stated annual salary. For salary figures, check the Internet or refer to journals like the *Journal of Medical Economics*. Also, many employment consultants can provide figures on the going rate of compensation for your market area. If you are an employee, you may be paid in equal biweekly installments and be subject to all tax withholding required by law. An independent contractor will not have the tax withholding requirements by the employer but will have their own, for which the rate is often higher.

Sign-on bonuses are becoming a thing of the past. With the fraud and abuse implications of the sign-on bonus, especially in light of the fact that there is no exchange of services for the bonus, it may not be a clean arrangement.

Obtain professional counsel before negotiating any bonus with a hospital that may have a relationship with you for referrals. The contractor or corporation usually provides to employed physicians any fringe benefits in accordance with the employer's flex benefit program. If you are independently contracted, you should take the differential value into account when negotiating your compensation. It will cost you more than it will cost an employer because of the differential in volume of business you bring to the insurance company or financial planner.

Physicians are usually entitled to time off for vacation, sick leave, and other approved leaves of absence. The contract should state how leave is accruable in hours per pay period. For independently contracted physicians, you must also factor this into your contract and compensation arrangements.

Often, if tied to a hospital benefit plan, combined time off may be offered. This may or may not be carried forward per corporation policy. Combined time off lumps together sick time, vacation time, and other approved leave to use at the physician's discretion.

CME benefit time and reimbursement may have certain stipulations tied to use. It must often be used in the year earned and may not be carried forward from year to year. This is done to prevent huge gaps in coverage and the potential need for locum tenens to be recruited and credentialed for longer coverage. Expect the contract to require advance written notice to be able to use combined time off and CME benefit time, except in cases of emergencies. You might also see a further stipulation that any dates selected must be reasonably satisfactory to your employer or contractor and approved in advance.

Disability periods may be a tough negotiation issue. Many contracts I have reviewed contain the stipulation that, if at any time during the term of the contract the physician becomes unable by reason of illness or physical or mental disability to perform the duties required of him or her under the contract, the employer or contractor "shall have no obligation to pay the physician's salary during the period of disability." Employers may pay for disability benefits provided to the physician in accordance with the employer's flex benefit program. Independent contractors will have to negotiate premium rates into their compensation rate or go it alone and perhaps go without coverage, as this coverage is very expensive.

GRIEVANCES

Grievance procedures are usually stipulated in the contract and are often required to be set for arbitration in the event the grievance is not internally resolved. See the arbitration chapter in this book for more details.

NONCOMPETE CLAUSES

Noncompete clauses are problematic in physician contracts as much as they are in every other type of business contract. There are issues of potential antitrust violations, public policy, and continuity of care, and the imposition on the sanctity of the doctor–patient relationship.

Often, as a requirement to engage in a contract with the employer or contractor, the physician agrees that during the term of contract and for a period of 1 year after the expiration or termination of the contract, by either party and for any reason, the physician will not individually or jointly, with any other physician, individual, or entity, directly or indirectly, whether as employer or employee, operator, agent, member, advisor, consultant, independent contractor, owner, stockholder, investor, partner, joint venturer, or otherwise,

1. Own, operate, or have any interest in any medical practice, medical clinic, or clinical laboratory
2. Provide professional medical services or related services, otherwise become involved in activities similar to or of the same type as the activities of the employer or in competition with the employer, or permit the physician's name to be used in connection with any activities similar to or of the same type as the activities of the employer or in competition with the employer
3. Solicit, hire, or employ, directly or indirectly, any person who is or was, at anytime during the physician's employment hereunder, an employee or independent contractor of the employer, or solicit, directly or indirectly, any patient of employer, including any patient treated by the physician during his employment hereunder, within a certain number of miles radius of the hospital, employer, or contractor's facilities or of any site to which the physician was assigned to provide services during the term of the contract

Additional requirements include that during the same time periods and within the same geographical area, the physician will not disclose or utilize for other than the employer's, contractor's, or corporation's benefit any proprietary or confidential information, including but not limited to patient lists, records, policies, and procedures.

These provisions usually remain in full force and effect if the agreement is terminated prior to its expiration, except in the event that the employer or contractor terminates this agreement without cause. In such a case, these provisions can be waived if the physician executes a separate written agreement providing that the physician will not solicit, directly or indirectly, any patient of the employer or contractor from the site or sites at which the physician practiced during the contract period, including any patient treated by the physician.

This is the part that may interfere with continuity of care and the doctor–patient relationship. "I agree that the covenants and undertakings contained in the non-compete section relate to matters which are of special, unique, and extraordinary importance to the employer or contractor and that violation of any of the terms may cause irreparable injury to the employer, the amount of which may be impossible to estimate or determine and which cannot be compensated adequately." This is a vague way of stating that the employer will pursue you for damages if you breach this. Check with an experienced health law attorney prior to agreeing with any non-compete terms and conditions of a contract.

As part of your reading, make sure that you obtain a copy of the Medicare program fraud alert titled "Hospital Incentives to Physicians" before undertaking any relationship with a hospital-related practice where there is a referral stream and a revenue stream present. Always seek out experienced counsel to explain the ramifications of any contract you may be offered. Hospital-managed or hospital-affiliated practice can be rewarding, but it is not for everyone.

14 Full Partnership Arrangements

When a physician has been an employee associate of a group practice for some time, invitation may be extended to become a full partner. This may also happen in the case of a new physician but is more uncommon, unless the physician is a family member of one of the partners or someone well known to the partnership.

Partnership arrangements are set up in a formal agreement with inherent tax and legal ramifications of the decisions of the partners, the partners' abilities to bind the partnership, and joint and several liabilities. This requires much more professional advice and is beyond the scope of this chapter.

In becoming a partner, you formalize your acceptance of an offer of partnership and your agreement to be bound by all the terms and provisions of the partnership agreement and any amendments to said partnership agreement that may be adopted in the future by a majority vote. You also further agree to be bound fully and to observe faithfully all the rules and regulations of partnership, which may have been adopted by existing partners or which are presently in force or which may be adopted pursuant to the terms of the said partnership agreement as amended.

DURATION OF PARTNERSHIP

Typically, the existing partnership continues until dissolved by written vote of two-thirds of the then active partners, and until so ended, the termination of interest of any partner does not dissolve the partnership with respect to the remaining members.

New partners may be admitted by a vote of two-thirds of the existing partners or whatever else is stated in the bylaws. New partners must execute a counterpart of the agreement, which is binding on the parties. Each new partner usually contributes an agreed upon sum in cash or in kind to the capital of the partnership. In kind is described as something having similar value but not a cash item.

Capital accounts must be maintained for each partner as required by section 704 of the Internal Revenue Code (IRC), as amended, and its regulations. Partners are usually not entitled to demand, receive, or withdraw any part of the partners' capital account or to receive any distribution from the partnership, except as provided in their partnership agreement. Any partner who receives a financial interest in the partnership, or whose interest in the partnership is increased or decreased by means of a transfer of all or part of the interest of another partner, should have a capital account that reflects the transfer. Capital accounts may also reflect elections in effect under IRC section 754 to the extent permitted under IRC section 704(b). This is the stuff that certified public accountants' (CPAs) dreams are made of (and practice administrators' nightmares).

The partnership is expected to keep complete and accurate records and accounts of the entire business and affairs of the partnership, which are maintained in the partnership office under the supervision of the partners, and are supposed to be available for inspection by each partner at all times. These records should include up-to-date accounts of all capital assets, income, receivables, liabilities, and disbursements. All professional fees received by the partners and their associates are mandated to be paid over to the partnership cashier. The books of the partnership are usually balanced and closed as of the last day of December in each year or a different time if stated in tax forms, at which time the profits and losses of the partnership and the indebtedness, if any, of the individual partners to the partnership are ascertained, settled, and paid. All patient charts are considered assets of the practice and treated as goodwill in financial dealings and valuations. They remain the exclusive property of the partnership, while the information contained in them belongs to the patient.

Each partner is supposed to devote his or her entire professional time and energy, to the utmost of his or her skill and ability, to the advantage of the partnership and is not expected to engage in any other activities such as moonlighting. This does not preclude an individual physician partner from joining any other organizations that do not require the practice of any medical, surgical, or specialized practice for private benefit or advantage. This would be a sticky situation if one partner wanted to join an independent practice association (IPA) or physician hospital organization (PHO) and the others did not because the revenues would go to the partnership, even if only one partner advanced personal funds for membership fees and stock.

Usually, the partnership provides for study time and continuing medical education (CME) expenses. There is usually some clarification of vacation time and sick time benefits in the partnership agreement. These must all comply with the Family Medical Leave Act (FMLA) and Americans with Disabilities Act (ADA), if applicable to the organization because of business size and other considerations. It is best to check with the appropriate counsel on the applicability of vacation and sick time benefits.

Payment of such CME expenses for courses, attendance at meetings, travel, and other expenses is usually accomplished through a special account of the partnership.

Policies on unused vacation time and unused study time should be spelled out in the agreement as well. If additional leave is required, expect to see a provision that the basic partnership draw is reduced by some amount. Sometimes when a partner will not be available for ordinary practice, other than on weekly days off or when prevented by illness or injury, the time is coupled as vacation time, as in a combined time-off scenario.

PARTNER DISABILITY BENEFITS

As an active partner prevented from conducting his or her ordinary practice as the direct result of illness or injury, or complications of pregnancy, a flat sum of money is often paid for the first 6 months of continuous disability. It is usually not too grand of a stipend but is just enough to get by. It all depends on how well the practice is doing and how much reserve is available to pay out higher amounts. This amount is paid to a partner who, at the commencement of the disability, might not have completed 1 full year's active membership in the partnership. The longer you are a partner, the more you get. Some agreements stipulate that after having completed 1 full year's active membership in the partnership, the partner might maintain the earnings ratio for the calendar year immediately preceding the one in which disability commences.

Disability benefits from the partnership usually are paid in addition to any benefits or income that would accrue to a partner where he or she then engaged in active practice. Any benefits accruing to the partner under disability insurance carried for the partner by the partnership, with premiums charged by the latter, would be held against the individual partner's distributable income.

Often, the partnership agreement stipulates some limit as to the time that a partner can continue to receive partnership disability benefits. Three years seems to be the norm in the business. If a partner's disability will continue longer than 1 year, the partnership may allow for termination of that partner on the grounds of impairment and carry out the termination either at the end of the year or at any subsequent time before resumption of active practice by the partner as a member of the partnership. If the partner is not so terminated, the value of the disabled partner's interest in accounts receivable might be determined as of the end of the second full month of disability, and the amount determined might be carried on the partnership's books, without interest, for a period of time set forth in the agreement. If the disabled partner is not terminated, he or she may usually resume active practice as a member of the partnership. Often, there is a provision for the automatic termination of a partner if the partner does not resume active practice within a certain time frame. In this case, his or her interest in the partnership is often liquidated in accordance with the partnership agreement.

If the partner's disability continues longer than the stated period of time in the agreement, and within the time permitted, the disabled partner can resume active practice as a firm member, the disabled partner is usually eligible for basic draw for the remainder of the calendar year in which he or she resumes active practice, if he or she was eligible for the basic draw for the calendar year in which the disability commenced.

If any controversy arises concerning the existence, cause, duration, or extent of disability claimed by any of the partners, a majority of the members of the partnership may designate two or more physicians who are not members of the partnership to examine the partner claiming disability and to report their findings. This again may come under ADA guidelines and would definitely intrude on the partner's right to privacy, as a copy of the report would be delivered to the partner claiming disability. Then, most likely, a decision that would be binding upon all members of the partnership would probably be made by vote of a majority of all partners at a meeting.

In most cases, membership in the partnership may be terminated in one of the following ways:

1. By resignation
2. By vote of two-thirds of all active partners to remove a partner
3. By the death of a partner

Usually, a partner will be deemed to have resigned from the partnership as of the effective date of his or her withdrawal from the partnership of which all the partners of the partnership are members. This leads to more administrator nightmares and CPA and legal expenses.

The partnership interest of a deceased partner is usually considered sold on the date of his or her death to the other members of the partnership, in equal shares. (How morbid!) In all likelihood, they get the funeral arrangements under way first and console the surviving spouse. Then, the purchase price for the sale of the deceased partner's interest in the partnership is computed and allocated as of the date of death. (I keep having this vision of vultures.)

The cash portion of the purchase price computed is then paid over a stated period of time to the estate, often with interest on each installment at the lowest annual rate permitted by the Internal Revenue Code of 1954, or successor provision, without the imputation of interest. The first monthly installment is then paid on a stated day following the deceased partner's death.

Each partner is party to this agreement, and it usually irrevocably constitutes the partnership as his or her agent to make the cash payments to the estate. The partnership then furnishes each partner with an annual report of any payments made on the partner's behalf, showing separately the principal and interest components thereof. Payments made under this situation on a partner's behalf are most often treated as distributions to that partner, and his or her capital account is adjusted accordingly, but that requires even more CPA involvement and guidance.

The capital account of any deceased partner as of the valuation date (taking into account the deceased partner's share of partnership income for the taxable year of the partnership closing as to the deceased partner on the date of his or her death) is usually divided equally among the partners purchasing his or her partnership interest. The capital accounts of the remaining purchasing partners are also adjusted to reflect any election in effect under IRC section 754.

(Many consultants have asked me to form a partnership with them. Having written this explanation of the trials and procedures, now I really know why I do not want to do this. Partnership is right for some folks but not for everyone.)

The partnership interest of a partner whose membership in the partnership has terminated for any reason except for his or her death is often completely liquidated by the partnership pursuant to the IRC. The payments to be made in liquidation of the interest of a partner are then computed and allocated as provided in their partnership agreement.

Payments for the liquidation of a partner's interest in the partnership will be made as follows: As of the effective date of termination of the outgoing partner's membership, the outgoing partner is usually relieved of his or her share of partnership liabilities. That is something you want to make sure of. Here is one instance where attorneys earn their fees.

The cash portion of the purchase price is computed by the agreement and is paid in monthly installments, without interest, beginning on a certain specified date in the agreement. Typically, the price for the sale or liquidation of a partner's interest in the partnership is calculated as the sum of (1) the ongoing partner's share of partnership liabilities as of the effective date of termination of his or her interest; plus (2) the balance of the outgoing partner's capital account, computed as of the end of the partnership's taxable year during which the partner's interest terminates; plus (3) the partner's share of the partnership's accounts receivable, computed as provided in the partnership agreement. This should be spelled out clearly for anyone to understand. The less clear the partnership agreement is, the more prone the partnership is to outsider intervention (in the form of arbitration or mediation).

The price for the sale or liquidation of a partner's interest is then allocated as follows: The portion of the price attributable to the partner's share of accounts receivable is usually in full payment for his or her interest in the unrealized receivables of the partnership, within the meaning of IRC regulations.

The balance of the price is customarily attributable to the partner's interest in the property of the partnership, consisting of the partnership's tangible assets, valued at their adjusted basis, and the cash and cash-equivalents of the partnership. In the case of a liquidation of a partner's interest, the portion of the price allocated is considered as paid in exchange for the partner's interest in partnership property, within the meaning of IRC regulations.

Payments made during any calendar year are usually apportioned as follows: Any assumption or release of the outgoing partner's share of the partnership liabilities is usually considered a payment. All other payments are considered made in the proportion that the total payments due under that provision, after reduction for liabilities assumed or released, bear to the total of all payments due after such reduction.

Unless another date is agreed upon in writing and signed by the outgoing partner and by a majority of the continuing partners within so many days following termination of a partner's membership, the date of valuation of a partner's interest in the partnership's accounts receivable is usually the last day of the calendar month within which falls the end of the second month after the termination of the partnership. At least that is usually what is stipulated in many agreements. Or, in cases where military active duty is involved, the date is the last day of the calendar month within which the date of discontinuing active practice with the partnership occurs in the case of a partner on active duty in the armed forces of the United States who will not resume full partnership practice by the end of so many (usually 3) years. In the face of what has happened with the war and reserve deployments since the first edition of this book was published, these terms may indeed be longer.

In the case of a resignation the value of the ongoing business is assessed on the last day of the calendar month within which the partnership business is concluded in all matters except as otherwise provided in the partnership agreement. The executive committee or any member thereof serves at the pleasure of the partners and may be replaced at any partnership meeting by vote of the majority of the partners. Members of the executive committee will receive such compensation for service on the executive committee as the partnership may from time to time determine appropriate.

The executive committee usually has the power to execute leases and contracts, other than contracts for the purchase of real estate, on such terms as it may determine to incur obligations on behalf of the partnership in connection with the business of the partnership, and in connection therewith to execute on behalf of the partners any and all documents necessary, incidental, and convenient to the carrying out of the intention and purpose of the partnership. As this includes the signing of managed care agreements, determine the experience of these partners before quietly agreeing to abide by their decisions. This could make or break the practice these days.

Actions requiring a vote of the partnership usually require a vote of the majority of all active partners. None of the partners, during the continuance of the partnership, should be required to assume any liability for another or others by means of endorsement, or by becoming guarantor or surety, without first obtaining the written consent of the other partners.

During the continuance of the partnership, each member, at his or her own expense, should carry personal liability insurance in the amount of at least $500,000 for injuries to one person and at least $1 million for any single accident on all automobiles owned or regularly operated by a partner or his or her family until the resignation is effective, except as otherwise provided by negotiation or the partnership agreement. In the case of a termination, it is often the last day of the calendar month within which a vote to terminate the membership of a partner occurs; for retirement, it is the last day of the calendar month during which a partner reaches the mandatory retirement age.

Many partnership agreements also contain language regarding noncompete restrictions. These should always be reviewed by counsel knowledgeable in antitrust law. A partner resigning or whose membership has been terminated in any manner authorized by the partnership agreement is restricted as to the practice of medicine or surgery within a certain mile radius of the partnership and within a period of time next following their resignation or other termination. In the event of a partner's noncompliance with the time period, there is usually a nasty court battle.

I remember three orthopedic surgeons who had a partnership agreement that dissolved. We will call them A, B, and C. A and B were long established in practice. When you thought of one, you thought of the other—A and B's practice. Then, they added C. C practiced with them as a partner for a few years. Then, one day, he struck out on his own. Yes, he had the typical noncompete language, but he defied it. Not only did he move immediately next door, but he arranged to have his telephone number different by only the first three numbers, and he took the established practice administrator with him. Then, a few years later, B moved out and took up office space less than a mile down the road and took the succeeding office administrator with him. A little bad blood goes a long way in a community. Think before you sign.

An executive committee appointed by a majority vote of the partners often manages partnerships. The executive committee exercises all the powers of the partnership in the conduct and operation living in the same household. Again, the attorneys earn their consultation fee here when giving good advice.

All expenses of a personal nature incurred by the several partners for membership fees in professional societies, medical and surgical publications, attendance at professional lectures or courses, operation and maintenance of automobiles, or otherwise are most often borne by the partners individually without reimbursement from the partnership.

The partnership often will carry malpractice insurance in the amount of $1 million to $3 million at the partnership's expense. In addition, the partnership will usually also provide "tail coverage" for any partner or employee who leaves the practice for any reason.

Partnership is something to aspire to only when you know you want to remain conjoined to the other members of the group for some time. As you can see by this chapter, it is complex, fiercely regulated, and paper intensive. It is not something to be entered into lightly or if there is any doubt that the arrangement might be temporary.

15 Medical Director Positions

The medical director is the individual responsible for the supervision of medical providers and assurance of adequate coverage and quality of services provided for center patients. This person reports to the executive director of a healthcare organization.

In 1995, the Medical Group Management Association (MGMA) collected data on medical directorships. Of the 545 groups who responded, only 168 had contracts. It is interesting to note that most of the medical directorships were in title only, and many received no extra compensation for their efforts. Many of the smaller one- to ten-physician practices did not pay their medical directors, and others paid a small honorarium. As the numbers grew into the 100-plus physician range, salaries hovered in the $200,000 annual salary range. One other observation I made was that areas with less managed care penetration paid their medical directors less in comparison to practices of similar size and specialty—perhaps because there were fewer dollars to spend on such roles?

As a leader, the medical director works in cooperation with the executive director and the clinical services director and is responsible for utilizing a balanced approach, which includes the perspectives of all disciplines involved in healthcare delivery.

The role requires flexibility to accommodate the diversity of the physicians, dentists, and midlevel providers employed. He or she supervises day-to-day clinical operations in conjunction with the clinic directors, administrative staff, and other professional staff. The position is that of a physician recommended to the executive director, and it is most often appointed by the board of directors with input from the executive director.

The duties and responsibilities of the medical director involve program planning and implementation. The medical director is expected to assist the clinical services director with development of annual goals and objectives for medical staff, ensure implementation of the healthcare plan, and most often direct day-to-day clinical operations through clinical directors and department heads.

In the organizational role, the medical director participates, is a voting member, and chairs the executive committee of the provider staff, and often appoints chairpersons of the medical staff committees.

Budgeting is another task often relegated to the medical director, who may recommend fee schedule changes to the executive director, and assist in the review of financial status on a monthly basis with the executive committee. The medical director often presents budget considerations to the executive committee and executive director.

In a supervisory role, the medical director provides for orientation of medical staff to the practice, prepares the provider schedule with input from the clinical services director and clinic directors, and often participates in the evaluations of performance of the provider staff annually and reviews performance with the clinical services director. Additionally, the medical director monitors the professional conduct and practices of all medical staff (including consultants and volunteers) and develops and implements the center's midlevel practitioner policies and goals.

In this directorship, the medical director plans in-service training for members of the professional staff through the staff education committee and develops and defines the roles and responsibilities of the medical staff.

The executive director, on relevant medical and legal aspects of the medical practice, expects regular consultation of the medical director.

A major role in the management of clinical quality and adherence to the standards of care is the responsibility of the medical director together with the clinical staff. He or she appoints the chairperson of the quality assurance committee, ensures the quality of medical care provided to patients, ensures proper credentialing of the clinical staff, and reviews annually the roles and responsibilities of the medical staff in conjunction with the clinical services director. In addition, the medical director is required to review and update treatment protocols annually as approved by the provider staff. The medical director's role is foremost in the oversight of the implementation of a peer review system that includes problem identification by the medical staff, patient care protocols, and reviewing quality assurance audits per state law and internal policy. The medical director also participates in and oversees the development of health risk management protocols.

As an internal liaison, the medical director facilitates communication and information flow with various committees and departments and sets goals with the committees and departments. The medical director also has a role as external liaison and coordinator in the performance or delegation of patient relations tasks. He or she initiates and promotes communication and information flow with external health agencies and organizations such as area hospitals, the county medical society, health departments, and various health-related agencies in coordination with the clinical services director.

Additionally, there are general administration duties that include oversight, administration, and delegation to clinic directors, including the tasks of coordination and troubleshooting medical and support services interface programs and procedures, and full participation in interviewing and qualifying candidates for the medical staff openings that arise. The medical director gets the highs and lows of personnel administration in the recommendation of hiring and firing of the provider staff to the executive director. He or she also recommends to the executive committee of the provider staff and participates in the final determination of disciplinary actions and terminations of the provider staff. Additionally, the medical director recommends merit or step increases and recognition or awards for provider staff to the executive director after consultation with the executive committee of the provider staff and reviews and updates the principles of practice and the policies and procedures for provider staff.

The medical directorship is evaluated by the board of directors in most cases, with input from the executive director and clinical services director.

The medical director must be an eligible physician licensed to practice medicine in the state in which he or she is employed, or making medical decisions on patients and the evaluation of other physicians in active practice. He or she should be board certified or eligible in a particular specialty and have at least 2 years' experience in active practice.

Interpersonal skills are a must for this position, as it is a people position rather than a secluded desk job. Therefore, the medical director should have good communication skills and problem-solving experience. What I hear most of all is that it is a thankless job, but somebody's got to do it.

16 Concierge Medicine: Contracting with the New Employer of Physicians—Consumers

Concierge care is a new and promising option for physicians who are tired of what has become the traditional managed care practice. I have heard the traditional managed care practice referred to as the "hamster wheel" practice when referred to by a concierge physician. What is it that they love so much about this style of privatized healthcare delivery?

For one, the money, if one builds a full private practice of about 600 patients. The traditional practice can have 3,000 to 4,000 patients per physician and, in primary care, a 75 percent overhead-to-gross ratio. Concierge practices generally run less than 30 percent overhead-to-gross ratios.

Second, the relationship with patients is distinctly different. There is more time to get to know patients, understand how they take care of themselves and others around them, what is important, lifestyle choices, and preventive health habits.

This mode of private practice is also referred to by different names, including

- Boutique practice
- Direct-care practice
- Platinum care practice
- Retainer practice
- Membership practice
- Premiere care

The models vary slightly, as do the terms, but for the most part, there is little to no managed care, capitation, and in many cases, no Medicare or Medicaid participation. In some cases, physicians actually render care to corporate executives at their places of business, or see patients at their homes when necessary.

Physicians can often also provide custom on site flu-shot programs as part of the corporate package they offer to local businesses to keep the company's entire office protected. This service is sometimes extended to all employees of any company providing three or more full corporate memberships to their staff. Corporate memberships also provide benefits to a company's visiting clients and executives should they need medical care while in town. They market the idea on the basis that keeping senior staff healthy and helping them do it conveniently and without unnecessary time lost from work is just good business.

These concierge practices often list a number of "membership benefits" for the price charged per year, including

- More time with the physician
- Same- or next-day appointments
- Appointment scheduling that reduces or eliminates time waiting to see the doctor
- "Open block" scheduling
- Arranging an appropriate amount of time for appointments rather than trying to fit patients into a 10-minute slot
- 24-hour, 7-day-a-week access to the physician or his or her covering physician in the event of absence
- Emergency, after-hours appointments
- Home and office visits when medically necessary
- Online access to your medical records in case of out-of-town emergencies
- Case management for chronic or complex medical issues
- Complimentary annual physical exam and wellness conferences
- Personalized wellness plans
- Patient education
- Coordination and facilitation of appointments and member patient care with specialists (in some cases, even visiting the specialist with the member patient when appropriate)
- Use of their patient lounge while at their office (entertainment and refreshment center, computer with broadband, and more)
- Online services such as medical information, prescription refills, secure online e-mail with the physician, online laboratory results, and more
- Many member privileges extended to the member's personal and business out-of-town guests while they are visiting
- Discounts for related health and wellness services and products
- Additional services to be added according to the needs of VIPs (built around patient needs, rather than managed care cost containment philosophies)

CONCIERGE PRACTICE FEE AGREEMENTS

In my experience establishing these practices for physicians as a consultant, the fee agreements vary. In some cases, the physicians would rather charge one price for the entire year inclusive of office visits. Others opt for a fee-for-service model where the members purchase an annual physical and access to the physician for longer office visits and a limited-access practice. In that case, each office visit has an associated charge for evaluation and management services, in addition to any related diagnostic testing or injections, medications, and so forth.

With both plans, a properly coded invoice is tendered to the patient so that the patient may file for reimbursements that may be due for out-of-network services covered by their insurance. In the case of Medicare patients, visits are always disclaimed as a noncovered service using the appropriate CMS forms if the physician has relinquished his or her Medicare participating provider status.

Also commonly seen in the concierge model is a reduction of the cost to collect fees. In most practices that I have established, a form is executed by the member patient that is a multiuse preauthorization to bill their credit card on file for services for the member and possibly the family if it is a family plan. This enables the practice to charge for visits, no-shows, and short-notice cancellations that may be addressed in the membership agreement.

One example of such an agreement appears below.

Sample Concierge Member Billing Agreement

DATE: _____/_____/_____

I acknowledge the following by my signature below:

1. I agree to pay my bill in full at the time services are provided, for any type of encounter, whether it is a traditional Office Visit, a Phone Visit, or an online Virtual Visit. For services performed at my request outside of an encounter (e.g., prescription refill, form completion, or referral), I agree to pay for these services in advance.
2. I understand that [Practice Name] and [Physician Name] are not contracted providers with any insurance companies, and are considered "out of network" and their services may not be covered by my insurance. I understand that [Physician Name] will attempt to work in the constraints of my insurance benefits if possible and at my request.
3. I agree to provide a valid driver's license or other form of identification to be kept securely on file at [Practice Name].
4. I agree to provide a valid credit or debit card to be kept securely on file at [Practice Name] and hereby authorize employees of [Practice Name] to charge this card for services provided to me and my dependents. I will be notified of these charges in advance of them occurring.
5. I verify that I have reviewed my insurance information listed with [Practice Name], and that it is correct. I understand that I am responsible for knowing what facilities or specialist physicians are preferred with my insurance, and what services may or may not be covered by my insurance. I will provide this information to [Physician Name] when I request he/she assist me in obtaining recommended services "in network" in the hopes my insurance will cover them.
6. I understand that [Practice Name] may provide a claim for me to file with my primary insurance carrier as a courtesy, but that it is my responsibility to follow up with my insurance company to ensure reimbursement. I understand that [Practice Name] cannot act as an intermediary between me and my insurance company to effect payment.
7. I hereby request and authorize [Practice Name]'s physician and personnel to deliver medical care to myself or my dependents.
8. I understand that medical records are the property of the physician of [Practice Name]; however, I am entitled to a copy, with sufficient advanced notice, upon my written request (patients aged 18 and older must sign their

own medical record release form). I understand that there may be a charge of $20 for copies of my medical records.

9. I acknowledge that I can obtain a copy of [Practice Name]'s Privacy Practices/Patient's Privacy Rights upon request.

10. I understand that a $60 fee will be charged for all appointments missed or not cancelled at least 24 hours in advance.

_____   _____
Patient/Guardian signature   Date

On the date of the first visit, often the practice has the patient complete the following authorization form for the first and future visits. The form is often worded as indicated below:

By my signature below, I authorize [Clinic Name] to make charges to my credit or debit card for medical services provided by [Clinic Name]. I will be notified in advance of these charges occurring, and may receive a copy of the receipt at my request.

Name as it appears on card: _____

Type of Card (circle):   Mastercard   VISA

Card # : _____ - _____ - _____ - _____

Expiration Date: _____/20 _____

Zip code where statements for this card are sent: _____

I authorize [Clinic Name] to securely store this credit/debit card information and charge it as listed above.

Signature: _____

Date: _____ / _____ /20 _____

In addition to myself, this card may be used for the following people:

_____
_____

ONLINE SERVICES

Busy patients like to interact with their physician online at times. In the concierge model, many physicians have a way to interact with patients through their choice of Google Health or Microsoft HealthVault, which integrates with their electronic medical records system. In addition, they often make available the following 24/7 online services:

- Medical Web links library
- Medical information library

- Prescription refill requests
- Laboratory results
- Patient medical records
- Send a message to your physician
- Request/change/cancel an appointment

In Appendix 7, I included a sample Concierge Physician Membership Agreement.

Appendix 1: Full Partnership Agreement

(All parties and names are intended to be fictitious.)

Warning: This agreement is problematic in that it may have several Stark II implications, Americans with Disabilities Act (ADA) concerns, and other matters of employment and health law. Always check with experienced legal counsel and your professional certified public accountant before proceeding with a partnership agreement. This is an example combining several partnership agreements I encountered in my research—a warning that they may not have been reviewed and maintained in accordance with current legal requirements. The purpose of the inclusion of this agreement is to provide a glimpse into the matters covered categorically, not substantively.

The undersigned acknowledges that he/she has been invited to become a partner in the group of physicians, surgeons, and dentists operating under the name and style of "The Masters Clinic."

The undersigned hereby accepts said offer of partnership and in becoming a partner in said partnership hereby agrees to be bound by all of the terms and provisions of the Partnership Agreement dated the 20th day of February, 2009. The undersigned, as a partner, also agrees to be bound by any amendments to said Partnership Agreement which may be hereafter adopted in the same manner as to the same extent as though the undersigned had been one of the parties to said Partnership Agreement as amended. The undersigned hereby further agrees to be bound fully and to observe faithfully all the rules and regulations of said partnership, which may have been adopted by said partners or which now are in force or which may hereafter be adopted pursuant to the terms of the said Partnership Agreement as amended.

IN WITNESS WHEREOF, the undersigned has hereunto subscribed his/her name and affixed his/her seal this 20th day of February, 2009.

(Seal)

Printed Name

WHEREAS, the parties have heretofore been conducting a medical practice in Partnership as "The Masters Clinic," and NOW, THEREFORE, the parties agree:

1.0 Duration of partnership
The existing Partnership shall continue until dissolved by written vote of two-thirds of the then active Partners, and until so ended, the termination of interest of any Partner shall not dissolve the Partnership with respect to the remaining members.

2.0 New partners

New Partners may be admitted by a vote of two-thirds of the existing Partners. New Partners shall execute a counterpart of this Agreement, which shall be binding on the parties. Each new Partner shall contribute $4,000.00 to the capital of the Partnership, as provided in Section 10.2.

3.0 Capital accounts

Capital accounts shall be maintained for each Partner as required by Section 704 of the Internal Revenue Code, as amended (hereinafter, "IRC"), and regulations thereunder. A Partner shall not be entitled to demand, receive, or withdraw any part of such Partner's capital account or to receive any distribution from the Partnership, except as provided in this Agreement. Any Partner who shall receive an Interest in the Partnership, or whose Interest in the Partnership shall be increased or decreased by means of a transfer of all or part of the Interest of another Partner, shall have a capital account which reflects such transfer. Capital accounts may also reflect elections in effect under IRC Section 754, to the extent permitted under IRC Section 704(b).

4.0 Records and accounts

Full and accurate records and accounts of the entire business and affairs of the Partnership shall be maintained in the Partnership office under the supervision of the Partners, and shall be available for inspection by each Partner at all times. Such records shall include up-to-date accounts of all capital assets, income, receivables, liabilities, and disbursements. All professional fees received by the Partners and their associates shall be paid over to the Partnership cashier. The books of the Partnership shall be balanced and closed as of the last day of December in each year at which time the profits and losses of the Partnership and the indebtedness, if any, of the individual Partners to the Partnership shall be ascertained, settled, and paid. All patient histories shall remain the exclusive property of the Partnership.

5.0 Duties of partners

Each Partner shall devote his/her entire professional time and energy, to the utmost of his/her skill and ability, to the advantage of Partnership and shall not engage in any medical, surgical, or specialized practice for private benefit or advantage.

6.0 Vacations; study time

6.1 Each Partner while regularly engaged in active practice shall be entitled during each calendar year to:

 (a) Four weeks vacation time; and
 (b) Provided he/she shall then be qualified for a Basic Draw under Section 11.2 hereof, an additional fifteen (15) days for postgraduate study, attendance at medical meetings, etc., herein termed "study time," and while in attendance, the Partner shall also receive such reimbursement for his/her expenses (including registration fees) as the Partnership may from time to time determine.

6.2 Unused vacation time and unused study time may be accumulated up to totals of eight (8) weeks, and thirty (30) days, respectively. Additional vacation time, as distinguished from disability privileges granted in Article 7.0, but not to exceed eight (8) weeks during a single calendar year, may be taken by a Partner on condition that for each seven (7) days or major portion thereof so taken, the amount of Basic Draw (as defined in Section 11.2[a] hereof) to which such Partner would otherwise be entitled under this Agreement for such calendar year shall be reduced by 1/52nd.

6.3 The time when a Partner shall not be available for ordinary practice, other than on weekly days off or when prevented by illness or injury, shall be coupled as vacation time, except as otherwise provided by this Agreement.

7.0 Disability benefits

An active Partner prevented from conducting his/her ordinary practice as the direct result of illness or injury (hereinafter, "disability"), other than one of the character described in Section 7.6 hereof, shall qualify for disability benefits as provided herein. For the purposes of this Article 7.0 "disability" shall include, without limitation, complications of pregnancy, and the period of recuperation following childbirth.

7.1 During the first six (6) months of continuous disability, One Thousand Dollars ($1,000.00) per month shall be paid (1) to a Partner who, at the commencement of such disability, shall not have completed one full year's active membership in the Partnership; and (2) to a Partner who, having completed one full year's active membership in the Partnership, shall have maintained the earnings ratio specified in Section 11.2(a) for the calendar year immediately preceding the one in which disability commences. Should such disability continue for more than one month, the sum of $2,000.00 per month shall be paid to a Partner who qualifies as above stated. Such payment of $2,000.00 per month shall be limited to a five-month period.

7.2 The benefits payable under Section 7.1 shall be in addition to (1) any income which would accrue to a Partner under Section 11.2, paragraphs (b), (c), or (d), were he/she then engaged in active practice, and (2) any benefits accruing to such Partner under disability insurance carried for said Partner by the Partnership, with premiums charged by the latter against the individual Partner's distributable income.

7.3 Payments under Section 7.1 shall be limited to a maximum of six (6) months during any period of three (3) consecutive years.

7.4 If a Partner's disability shall continue longer than one (1) year, such fact shall constitute a sufficient ground for termination of the Partner's membership, either at the end of such year or at any subsequent time before resumption of active practice by such Partner as a member of the Partnership. If not so terminated in the manner provided in Section 8.1, the value of the disabled Partner's interest in accounts receivable shall be determined as of the end of the second full month of disability and the amount so determined shall be carried on the Partnership books, without interest, for a period not to exceed three (3) years. Until termination of a disabled Partner's membership, he/she may resume active practice as a member of the Partnership. Failure to do so within three (3) years from the commencement of disability shall automatically terminate the Partner's membership.

Upon the termination of a Partner's membership pursuant to this Section 7.4, his/her interest in the Partnership shall be liquidated in accordance with Articles 8.0 and 9.0 hereof.

7.5 If disability shall continue longer than one (1) year, and within the time permitted, the disabled Partner shall resume active practice as a firm member, he/she shall be eligible for a Basic Draw under the provisions of Section 11.2(a) for the remainder of the calendar year in which he/she resumes active practice if he/she was eligible for such Basic Draw for the calendar year in which such disability commenced.

7.6 No Partner shall be entitled to any benefit under Section 7.1 if his/her disability shall be occasioned directly or indirectly by alcohol, drug addiction or by psychiatric disorder.

(Author's note: All these disability issues may be ADA issues. If you see this, check with counsel.)

7.7 If any controversy shall arise concerning the existence, cause, duration, or extent of disability claimed by any Partners, a majority of the members of the Partnership may designate two (2) or more physicians, not members of the Partnership, to examine the Partner claiming disability and to report their findings. A copy of this report shall be delivered to the Partner claiming disability and thereafter a decision, binding upon all members of the Partnership, shall be made by vote of a majority of all Partners at a meeting to be held on at least ten (10) days' notice.

8.0 Resignation, removal, or death of partner; sale or liquidation of partnership interest

8.1 In addition to the provisions contained in Articles 7.0, 16.0, and 20.0, membership in the Partnership may be terminated (1) by resignation, by vote of two-thirds of all active Partners to remove a Partner, or (2) by the death of a Partner. For purposes of this Article 8.0, a Partner shall be deemed to have resigned from the Partnership as of the effective date of his/her withdrawal from, a Partnership of which all the Partners of this Partnership are members.

8.2

(a) The Partnership interest of a deceased Partner shall be sold on the date of his/her death to the other members of the Partnership, in equal shares. The purchase price for the sale of a deceased Partner's interest in the Partnership shall be computed and allocated as provided in Article 9.0.

Payments for the purchase of the interest of a deceased Partner shall be made as follows:

(i) As of the date of the deceased Partner's death, the other members of the Partnership shall assume, in equal shares, the deceased Partner's share of the liabilities of the Partnership on that date.

(ii) The cash portion of the purchase price computed under Article 9.0 shall be paid in sixty (60) equal monthly installments, with interest on each installment at the lowest annual rate permitted by the Internal Revenue Code of 1954, or successor provision, without the imputation of interest. The first monthly installment shall be paid on the last day of fourth full calendar month following the deceased Partner's death.

(c) Each party to this Agreement hereby irrevocably constitutes the Partnership as his/her agent to make the cash payments due under this Article 8.0. The Partnership shall furnish each Partner with an annual report of any such payments made on the Partner's behalf, showing separately the principal and interest components thereof. Payments made under this paragraph (c) on a Partner's behalf shall be treated as distributions to that Partner, and his/her capital account shall be adjusted accordingly.

(d) The capital account of any deceased Partner as of the valuation date (taking into account the deceased Partner's share of Partnership income for the taxable year of the Partnership closing as to the deceased Partner on the date of his/her death) shall be divided equally among the Partners purchasing his/her Partnership interest under this Section 8.2. The capital accounts of such purchasing Partners shall also be adjusted to reflect any election in effect under IRC Section 754.

8.3

(a) The Partnership interest of a Partner whose membership in the Partnership has terminated for any reason under this Agreement, except for his/her death, shall be completely liquidated by the Partnership pursuant to IRC Section 736. The payments to be made in liquidation of the interest of such a Partner shall be computed and allocated as provided in Article 9.0.

  Payments for the liquidation of a Partner's interest in the Partnership shall be made as follows:

(i) As of the effective date of termination of the outgoing Partner's membership, the outgoing Partner shall be relieved of his/her share of Partnership liabilities.

(ii) The cash portion of the purchase price computed under Article 9.0 shall be paid in sixty (60) equal monthly installments, without interest, beginning on the last day of the fourth full calendar month following the month in which the effective date of the termination occurred, and continuing monthly thereafter. An outgoing Partner's noncompliance with Article 12.0 of this Agreement shall postpone for a period equal to the duration of such noncompliance the Partnership's obligation to make payments under this Section 8.3.

9.0 Computation and allocation of price sale or liquidation of partnership interest

9.1 The price for the sale or liquidation of a Partner's interest in the Partnership shall be the sum of (1) the ongoing Partner's share of Partnership liabilities as of the effective date of termination of his/her interest; plus (2) the balance of the outgoing Partner's capital account, computed as of the end of the Partnership taxable year during which the Partner's interest terminates; plus (3) the Partner's share of the Partnership's accounts receivable, computed as provided in Section 9.5.

9.2 The price for the sale or liquidation of a Partner's interest, computed under Section 9.1, shall be allocated as follows:

(a) The portion of the price attributable to the Partner's share of accounts receivable shall be in full payment for his/her interest in the unrealized receivables of the Partnership, within the meaning of IRC Section 751.

(b) The balance of the price shall be attributable to the Partner's interest in the property of the Partnership, consisting of (1) the Partnership's tangible assets, valued at their adjusted basis, and (2) the cash and cash equivalents of the Partnership. In the case of a liquidation of a Partner's interest, the portion of the price allocated under this paragraph (b) shall be considered as paid in exchange for the Partner's interest in Partnership property, within the meaning of Section 736(b).

9.3 Payments made pursuant to this Article 9.0 during any calendar year shall be apportioned as follows:

(a) Any assumption or release of the outgoing Partner's share of the Partnership liabilities shall be considered a payment under Section 9.2(b).

(b) All other payments shall be considered made under Section 9.2(b) in the proportion that the total payments due under that provision, after reduction for liabilities assumed or released, bear to the total of all payments due under Section 9.2, after such reduction.

9.4 Unless another date shall be agreed upon in writing, signed by the outgoing Partner and by a majority of the continuing Partners within ten (10) days following termination of a Partner's membership, the date of valuation of a Partner's interest in the Partnership's accounts receivable shall be:

(a) The last day of the calendar month within which falls the end of the second month of continued disability in the case of a Partner covered by Section 7.4 whose membership shall be terminated by reason of continued disability for longer than one (1) year or, if not previously terminated for that reason, shall be later terminated either by the Partner's resignation or because of failure to resume active practice within three (3) years following commencement of his/her disability;

(b) The last day of the calendar month within which the date of discontinuing active practice with the Partnership occurs in the case of a Partner on active duty in the Armed Forces of the United States who shall not resume full Partnership practice by the end of three (3) years;

(c) The last day of the calendar month within which a Partner's resignation is effective, except as otherwise provided in paragraphs (a) or (b) of this Section 9.4;

(d) The last day of the calendar month within which a vote to terminate the membership of a Partner occurs under Section 8.1;

(e) The last day of the calendar month during which the membership of a Partner is terminated by death, except as provided in paragraphs (a) or (b) of this Section 9.4; or

(f) The last day of the calendar month during which a Partner reaches the mandatory retirement age.

9.5 The interest of a Partner in the accounts receivable of the Partnership as of the applicable valuation date shall be determined as follows:

Compute a gross receivable value as follows:

   (i) No value shall be attributed to accounts more than one (1) year old;

  (ii) Accounts one (1) year old, or less, shall be valued at seventy-five percent (75 percent) of face amount;

 (iii) Multiply the amount determined in subdivision (ii) hereof by a fraction whose numerator shall equal the adjusted gross charges (including laboratory, x-ray, and audiology), as customarily computed by the Partnership, earned by such member during the twelve (12) months immediately preceding the valuation date, and the whole denominator shall equal the total adjusted gross charges (including laboratory, x-ray, and audiology), as customarily computed by the Partnership, earned during the same period by all Partners (including the outgoing Partner) who are active Partners on the valuation date.

Multiply the gross receivable value determined in paragraph (a) hereof by a fraction the numerator of which is the number of full years in excess of five (5) the Partner has been a member of the Partnership (which numerator shall be zero if the Partner has not been a Partner for six full years) and the denominator of which is ten (10); provided, however, that such fraction shall not exceed one (1).

10.0 Distributions

10.1 Partnership income in excess of any reserve deemed necessary by the Executive Committee shall be distributed among the Partners in accordance with Article 11.0.

10.2 The capital contribution required of a new Partner shall be made by withholding from the distribution of the income allocated to such new Partner the annual sum of $800.00 for each of the first five years of the new Partner's membership in the Partnership.

11.0 Income allocations

(Author's note: There may be a few contradictions to Stark II in this section. On older partnership agreements, it would be wise to have this reviewed by a health law attorney well versed in the latest developments of Stark II. Each set of circumstances must be studied on its own merits.)

11.1 Except as otherwise provided in Articles 6.0, 7.0, and 16.0, the right to share in Partnership income shall be limited to those Partners who are regularly engaged in active practice in the Partnership.

11.2 The respective shares of active Partners in Partnership income for each calendar year shall be allocated as follows:

  (a) A Basic Draw of One Thousand Dollars ($1,000.00) (Author's note: Just a number!) per month shall be allocated (1) to each Partner during the first full calendar year of his/her active membership in the Partnership; and (2) to each other active Partner who earned cumulative total charges (including charges under paragraph [d] hereof) during the preceding calendar year equal to or in excess of one-half the amount that would result from dividing the cumulative total charges (including charges under paragraph [d] hereof) earned during the same period by all Partners who were active Partners throughout that period by the number of such Partners. In making the computation described in this subparagraph with respect to any Partner, any portion of the year during which that Partner did not conduct his/her ordinary practice while on disability status under Article 7.0, while on active duty in the Armed Forces under Article 16.0, or while absent on vacation or study time in excess of the time specified in Section 6.1, shall be excluded from the computation for all purposes.

(b) Any Partner who does not qualify for a Basic Draw under paragraph (a) hereof shall be allocated a share of Partnership net income, to be computed after deduction of study-time allowances under Article 6.0, but before deduction for the Basic Draw of any Partner, in the same proportion as the total of charges for services performed by him or her during that period bears to the total charges for services performed by all Partners during the same period.

(c) All remaining Partnership net income (after the allocations specified in paragraphs [a] and [b] for each calendar year) shall be allocated among all Partners eligible for a Basic Draw in the same proportions as the totals of their respective contributions to Partnership charges for services performed during the same period by all Partners entitled to benefits under this paragraph (c).

(Author's note: The following paragraph has a very loud potential "Stark Alarm.")

(d) For purposes of paragraphs (b) and (c) hereof, the term "Partnership net income" shall not include the net income from ancillary services. The net income from each ancillary service, such as laboratory, x-ray, and audiology, shall be allocated to each Partner based on the ratio of the charges for such service ordered by that Partner to the charges for such service ordered by all Partners.

11.3

(a) The annual income otherwise allocated under Section 11.2 for any Partnership fiscal year to any Partner who has been a member of the Partnership for fewer than five (5) full years as of the beginning of that Partnership fiscal year shall be reduced by (1) in the case of a Partner admitted to the Partnership before 1996, $1,000.00; or (2) in the case of a Partner admitted to the Partnership in 1986 or thereafter, $2,000.00.

(b) The amount of income by which any Partner's income allocation is reduced under Section 11.3(a) for any Partnership fiscal year shall be reallocated, using the formula specified in Section 11.2(b), among all active Partners who have been members of the Partnership for at least five (5) full years as of the beginning of that Partnership fiscal year.

11.4 The income allocation of a deceased Partner for the taxable year of his/her or her death shall be computed under Section 11.2 by substituting for the calendar year, in each paragraph hereunder, the portion of the calendar year ending on the valuation date specified in Section 9.4(e).

12.0 Agreement not to compete

12.1 A Partner resigning or whose membership shall be terminated in any manner authorized in this Agreement shall not practice medicine or surgery within a ten (10) mile radius within a period of five (5) years next following such resignation or other termination. In the event of a Partner's noncompliance with said Agreement during such five (5) year period, or any portion thereof, the effective period of the restriction shall be automatically extended for a period equal to the combined period or periods of noncompliance.

(Author's note: This may not be enforceable—always check with counsel.)

12.2 Each of the undersigned expressly agrees to accept and comply with said restrictions, and further that:

(a) Said restrictions are reasonable and just.
(b) Said restrictions shall survive the termination of membership of any Partner or Partners, so long as one or more of the present Partners shall continue the practice of medicine or surgery under the named entity;
(c) Enforcement of said restrictions is essential to the continued existence and growth of the Partnership and to maintain and improve the quality of scope of present and future members' professional services to the public.
(d) Violation would cause great, immeasurable, and irreparable damage to all remaining active Partners, which damage would continue at least throughout the entire period of violation.
(e) Each of the undersigned approved, accepted, and agreed to abide by substantially similar restrictions at the time of becoming a member of the existing Partnership or one of its predecessor organizations.
(f) Actual or threatened violation by any member or members may be enjoined by appropriate Court decree.

13.0 Partnership name

In the event of the termination of the interest of a Partner, the continuing Partners shall have the exclusive right to use the name.

14.0 Management

14.1 The Partners shall, by a majority vote, appoint an Executive Committee consisting of not fewer than three (3) and not more than five (5) Partners. The Executive Committee shall exercise all the powers of the Partnership in the conduct and operation of the Partnership business in all matters except as otherwise provided by this Agreement. The Executive Committee or any member thereof shall serve at the pleasure of the Partners, may be replaced at any Partnership meeting by vote of the majority of the Partners, and shall serve from year to year or until successors are appointed. Members of the Executive Committee shall receive such compensation for service on the Executive Committee as the Partnership may from time to time determine.

14.2 The Executive Committee shall, without limiting the foregoing Section 14.1, have the power to execute leases and contracts, other than contracts for the purchase of real estate, on such terms as it may determine; to incur obligations on behalf of the Partnership in connection with the business of the Partnership; and in connection therewith to execute on behalf of the Partners any and all documents necessary, incidental, and convenient to the carrying out of the intention and purpose of the Partnership.

14.3 Except as otherwise provided in this Agreement, actions requiring a vote of the Partnership shall require a vote of the majority of all active Partners.

15.0 Partners not to become sureties, etc.

None of the Partners, during the continuance of the Partnership, shall assume any liability for another or others by means of endorsement, or by becoming guarantor or surety, without first obtaining the written consent of all other Partners.

16.0 Service in the Armed Forces

In the event that one or more Partners shall be prevented from continuing active practice with the Partnership by reason of being on active duty as a member of any branch of the Armed Forces of the United States, and such Partner shall not resign from the Partnership, then, during the continuance of such tour of duty, but not longer than three (3) years, and during the continuance of this Partnership, such Partner shall be entitled to receive Two Hundred Dollars ($200.00) per month as his/her entire share of Partnership earnings during that period. If the Partner shall not resume full practice by the end of three (3) years, his/her membership in the Partnership shall then terminate. If the total of monthly payments theretofore made by the Partnership in accordance with this section have exceeded Two Thousand Four Hundred Dollars ($2,400.00), the amount of such excess shall be credited against the amount of the purchase price payable by the Partnership for his/her interest in the Partnership's accounts receivable. If within the three (3) year period the Partner shall resume active practice with the Partnership, such resumption shall be upon the same terms as to compensation set forth in Section 7.5.

(Author's note: If there's any question on military service or reserve duty clauses and you are in the military, check with the Military Judge Adjutant General's [JAG's] office for guidance and review.)

17.0 Liability insurance

During the continuance of this Partnership, each member, at his/her own expense, shall carry personal liability insurance in the amount of at least Five Hundred Thousand Dollars ($500,000.00) for injuries to one person and at least One Million Dollars ($1,000,000.00) for any single accident on all automobiles owned or regularly operated by him or her.

18.0 No reimbursement of personal expenses

All expenses of a personal nature incurred by the several Partners for membership fees in professional societies, medical and surgical publications, attendance at professional lectures or courses (except as otherwise provided in Article 6.0), operation and maintenance of automobiles, or otherwise, shall be borne by them individually without reimbursement from the Partnership.

19.0 Malpractice insurance

The group shall carry malpractice insurance in the amount of One Million Dollars ($1,000,000.00)/Three Million Dollars ($3,000,000.00) at the Masters Group's expense. In addition, the Masters Group shall also provide "Tail Coverage" for any Partner or employee who leaves the Masters Group for any reason.

20.0 Mandatory retirement

Retirement of a Partner shall be mandatory upon his/her reaching the age of Seventy (70) years. Such retirement shall be effective on the last day of the month in which the Partner's 70th birthday occurs. This provision, however, shall not apply to [name].

21.0 Amendment

Except as provided in Article 2.0 hereof, this Agreement may be altered or amended only by the affirmative vote of two-thirds of the Partners. Such amendment shall be effective as of the date adopted by the Partnership.

22.0 Assignment, sale, or transfer

Except as otherwise provided in the foregoing provisions Agreement, no assignment, sale, or transfer of the whole of any part of the Partnership interest of any member shall be effective.

23.0 Dispute resolution

23.1 Any dispute, claim, or controversy arising under or in connection with the terms of this Agreement shall be deemed for purposes of this Agreement to be a "Grievance."

   (a) Any and all Grievances shall be resolved exclusively through arbitration in accordance with the Voluntary Labor Arbitration Rules of the American Arbitration Association then in effect.
         The Arbitrator's decision will be final and binding and any and all Grievances shall be disposed of as follows:
   (i)   Any and all Grievances must be submitted in writing by the aggrieved party.
   (ii) Within thirty (30) days following the submission of the written Grievance, the party to whom the Grievance is submitted shall respond in writing. If no written response is submitted, or the Grievance is otherwise not resolved, within thirty (30) days, the Grievances shall be deemed denied.
   (iii) If the Grievance is denied, either party may, within thirty (30) days of such denial refer the Grievance to arbitration in Denver City and County, Colorado, by filing a Demand for Arbitration with the American Arbitration Association office in such county and serving a copy thereof on the other party to this Agreement.
   (iv) The arbitrator shall be chosen in accordance with the Voluntary Labor Arbitration Rules of the American Arbitration Association then in effect, and the expense of the arbitration shall be shared equally by the Partner and the other members of the Partnership.

(v)   Any Grievance shall be deemed waived unless presented within the time limits specified above.

(vi)   The arbitrator shall not have jurisdiction or authority to change, add to, or subtract from any of the provisions of this Agreement.

(vii)   The arbitrator's sole authority shall be to interpret or apply the provisions of this Agreement.

(viii) Judgment upon the award rendered may be entered in any court having jurisdiction.

(ix)   The parties hereby acknowledge and agree that since arbitration is the exclusive remedy with respect to any Grievance, as defined above, neither party has the right to resort to any federal, state, or local court or administrative agency for the resolution of any Grievance. The parties further acknowledge and agree that any suit, action, or proceeding instituted in any federal, state, or local court or before any administrative agency with respect to any Grievance shall be dismissed with prejudice immediately upon submission to such court or agency of an executed copy of this Agreement.

(x)   The arbitration provisions hereof shall, with respect to any Grievance, survive the termination or expiration of this Agreement for any reason.

24.0 Confidentiality

The terms of this Agreement shall be kept confidential by the Partners except that each may disclose the contents to their attorneys and/or accountants provided that each agrees to retain the confidentiality of the Agreement.

25.0 Entire Agreement

This Agreement contains the complete, full, and exclusive understanding of Partners with respect to the Partnership and supersedes any and all other oral and written agreements between the parties hereto with respect to this subject matter.

26.0 Notice

Any notice given under this Partnership Agreement shall be effective only if in writing and given by personal delivery or certified mail, return-receipt requested, to the intended recipient at the following addresses:

(a) If to Partnership:
     Name
     Organization
     Address
     City, State, Zip
     Telephone

(b) If to Partner, at the residence of record, as follows:
     Name
     Address
     City, State, Zip
     Telephone

Partners shall provide the Partnership written notice of all changes in residence in the manner specified in this Section 26.0.

27.0 Enforceability

The invalidity or unenforceability of any particular provision of this Partnership Agreement shall not affect the other provisions hereof and this Partnership Agreement shall be construed in all respects as if such invalid or unenforceable provision were omitted, unless any of the material purposes for entering into this Partnership Agreement ceases for either party to exist.

28.0 Venue and governing law

This Partnership Agreement shall be deemed executed in Colorado and shall be governed by the laws of the State of Colorado.

Appendix 2: Full-Time Faculty Member—University Medical Corporation

PHYSICIAN EMPLOYMENT AGREEMENT

(All parties and names, terms, and conditions are intended to be fictitious.)

THIS AGREEMENT made as of the day of the 20th day of January, 2009, by and between the University Medical Corporation, a Colorado nonprofit corporation, hereinafter called "Corporation," and John Doe, MD, a member of the faculty of the University School of Medicine, hereinafter called "Employee."

1. RECITALS

WHEREAS, this Agreement is consistent with American Medical Association and Association of American Medical Colleges policy governing the care of paying patients in medical school hospitals and with the Bylaws governing the compensation and status of the Faculty of the University School of Medicine, and the rendering of professional services to patients; and

WHEREAS, Employer agrees to and does hereby employ Physician in the specialty of Internal Medicine; and

WHEREAS, Physician agrees to become and does become, with his or her signing of this Agreement, a full-time employee of Employer; and

WHEREAS, Physician shall render professional services for which he or she is qualified on behalf of Employer and shall perform such other duties on behalf of Employer as may be assigned by the Manager of Clinical Services or a Corporation designee.

NOW, THEREFORE, it is mutually agreed by and between the parties hereto as follows:

2.0 Employment and Duties

2.1 The Corporation hereby employs Employee to perform professional services at the University Medical Center in Denver, Colorado, or elsewhere as is directed by the Dean of the School of Medicine, and Employee hereby accepts such employment.

2.2 Employee agrees to obtain and maintain hospital staff privileges at University Hospitals, or elsewhere directed by the Dean of the School of Medicine.

143

2.3 The Dean of the School of Medicine or his or her designated representative will prescribe employee's specific duties.

2.4 The Employee agrees to perform such assigned duties in accordance with the provisions of the Bylaws of the University Medical Corporation, which Bylaws are hereby incorporated by reference into, and made a part of, this Agreement.

2.5 Physician shall not participate in any third-party payment or health delivery plan (such as Medicare, Medicaid, Blue Cross/Blue Shield, HMOs, and PPOs) in connection with his or her professional practice without the prior consent of Employer.

2.6 Physician shall participate in any third-party payment or health delivery plan designated by Employer. Physician shall abide by all applicable requirements and guidelines of each third-party payment or health delivery plan in which he or she participates.

3.0 Duties of the Employer

3.1 Employer shall provide office and clinical space for the Physician to provide professional services and shall furnish and maintain all equipment and supplies necessary for the proper rendering of services by Physician. Physician shall promptly notify Employer of any perceived deficiency in any equipment or deficit of supplies.

3.2 Employer shall provide such clerical and clinical support staff for the Physician as Employer determines is appropriate to enable Physician to perform his or her responsibilities pursuant to this Agreement and in accordance with accepted standards of medical practice.

4.0 Duties Not Assignable

Neither party shall assign its rights or delegate its duties or performance under this Agreement without the prior written approval of the other party. Any purported assignment or delegation without prior written approval shall be void.

5.0 Employee Performance

Employee agrees that he or she will at all times, faithfully, industriously, and to the best of his or her ability, experience, and talents, perform all of the duties that may be required of him or her, including but not limited to the recording of all information necessary for patient charts and other records and the billing of patients services rendered them by Employee, and that, in the event this contract is terminated for any cause, Employee will, at a negotiated additional cost to the Corporation, provide to the Corporation all reasonable assistance and information necessary to complete all such records and the billing of patients for services rendered them by Employee up to and including the termination of this Agreement.

6.0 Term

The term of this Agreement shall be from the 20th day of January, 2009, to (but not including) the first day of February, 2010, unless sooner terminated as provided elsewhere in this Agreement. This Agreement shall not be in effect during any time when Employee is not a member of the Medical Staff of University Hospitals, or the Medical Staff of another medical facility or facilities consistent with the Employee's duties as specified in Section 2, above.

7.0 Termination

7.1 In the event that Employee ceases to practice at University Hospital, or elsewhere as directed by the Dean of the School of Medicine, or fails to faithfully, industriously, and to the best of his or her ability, experience, and talents perform all of the duties that may be required of him or her including but not limited to the recording of all information necessary for patient charts and other records and the billing of patients for services rendered them by Employee, the Corporation may terminate this Agreement upon fifteen (15) days' written notice to the Employee.

7.2 This Agreement shall terminate upon the death of the Physician.

7.3 Either party may terminate this Agreement at any time, with or without cause, upon one hundred and twenty (120) days' prior written notice to the other party.

7.4 In the event of termination pursuant to this provision, Physician agrees that Employer shaft have the option of paying the Physician in lieu of the Physician performing his/her duties for the 120-day period or any portion thereof.

7.5 In the event that the Physician terminates his/her employment without providing the notice required by this provision or if Physician is terminated pursuant to paragraph 7.3, Physician consents to the Employer's retention of six (6) weeks' pay.

  (a) In the event this Agreement is terminated for any reason, as herein set forth, all obligations on the part of either party shall cease on the date of such, except where indicated to the contrary.
  (b) Nothing contained herein shall relieve the Employer of the payment of any amounts owed to Physician (including any applicable bonus or incentive payments) which have accrued and are unpaid as of the date of such termination.

8.0 Compensation

For the services to be rendered by Employee hereunder, the Corporation agrees to pay Employee salary of $ per annum. Salary payments will be made in installments of 1/26 of the above annual salary, less the usual amounts withheld for taxes, Social Security, and the like.

9.0 Restrictive Covenant

9.1 Employee agrees that he or she will not, within a period of one (1) year after leaving the employ of the Corporation, engage, directly or indirectly, either personally or as an employee, associate partner, partner, manager, agent, or otherwise, or by means of any corporate or other device, in the practice of medicine within a radius of fifty (50) miles of the practice site(s) at which he or she is practicing, or has practiced within the preceding two (2) years, while employed by the

Corporation, without the express written authorization of the President and Chief Executive Officer of the Corporation.

9.2 Employee understands that violation of this covenant will cause substantial damage to the Corporation and that such violation will entitle the Corporation to apply to any court of competent jurisdiction for:

(a) Its order or decree enjoining any such violation, threatened or actual, of this Agreement; and

(b) Such violation, a sum to be paid by Employee to the Corporation equal to seventy percent (70 percent) of the average of Employee's gross charges from the practice of medicine for the two (2) years preceding the violation of this covenant or the sum of One Hundred Thousand Dollars ($100,000), whichever is the greater amount, plus reasonable attorneys' fees incurred by the Corporation in securing such equitable or legal relief or in the collection of such sum.

10.0 Income from Other Professional Services

Employee understands that, in accordance with the Bylaws of the Corporation, which have heretofore been made a part of this Agreement, he or she is prohibited from receiving other income as a result of performing professional services, unless specifically authorized in writing by the Employee's departmental chairperson and the Dean of the School of Medicine or permitted by the Bylaws.

11.0 Disability

In the event of disability of Employee, he or she shall continue to receive for six (6) months following the onset of the disability any salary he or she would have been entitled to receive from the Corporation and from the University if the disability had not occurred, provided that the Employee shall be entitled to receive this disability benefit only one time during his or her employment with the Corporation if the disability is the result of alcohol or drug abuse. Determination of the date of the onset of Employee's disability shall be made by the Corporation in cooperation with Employee's departmental chairperson.

12.0 Other Benefits

12.1 The Corporation agrees to provide Employee all fringe benefits which are generally provided for other employees of the Corporation who are members of the faculty of the University School of Medicine, upon the same terms and conditions as are offered to such other employees.

12.2 Physician shall be entitled to Combined Time Off (CTO) accruable at the rate of 4.6 hours per pay period in addition to the benefits described in Exhibit A, attached hereto and incorporated herein by reference. (Combined Time Off may be carried forward per Corporation policy, a copy of which will be provided to Employee on the Effective Date).

12.3 Continuing Medical Education (CME) benefit time and reimbursement must be used in the year earned and may not be carried forward from year to year.

12.4 Physician shall give Employer thirty (30) days advance written notice of any CTO/CME time and agrees that any dates selected must be reasonably satisfactory to Employer and approved in advance.

13.0 Amendments and Notice

This Agreement may not be modified or changed orally, but only a writing signed by both parties. Any notice given under this Agreement shall be effective only if in writing and given by personal delivery or certified mail, return-receipt requested, to the intended recipient at the following addresses:

  (a) If to Employer, to "Manager, Clinical Services" at the Corporation's administrative offices set forth below.
       Manager, Clinical Services, University Medical Corporation 14 University Avenue, Denver, Colorado 80202; Telephone
  (b) If to Physician, to Physician's residence of record, as follows:
       Name, Address, City, State, Zip, Telephone
       Physician shall give Employer written notice of all changes in residence in the manner specified.

14.0 NO THIRD PARTY

This Agreement is for the benefit of the parties hereto, and is not entered into for the benefit of any other person or entity, including but not limited to patients and their representatives.

15.0 Captions and Construction

The underlined heading of any Section contained in this Agreement is for convenience only and shall not be deemed a part of this Agreement or a representation as to the contents of the Section.

16.0 Interpretation and Severability

The parties agree that the law of the State of Colorado shall govern the interpretation and legal effect of this Agreement. If any provision of this Agreement is held invalid or otherwise unenforceable, the validity and enforceability of the other provisions shall not be impaired thereby.

WITNESS the signatures of Employee and the duly authorized of the Corporation.
UNIVERSITY MEDICAL CORPORATION

    By:
    Name:
    Date:

PHYSICIAN

    Signature:
    Print Name:
    Date:

CONSENT FOR BILLING

I hereby consent to and authorize Jones Corporation or its designee to bill for all services rendered by me at all sites designated pursuant to the foregoing Agreement, and hereby assign to University Medical Corporation, and agree to its receipt of all payment for such services.

Date:
Signature:
Printed Name:

Appendix 3: Physician Employment Agreement

SAMPLE Hospital-Affiliated Practice/Physician

PHYSICIAN EMPLOYMENT AGREEMENT

(All parties and names are intended to be fictitious.)

This Agreement is made and entered into as of this day of , 2009, by and between Jones Corporation, a Colorado nonprofit corporation (hereinafter the "Employer" or the "Corporation") and John Smith, DO (hereinafter the "Physician") of Denver, Colorado, and is effective August 1st, 1999 (the "Effective Date").

I. RECITALS

WHEREAS, Employer agrees to and does hereby employ Physician in the specialty of Internal Medicine; and

WHEREAS, Physician agrees to become and does become, with his/her signing of this Agreement, a full-time employee of Employer; and

WHEREAS, Physician shall render professional services for which he/she is qualified on behalf of Employer and shall perform such other duties on behalf of Employer as may be assigned by the Manager of Clinical Services or a Corporation designee.

NOW THEREFORE, in consideration of this covenants set forth herein, the parties agree as follows:

II. DUTIES OF THE PHYSICIAN

1. Physician's full time and effort shall be devoted to the performance of his/her duties for Employer pursuant to this Agreement. Physician will spend, on the average, not less than 40 hours per week carrying out his/her duties which generally include providing professional services and related activities in the office and hospital setting, and being actively involved in corporate, departmental, and medical staff meetings and activities. From time to time the Physician may be required to work longer than the foregoing stated hours.
2. Physician will spend on average not less than 30 hours per week seeing patients in the office.
3. Physician shall not, except as otherwise expressly authorized by Employer in advance, undertake any professional obligations of any kind, medical, administrative, executive, or otherwise, for any entity except Employer.

4. Employer, in consultation with Physician, shall set Physician's work schedule and the sites at which professional services are to be rendered by Physician.
5. Physician shall be available on an on-call basis in accordance with Employer's standard on-call policies and will arrange coverage for scheduled time off with other physicians employed by Corporation.
6. Throughout the term hereof, Physician shall:
    a. Maintain membership on the medical staff of, and full clinical and admitting privileges at Jones Hospital.
    b. Should, for any reason, Physician cease to be a member of the medical staff of Jones Hospital, or should, for any reason, Physician's clinical and/or admitting privileges expire without renewal or be suspended or revoked, or Physician's license to practice medicine in the State of Colorado be suspended, revoked, or canceled, then, effective as of the date Physician ceases to be a member of the medical staff or as of the date of expiration, suspension, revocation, or cancellation of such clinical and/or admitting privileges or license.
7. Employer may terminate this Agreement if Physician's clinical and/or admitting privileges at Jones Hospital are restricted or made subject to supervision in accordance with the applicable medical staff bylaws, rules, and regulations or comparable rules, regulations, or policies applicable to the practices of physicians.
8. Physician may continue to render services hereunder only in accordance with such restriction or supervision. If Employer determines in its sole reasonable discretion that imposition of such restriction or supervision of Physician's privileges unreasonably interferes with the performance of Physician's duties under this Agreement, Employer may terminate this Agreement effective immediately by written notice to Physician.
9. Throughout the term of this Agreement, Physician agrees to maintain his/her clinical skills as evidenced by participating in appropriate continuing medical education activities and maintaining good standing in professional associations.
10. Physician further agrees with all applicable federal and state statutes and regulations and compliance policies and all Joint Commission accreditation standards applicable to Corporation and/or to Jones Hospital.

III. COMPENSATION

1. Employer shall compensate Physician for the services rendered pursuant to this Agreement at an annual salary of $115,000.00 payable in equal biweekly installments and subject to all tax withholding required by law, plus a five thousand dollar ($5,000.00) sign-on bonus payable on the Effective Date.
2. Employer shall provide to Physician any fringe benefits in accordance with Employer's flex benefit program as it may exist from time to time.
    a. Physician shall be entitled to Combined Time Off (CTO) accruable at the rate of 4.6 hours per pay period in addition to the benefits described in Exhibit A, attached hereto and incorporated herein by reference. (Combined Time Off may be carried forward per Corporation policy a copy of which will be provided to Employee on the Effective Date.)

b. Continuing Medical Education (CME) benefit time and reimbursement must be used in the year earned and may not be carried forward from year to year.

c. Physician shall give Employer thirty (30) days advance written notice of any CTO/CME time and agrees that any dates selected must be reasonably satisfactory to Employer and approved in advance.

3. If at any time during the term of this Agreement Physician becomes unable by reason of illness or physical or mental disability to perform the duties required of him under this Agreement, Employer shall have no obligation to pay Physician's salary during the period of disability. Disability benefits will be provided to Physician in accordance with Employer's flex benefit program, as it exists from time to time and as described in Exhibit A.

IV. OBLIGATIONS OF THE EMPLOYER

1. Employer shall provide Physician with professional inability insurance coverage through Employer's self-insurance program for professional inability claims that may arise from services rendered by Physician on behalf of Employer pursuant to this Agreement.

2. Employer solely may bill for professional services rendered by Physician pursuant to this Agreement.

3. Any and all fees received in connection with such billed services belong to Employer and shall be paid as received to Employer and, if payable to Physician, shall be assigned or endorsed over promptly to Employer by Physician.

4. Employer or its delegate shall have responsibility for billing or collecting any amounts owed for services provided by Physician pursuant to this Agreement.

5. Physician shall timely provide Employer with all accurate and complete information and documentation, including but not limited to, completion of all medical records, to assist the Corporation to bill and collect amounts owed.

6. Physician shall not participate in any third-party payment or health delivery plan (such as Medicare, Medicaid, Blue Cross/Blue Shield, HMOs, and PPOs) in connection with his/her professional practice without the prior consent of the Employer.

7. Physician shall participate in any third-party payment or health delivery plan designed by Employer. Physician shall abide by all applicable requirements and guidelines of each third-party payment or health delivery plan in which he/she participates which does not conflict or create fiduciary conflicts with the Physician's independent professional medical judgment in caring for his/her patients.

8. Employer shall provide office and clinical space for the Physician to provide professional services and shall furnish and maintain all equipment and supplies necessary for the proper rendering of services by Physician. Physician shall promptly notify Employer of any perceived deficiency in any equipment or deficit of supplies.

9. Employer shall provide such clerical and clinical support staff for the Physician as Employer determines is appropriate to enable the Physician to perform his/her responsibilities pursuant to this Agreement and in accordance with accepted standards of medical practice.

V. TERM AND TERMINATION

1. The term of this Agreement shall commence on the Effective Date set forth above and thereafter remain in full force and effect for a period of two (2) years with automatic renewal for additional one (1) year terms unless either party notifies the other in writing of its intent not to renew at least ninety (90) days prior to the expiration of the then current term.
2. Any other provision to the contrary notwithstanding.
3. This Agreement shall terminate upon the death of the Physician.
4. Either party may terminate this Agreement at any time, with or without cause, upon one hundred and twenty (120) days' prior written notice to the other party.
   a. In the event of termination pursuant to this provision, Physician agrees that Employer shall have the option of paying the Physician in lieu of the Physician performing his/her duties for the 120-day period or any portion thereof.
   b. In the event that the Physician terminates his/her employment without providing the notice required by this provision or if Physician is terminated pursuant to paragraph II.6, Physician consents to the Employer's retention of six (6) weeks' pay.
   c. In the event this Agreement is terminated for any reason, as herein set forth, all obligations on the part of either party shall cease on the date of such termination except as set forth in Paragraphs VI.1 (a) and VI.2; provided, however, that, subject to the provisions of paragraph 4 (b), nothing contained herein shall relieve the Employer of the payment of any amounts owed to Physician (including any applicable bonus or incentive payments) which have accrued and are unpaid as of the date of such termination.
   d. In the event this Agreement is terminated by reason of the death of the Physician any unpaid compensation shall be paid to the Physician's estate, and any unpaid amount owed by Physician to Employer shall be paid to the Physician's estate.

VI. NONCOMPETE

1. In consideration of the terms and conditions of this Agreement, and Physician's resulting access to Employer's patients, business and goodwill, Physician agrees that, during the term of this Agreement and for a period of one (1) year after the expiration or termination of this Agreement, by either party and for any reason, Physician shall not, individually or jointly, with any other physician, individual or entity, directly or indirectly, whether as employer or employee, operator, agent, member, advisor, consultant, independent contractor, owner, stockholder, investor, partner, joint venturer, or otherwise:
   a. Own, operate, or have any interest in any medical practice, medical clinic, or clinical laboratory;
   b. Provide professional medical services or related services;
   c. Otherwise become involved in activities similar to or of the same type as the activities of Employer and/or in competition with Employer;

     d. Permit Physician's name to be used in connection with any activities similar to or of the same type as the activities of Employer and/or in competition with Employer;

     e. Solicit, hire, or employ, directly or indirectly, any person who is or was, at anytime during Physician's employment hereunder, an employee or independent contractor of Employer, or solicit, directly or indirectly, any patient of Employer, including any patient treated by Physician during his/her employment hereunder, within a three (3) mile radius of Jones Hospital or of any site to which Physician was assigned to provide services during the term of this Agreement. Nor during the same time periods and within the same geographical area, shall Physician disclose or utilize for other than Employer's benefit any of Employer's confidential information, including, but not limited to, Employer's patient lists, records, policies, and/or procedures.

2. The foregoing provisions of paragraph VI.1 shall be of full force and effect if this Agreement is terminated prior to its expiration, except in the event that Employer terminates this Agreement without cause pursuant to paragraph V.4. In such case, the provisions of paragraph VI.1 shall be waived if Physician executes a separate written agreement providing that Physician will not solicit, directly or indirectly, any patient of Employer from the site(s) at which Physician practiced pursuant to this Agreement, including any patient treated by Physician during employment under this Agreement.

3. Physician acknowledges and agrees that the covenants and undertakings contained in this paragraph VI.1 relate to matters which are of special, unique, and extraordinary importance to Employer and that violation of any of the terms hereof may cause irreparable injury to Employer, the amount of which may be impossible to estimate or determine and which cannot be compensated adequately.

4. Physician further acknowledges and agrees that the provisions of this paragraph VI.1 are reasonable and necessary for the protection of Employer, and that without them, Employer would not be willing to execute this Agreement or hire Physician.

5. Physician further acknowledges and agrees that the remedy at law for a breach or threatened breach of such covenants would be inadequate, and that Employer shall be entitled, without prior notice and without necessity of proving actual damages, to immediate, permanent injunctive, and other equitable relief from any court of competent jurisdiction, restraining any violation or threatened violation of any such covenants by Physician and such other persons as the court shall order.

6. The rights and remedies provided for herein are cumulative and are in addition to rights and remedies otherwise available to the Employer under any other agreement or applicable law.

7. Physician agrees that if any portion of the restrictive covenants set forth in paragraph VI.1 is held to be unreasonable, arbitrary, or against public policy, then each covenant shall be considered divisible as to time, geographic area, and other relevant feature, with each month of a specified period being deemed a separate period of time.

8. Physician further agrees that if any court of competent jurisdiction determines that a specified time period, a specified geographical area, a specified occupational limitation, other relevant feature, or any provision of

paragraph VI.1 is unreasonable, arbitrary, or against public policy, a lesser time period, geographical area, occupational limitation, or other relevant feature shall be enforced against Physician to the maximum extent which is determined by such court to be reasonable, not arbitrary, and not against public policy, and that the remaining provisions of this paragraph VI shall be construed and enforced so as to provide Employer with the maximum protection permitted by law.

VII. DISPUTE RESOLUTION

1. Any dispute, claim, or controversy arising under or in connection with the terms of this Agreement, other than any arising under or in connection with Section VI hereof, shall be deemed for purposes of this paragraph VII to be a "Grievance."

2. Any and all Grievances shall be resolved exclusively through arbitration in accordance with the Voluntary Labor Arbitration Rules of the American Arbitration Association then in effect. Any dispute, claim, or controversy arising under or in connection with Section VI of this Agreement shall be subject to resolution as provided in Section VI.

   The Arbitrator's decision will be final and binding and any and all Grievances shall be disposed of as follows:

   a. Any and all Grievances must be submitted in writing by the aggrieved party;

   b. Within thirty (30) days following the submission of the written Grievance, the party to whom the Grievance is submitted shall respond in writing. If no written response is submitted, or the Grievance is otherwise not resolved, within thirty (30) days, the Grievances shall be deemed denied;

   c. If the Grievance is denied, either party may, within thirty (30) days of such denial, refer the Grievance to arbitration in Denver City and County, Colorado, by filing a Demand for Arbitration with the American Arbitration Association office in such county and serving a copy thereof on the other party to this Agreement;

   d. The arbitrator shall be chosen in accordance with the Voluntary Labor Arbitration Rules of the American Arbitration Association then in effect, and the expense of the arbitration shall be shared equally by the Physician and the Corporation;

   e. Any Grievance shall be deemed waived unless presented within the time limits specified above;

   f. The arbitrator shall not have jurisdiction or authority to change, add to or subtract from any of the provisions of this Agreement;

   g. The arbitrator's sole authority shall be to interpret or apply the provisions of this Agreement;

   h. Judgment upon the award rendered may be entered in any court having jurisdiction;

   i. The parties hereby acknowledge and agree that since arbitration is the exclusive remedy with respect to any Grievance, as defined above, neither party has the right to resort to any federal, state, or local court or administrative agency for the resolution of any Grievance. The parties further acknowledge and agree that any suit, action, or proceeding

instituted in any federal, state, or local court or before any administrative agency with respect to any Grievance shall be dismissed with
prejudice immediately upon submission to such court or agency of an
executed copy of this Agreement;

j. The arbitration provisions hereof shall, with respect to any Grievance,
    survive the termination or expiration of this Agreement for any reason.

VIII. CONFIDENTIALITY

The terms of this Agreement shall be kept confidential by Physician and Employer
except that each may disclose the contents to their attorneys and/or accountants
provided that each agrees to retain the confidentiality of the Agreement. Physician
shall not ask any physician employed by Employer to disclose the contents of their
agreement.

IX. ASSIGNMENT

No portion of this Agreement, nor any portion of either party's rights or obligations hereunder may be assigned without the prior written consent of the other
party; provided, however, that Employer may, upon written notice to Physician,
assign this Agreement to any entity which either controls Employer or is under
Employer's control.

X. ENTIRE AGREEMENT

This Agreement, including Exhibit A hereto, contains the complete, full, and exclusive understanding of Employer and Physician with respect to Physician's employment by Employer and supersedes any and all other oral and written agreements
between the parties hereto with respect to this subject matter. Furthermore, all
policy statements, manuals, or documents issued by Employer shall be interpreted
in a manner consistent with and subject to this Agreement.

XI. AMENDMENT

Any amendment, modification, addition, or supplement to this Agreement shall
be effective and binding upon Physician and Employer only if in writing and
signed by both Physician and Employer through Employer's duly authorized
representative.

XII. NOTICE

Any notice given under this Agreement shall be effective only if in writing and
given by personal delivery or certified mail, return-receipt requested, to the
intended recipient at the following addresses:

If to Employer, to:
    Manager, Clinical Services
    at the Corporation's administrative offices set forth below:
Manager, Clinical Services
Jones Corporation
    14 Jones Road
    Denver, Colorado 80202
    Telephone

If to Physician, to:
    Physician's residence of record, as follows:
    Name
    Address
    City, State, Zip
    Telephone

Physician shall give Employer written notice of all changes in residence in the manner specified in this Section XII.

XIII. NO THIRD PARTY

This Agreement is for the benefit of the parties hereto, and is not entered into for the benefit of any other person or entity, including but not limited to patients and their representatives.

XIV. ENFORCEABILITY

The invalidity or unenforceability of any particular provision of this Agreement shall not affect the other provisions hereof and this Agreement shall be construed in all respects as if such invalid or unenforceable provision were omitted, unless any of the material purposes for entering into this Agreement cease for either party to exist.

XV. VENUE AND GOVERNING LAW

This Agreement shall be deemed executed in Colorado and shall be governed by the laws of the State of Colorado.

IN WITNESS WHEREOF, the Employer has caused this Agreement to be executed by its duly authorized officer, and Physician has executed this Agreement, on the date(s) specified below but effective as of the Effective Date specified above.

CONSENT FOR BILLING

I hereby consent to and authorize Jones Corporation or its designee to bill for all services rendered by me at all sites designated pursuant to the foregoing Agreement, and hereby assign to Jones Corporation, and agree to its receipt of all payment for such services.

Appendix 4: Independent Contractor Agreement

SAMPLE INDEPENDENT CONTRACTOR AGREEMENT

(All parties and names are intended to be fictitious.)

This Agreement is made and entered into as of this 20th day of February, 2009, by and between Jones Clinic ("Clinic"), a for-profit professional limited liability corporation incorporated under the laws of the state of Colorado, and John Smith, DO (hereinafter the "Physician") of Denver, Colorado, and is effective this 20th day of February, 2009 (the "Effective Date").

RECITALS

WHEREAS, Clinic desires to engage Physician to be readily available to perform medical services for patients at the Medical Center, and Physician desires to obligate himself to be available to perform such services, all on the terms and conditions specified in this Agreement; and

WHEREAS, Physician is licensed to practice medicine in the state of Colorado and is qualified to perform the services required by this Agreement.

NOW, THEREFORE, in consideration of the mutual covenants herein contained, the parties hereto agree as follows:

1. Services to be Provided by Physician

Physician agrees to provide services to patients at the Medical Center including (but not limited to) the following:

   (a) Physician shall be on duty at the Center during business hours, Monday through Friday, except for vacations, illness, and attendance at seminars and meetings, and except as modified in an on-duty schedule mutually agreed to by Physician and the Medical Director of Clinic.

   (b) Physician shall make his medical services available to all patients who come to the Medical Center in need of and seeking immediate physician services during the hours he is scheduled to be on duty at the Medical Center. Physician shall, when appropriate in his medical judgment, seek appropriate consultations and refer patients for additional medical care to specialists who are members of the Consulting Medical Staff of the Center. (Author's note: This may or may not be legal in light of Stark II and antikickback regulations, depending upon the circumstances of the contract.)

(c) Physician shall keep or cause to be kept accurate and complete records, including an adequate filing system. Physician shall cause his practice to comply with all governmental record-keeping and reporting requirements.

(d) Physician and Clinic acknowledge and agree that the responsibilities of Physician and Clinic pursuant to this Agreement are separate and distinct. Physician has full responsibility for and authority over the medical functions of his practice, such functions being defined as engaging in the diagnosis and treatment of disease, defects, or injuries and recommending or prescribing treatments for the relief or cure of physical, mental, or functional ailments or defects. Clinic has full responsibility for and authority over the administrative and related medical business aspects of the operation of the Center and may advise Physician as to the relationship between his performance of medical functions and the overall administrative and business functioning of his practice.

2. Insurance

Physician shall obtain and maintain general and professional liability insurance, including malpractice insurance, for himself in the amount of not less than $1 million for each occurrence and $3 million annual aggregate. Physician shall, within five (5) days after execution of this Agreement and thereafter on the first day of each year of the term of this Agreement, furnish appropriate evidence to Clinic of the existence of such insurance and the payment of premiums by Physician for the ensuing year. In the event that Physician pays professional insurance premiums more frequently than annually, Physician shall, promptly upon the making of each premium payment, provide evidence thereof to Clinic.

3. Physician's Warranties

Physician represents and warrants to Clinic that he:

(a) Is duly licensed to practice medicine in the State of Colorado;
(b) Is certified in the specialty of emergency medicine by the Board or is otherwise able to provide satisfactory evidence to Clinic that he has sufficient experience in providing emergency medical services; and
(c) Has all customary narcotics and controlled substances numbers and licenses.

Physician further represents and warrants to Clinic that:

(a) His license to practice medicine in any state has never been suspended or revoked;
(b) He has never been reprimanded, sanctioned, or disciplined by any licensing board or state or local medical society or specialty board;
(c) There has never been entered against him a final judgment in a malpractice action having an aggregate award to the plaintiff in excess of $10,000, ever been settled by payment to the plaintiff of an aggregate of more than $10,000; and
(d) He has never been denied membership or reappointment to membership on the medical staff of any hospital and none of his hospital medical staff membership or clinical privileges have ever been suspended, curtailed, or revoked.

4. Supporting Facilities and Services by Clinic

Clinic shall provide to Physician a suitably equipped office suite and examination and treatment facilities (the "Offices"), served by an adequate number of employees, both as determined in the discretion and judgment of Clinic.

(a) *Employees.* Employees in the Offices shall be obtained by Clinic and shall be required to comply with all rules and regulations established by the administration of Clinic. The compensation, discharge, or transfer of employees shall be the sole responsibility of Clinic, after such consultation with Physician as it deems necessary. Physician shall not alter or vary Clinic's policies and procedures with respect to personnel in any way.

(b) *Equipment and Supplies.* Clinic shall furnish such equipment and apparatus as is necessary in the judgment of Clinic for the operation of the Offices and shall keep the same in good repair. Additional equipment shall be obtained by Clinic from time to time if deemed necessary or desirable by Clinic after consultation with Physician. Supplies for the emergency medical practice shall be purchased by Clinic, and the type of services and the quantities maintained shall be determined by Clinic after consultation with Physician.

5. Financial Matters

(a) *Charges for Services.* The charges for services provided to patients shall include fees for use of the facility, equipment, supplies, and physician professional fees in a single comprehensive charge.

(b) *Physician Compensation.* In order for the compensation to Physician for services rendered pursuant to this Agreement to vary based on the amount of work performed by Physician, records shall be kept of all services to patients performed by Physician and of the hours Physician is on duty at the Medical Center. The Physician shall be compensated on a monthly basis.

  (i) *Base Rate.* Compensation to Physician shall be based on the fixed rate of one hundred twenty dollars ($120) per hour for the services performed during the preceding month by Physician ("the Base Rate").

  (ii) *Incentive Rate.* If Physician completes at least six entire months of performing medical services under this Agreement and the average number of hours Physician was on duty at the Medical Center during such months equals or exceeds one hundred and twenty (120) hours.

Physician shall be compensated at the Base Rate each month, and at the end of each calendar quarter thereafter, Clinic shall determine the amount that equals the rate of twenty-three dollars ($23.00) per hour for the services performed during such quarter by Physician, plus fourteen percent (14 percent) of the Gross Revenues for such quarter. If such amount exceeds the total compensation paid to Physician during that quarter under (i), then Physician shall be paid the difference. "Gross Revenues" means the amount of gross patient charges billed for services rendered by Physician to patients at the Medical Center during the calendar quarter, including the lab charges and the technical component of the radiology charges.

(c) Benefits. Clinic will not provide Physician with any health, life or dental insurance, paid vacation, or paid sick leave. Clinic will pay the costs of any continuing education or other program attended by Physician which Clinic requests the Physician to attend.

6. Covenants and Responsibilities of Physician

   (a) Nothing herein shall be construed as giving control over, or the right to control, the professional judgment, treatment, or actions of Physician performing services hereunder, and Physician shall at all times act as and be an independent practitioner of medicine. The interest and responsibility of Clinic is to ensure that the Medical Center is operated and the services rendered hereunder are performed in a competent and satisfactory manner. Physician is not and shall not be an employee, agent, or servant of Clinic; instead, Physician is an independent contractor who has agreed to make himself available to provide professional services to patients in the Offices operated and managed by Clinic.

   (b) In performing services under this Agreement, Physician covenants and agrees that he:
       (i) Shall use diligent efforts and professional skills and judgment,
       (ii) Shall perform professional and supervisory services and shall render care to patients in accordance with and in a manner consistent with customary and recognized standards of the medical profession,
       (iii) Shall conduct himself in a manner consistent with the Principles of Medical Ethics of the American Medical Association, and
       (iv) Shall comply with the policies, rules, and regulations of Clinic in conjunction with the facility administrator.

   (c) Physician shall promptly notify the Clinic facility administrator if any equipment in the Offices of the emergency medical practice is defective, inoperative, or in disrepair and if any employee of the practice, to the best judgment of Physician, is incompetent, inadequately trained, or absent without proper excuse.

   (d) Physician shall not disclose information relating to the business, affairs, or operations of Clinic to persons other than governmental licensing authorities without obtaining the prior written consent of Clinic. Physician shall not disclose such information to third-party reimbursement agencies (whether public or private) unless such disclosure is required by applicable law and regulations or by the terms and conditions of an applicable contract or agreement for reimbursement.

7. Indemnification of Clinic

Physician hereby indemnifies and holds harmless Clinic and its directors, officers, employees, and agents from and against any claim, loss, damage, cost, expense (including reasonable attorneys' fees), or liability arising out of or related to the performance or nonperformance by Physician of any services to be performed or provided by Physician under this Agreement. (Author's note: This should be replaced with an each responsible for own acts language crafted by your attorney. Your malpractice policy may not provide for liability by contract.)

8. Term

The term of this Agreement shall be for twelve (12) months from the date hereof, and this Agreement shall be self-renewing for additional one-year terms unless

Clinic or Physician terminates this Agreement by giving written notice to the other party at least sixty (60) days prior to the last day of any one-year term. Any provision of the preceding sentence to the contrary notwithstanding, this Agreement may be terminated by either party (a) during the first ninety (90) days from the date hereof on ten (10) days' notice to the other party, and (b) thereafter on ninety (90) days' notice to the other party. Notice may be given and this Agreement may be terminated pursuant to this Section 3 with or without cause.

9. Early Termination by Clinic

Clinic may terminate this Agreement immediately upon written notice to Physician in the event that:

(a) Physician fails to obtain or maintain insurance as provided herein;

(b) Physician's license to practice medicine in any state is suspended, revoked, or terminated, or the State Board of Medical Examiners or other governmental agency having jurisdiction over Physician initiates any proceeding or investigation for the purpose of suspending, terminating, or revoking any such license or for the purpose of considering any of the foregoing; or

(c) Physician's right or license to use or prescribe any controlled substance is suspended, revoked, or terminated or any governmental agency having jurisdiction over controlled substances initiates any proceeding or investigation for the purpose of suspending, terminating, or revoking any such right or license or for the purpose of considering any of the foregoing.

(d) In any such event, if Clinic terminates this Agreement, all obligations of Clinic hereunder shall cease upon termination. Clinic may also terminate this Agreement, upon ten (10) days' written notice to Physician, in the event that Physician fails, after thirty (30) days' written notice of default or failure to comply, to provide the professional services required to be provided under this Agreement or fails to comply with any other provision of this Agreement.

10. Assignment

This is a contract for professional and specialized services and shall not be assigned by Physician or by Clinic in any manner or by operation of law.

11. Negation of Partnership, Joint Venture, and Equity Interest

Nothing in this Agreement shall constitute or be construed to be or to create a partnership, joint venture, or lease between Physician and Clinic with respect to Physician's practice or the offices of the Medical Center or any equity interest in the Medical Center on the part of Physician or in Physician's practice on the part of Clinic. Nothing herein shall give any party any right or duty to share in the losses or profits of the other party.

12. Prohibition on Outside Practice

Physician shall not, during the term of this Agreement, engage in the private practice of medicine other than the providing of services pursuant to this Agreement, unless Physician shall have first obtained the consent of Clinic.

(Author's note: This may not pass muster under IRS regulations for determination of Independent Contractor status.)

13. Modification of Agreement

This Agreement contains the entire understanding of the parties and shall be modified only by an instrument in writing signed on behalf of each party hereto.

14. Governing Law

This Agreement is made in the State of Colorado, and shall be construed, interpreted, and governed by the laws of State.

15. Notices

Any notices required or permitted hereunder shall be sufficiently given if sent by registered or certified mail, postage prepaid, or personally delivered, addressed or delivered as follows:

> If to the Clinic:
>   Attention Name
>   Address
>   City, State, Zip
>   Telephone
> If to the Physician:
>   Name
>   Address
>   City, State, Zip
>   Telephone

or to such other addresses as shall be furnished in writing by the parties to each other, and, any such notice shall be deemed to have been given, if mailed, as of the date received, and, if personally delivered, as of the date delivered.

16. No Waiver

No waiver of a breach of any provision of this Agreement shall be construed to be a waiver of any breach of any other provision of this Agreement or of any succeeding breach of the same provision. No delay in acting with regard to any breach of any provision of this Agreement shall be construed to be a waiver of such breach.

17. Rights in Property

All title to supplies, fiscal records, patient charts, patient records, patient information, equipment, and furnishings shall remain the sole property of Clinic. Physician may, however, secure copies of patient charts at his own expense.

IN WITNESS WHEREOF, Physician and Clinic have executed this Agreement on the day and year first above written.

CONSENT FOR BILLING

I hereby consent to and authorize Clinic or its designee to bill for all services rendered by me at all sites designated pursuant to the foregoing Agreement, and hereby assign to Clinic, and agree to its receipt of all payment for such services.

INDEPENDENT CONTRACTOR STATUS

Before leaving this appendix, I want to include the 20 questions often considered before determining status as an independent contractor compared to an employee. These questions follow Revenue Ruling 87-41 of the Internal Revenue Code. Whenever I hire an independent contractor, I always provide a copy of this question and answer sheet with the contract. If you have questions, always ask competent tax and legal counsel.

FACTORS IN REVENUE RULING 87-41

1. Is the worker subject to the employer's instructions?

   A worker who is required to comply with the employer's instructions as to when, where, and how work is to be done is most likely an employee. It is only required that an employer have the right to control the worker; whether or not the control is implemented is irrelevant.

2. Does the employer provide training?

   Any form of employer-provided training suggests an employee–employer relationship, because training implies that the work needs to be performed in a particular manner. The Internal Revenue Service (IRS) defines training in very broad terms.

3. What is the degree of integration of the services into the business?

   If the success of the services performed by the individual is crucial to the success of the business as a whole, control over the services is presumed to exist. The greater is the degree of integration of the work into the business, the greater is the likelihood that an employer–employee relationship exists.

4. Are the services rendered personally by the worker?

   Services required to be performed in person by the worker tend to indicate control, especially when the employer has an interest in how the results are achieved.

5. Who is responsible for hiring, supervising, and paying assistants?

   Hiring, directing, or paying assistants, when done by the employer, shows an employee–employer arrangement. Independent contractors hire, direct, and pay their own people.

6. Does a continuing relationship exist?

   Continuing work by the individual, even if not regular, points toward an employer–employee relationship.

7. Does the employer set hours of work?

   Designating hours of work demonstrates control over the worker.

8. Is full-time work required?

   Utilizing a worker on a full-time basis precludes the worker from pursuing other work and is an indication of control.

9. Is the person doing work on the employer's premises?

   Performing work away from the employer's offices reduces the thread of control. Although some independent contractors do work on the employer's premises, this tends to indicate greater control by the employer.

10. Is the work order or sequences set by the employer?

    Following routines or work patterns established by the employer is indicative of employee status.

11. Are oral or written reports required?

    The requirement of regular progress reports demonstrates control.

12. Is payment by the hour, week, or month?

    Payment on a fixed periodic basis, rather than upon completion of the work, is an indicator of employee status.

13. Does the employer make payment of business or traveling expenses?

    The payment of these expenses by the employer points to regulation of business activities and thus indicates employee status.

14. Is the employer responsible for the furnishing of tools and materials?

    Independent contractors normally provide their own tools and materials.

15. Is the worker required to make a significant investment to perform the work?

    The making of a substantial investment by the worker (e.g., rental of a facility) tends to support the existence of independence.

16. Does performance result in realization of profit or loss?

    The ability to realize either a profit or a loss in performing the work is a characteristic of an independent contractor.

17. Is the individual working for more than one firm at a time?

    The performance of services for several customers simultaneously is typical of an independent contractor.

18. Is the individual engaged in making service available to the general public?

    Marketing one's services to the general public indicates independence.

19. Does the employer have a unilateral right to discharge the worker?

    The right to discharge at will indicates an employer–employee relationship. Independent contractors typically can only be discharged for failure to meet contract requirements.

20. Does the worker have a unilateral right to terminate his or her services?

    An employee may resign at will, but an independent contractor may be contractually obligated to perform.

Appendix 5: Medical Director Employment Agreement

(All parties and names are intended to be fictitious.)

AGREEMENT is made and entered into this 21st day of January, 2009, by and between Central Health Services, Inc. ("CHS"), a corporation organized under the provisions of the Colorado Statutes, as amended (hereinafter called the "Center") and John Doe, MD (hereinafter called the "Physician").

WITNESS:

WHEREAS, the Center requires the services of Physicians and surgeons and conducts the practice of medicine generally; and

WHEREAS, John Doe, MD, is a licensed and expert primary care physician; and

WHEREAS, the Center desires to retain the services of the Physician in the performance of the Center's obligations; and

WHEREAS, the Physician, as well as the Center desire to enter into an employment agreement, which recognizes fully the contributions of the Physician and assures continuous harmonious management of the affairs of the Center.

NOW THEREFORE, in consideration of the premises and the mutual covenants herein contained and other good and valuable considerations, receipt, and sufficiency whereof are hereby acknowledged, it is mutually covenanted and agreed by and between the parties hereto as follows:

I. TERM OF THE AGREEMENT
The term of this Employment Agreement shall commence on February 1, 2009, and shall continue until January 31, 2010, at which time it shall terminate unless extended, renewed or changed by a written instrument signed by both parties to this Agreement.

II. ASSIGNMENT
This Agreement is personal to each of the parties hereto and neither party may assign nor delegate any of his/her rights or obligations hereunder without first obtaining the written consent of the other party.

III. GOVERNING LAW
This Agreement shall be subject to and governed by the laws of the State of Colorado and pertinent regulations of the U.S. Department of Health and Human Services. The invalidity or unenforceability of any particular provision of this Agreement shall be construed in all respects as if such invalid and unenforceable

provisions. This Agreement shall be binding and inure to the benefits of the Center and the Physician.

IV. DUTIES AND PERFORMANCE

The Physician shall attend punctually at the office of said Center as his/her duties may require and shall devote his/her time and attention to and diligently perform the functions of a Primary Care Physician, and conform to the published rules, regulations, and policies of the Center as provided in the then current Principles of Practice of CHS, the ethics and professional conduct as laid down in the Principles of Medical Ethics of the American Medical Association, and such other statutes, ordinances, rules, and regulations as may be applicable to Physician practicing with the Center. The Personnel Policies of the Center will guide in administrative personnel matters not specifically mentioned in this Agreement. In the event of a conflict between the terms of this Agreement and provisions of the Principles of Practice or the Personnel Policies, the Agreement will prevail.

The Physician further agrees to carry out and perform reasonable orders and directions as the Executive Director of the Center may from time to time, state them to him either orally or in writing. The Physician understands that he/she may not refuse to accept a patient on the basis of race, color, religion, gender, national origin, age, disability, martial or veteran status, ability to pay, or any other legally protected status.

The Physician further understands that the Center shall have final authority over the amount of fee to be charged any patient for professional services.

The Physician affirms that he/she understands that he/she may be assigned responsibility for supervision of the medical care activities of a Nurse Practitioner or Physician's Assistant in accordance with the terms of this Agreement. The Nurse Practitioner or Physician's Assistant assigned must be acceptable to the Physician. Professional liability coverage for Nurse Practitioners and Physician's Assistants is included under the Center's general medical liability policy.

The Physician will provide after-hours, weekend, and holiday coverage according to a rotation schedule with the other staff physicians. Coverage will include being available for phone consultation or, as appropriate, meeting the patient at the Center.

V. EXCLUSIVE PRACTICE

The Physician hereby does agree to and with the Center that during the term of this agreement he/she will devote his/her professional ability, services, skill, labor, and attention to said employment, agreeing to perform his/her professional services to the best of his/her ability and for the benefit of the Center and its patients only unless such activity in no way interferes with the fulfillment of the Physician's obligations to the Center as determined by the Board of Directors.

VI. COMPENSATION AND FRINGE BENEFITS

A. SALARY

The Physician will be paid a base salary of $200,000 (two hundred thousand dollars) during the first year of this Agreement. There will be additional fifteen (15) percent paid for the administrative responsibilities. There will be a four (4) percent increase of the base for each subsequent year. This contract may, however, be renegotiated sixty (60) days before the end of each contract year. Employment consists of forty (40) hours of patient care time per week, including related administrative duties as Director of Medical Services, leave and paid holidays, but excluding after-hours, weekend, or holiday call. The Physician's salary will be paid biweekly.

B. INCENTIVE PAY AND AFTER-HOURS PAY

In addition to salary and fringe benefits, incentive and after-hours pay shall be made in accordance with the attached Physician Incentive and After-Hours Plans, and both parties to the Agreement acknowledge that the Physician Incentive and After-Hours Plans shall form part of this Agreement, although separately signed. Changes in the above plans will not be retroactive.

C. FRINGE BENEFITS

The Center shall provide to the Physician such benefits as the Board of Directors may from time to time determine to be in effect including but not limited to the following:

1. Health and Insurance benefits will be provided according to the flex benefit policy as provided by the Center.
2. Professional liability insurance: The Center will pay the premiums of a professional liability insurance policy with coverage of $2,000,000 per claim, $2,000,000 per year aggregate on behalf of the Physician for activities in the performance of duties under this agreement. The Center will pay the premium of tail insurance at the end of employment.
3. Tax-sheltered annuity: The Center shall arrange for participation in an interest-bearing, tax-sheltered annuity plan for the Physician. The Center will match an amount of 3 percent of the Physician's gross base salary to the annuity.
4. Professional and continuing education expenses: CHS will allow the Physician $1,000.00 dollars annually, to cover the costs of professional journals, memberships, books, software, and expenses incurred by the Physician only in the pursuit of approved continuing education opportunities. Such payments will be made as approved by the Executive Director.
5. Holidays: The Physician is entitled to time off with pay on official CHS holidays (listed in the Personnel Policies) providing such holiday leave does not unreasonably interfere with the medical care activities of CHS.
6. Vacation leave: The Physician is entitled to twenty (20) working days vacation leave with pay per year to the extent that his/her absence does not unreasonably interfere with the medical care activities of CHS. Vacation leave may be accrued up to a maximum of forty (40) days during continued employment. Only twenty (20) days may be carried over from one contract year to the next. Upon termination of employment with CHS, payment will be made to the Physician for up to twenty (20) days accrued annual leave.
7. Sick leave: The Physician is entitled to up to twelve (12) working days sick leave with pay per year during the term of this agreement. If the Physician shall become medically disabled the Center shall provide, from the date of disability, a maximum of ninety (90) days leave including any available

sick leave. In no single contract year shall the total leave provided for disability be more than 90 days. To qualify for leave (in excess of allocated sick leave) due to disability, it shall be necessary for the Physician to tender to the Center a medical statement, acceptable to the Center, confirming the disability. The Physician is encouraged to obtain a long-term disability policy that provides benefits after the 90th day.

8. Continuing education leave: In addition to vacation leave, the Physician is entitled to a maximum of eight (8) working days continuing education leave per year for attendance at medical meetings, conventions, or postgraduate educational meetings at no loss of salary or benefits. The Physician is required to devote at least four (4) days of the eight (8) days allowed per year in actual attendance at continuing education conferences, meetings, or seminars. Continuing education leave may not be accumulated from year to year.

VII. MEDICAL PRACTICE EXPENSE AND OPERATIONS

A. EXPENSE

During the period of his/her employment, the Physician will be reimbursed for such reasonable expenses in accordance with established policy of the Center as adopted by the Center's Board of Directors from time to time.

B. FACILITIES AND SUPPORT SERVICES

The Center shall provide and maintain (or cause to be provided and maintained by any hospital, corporation, or practice, if appropriate) such facilities, equipment, supplies, technical, clerical, and stenographic support services as are reasonably necessary for the Physician's performance of his/her professional duties under this Agreement.

VIII. MEDICAL RECORDS

Each Physician shall prepare and maintain medical records as directed by the Board of Directors of Central Health Services, Inc., and all medical records shall be the sole property of the Center only.

IX. TRANSPORTATION

During the term of this agreement, the Physician shall be reimbursed for the business use of his/her automobile. The Board of Directors may establish the use of his/her personal automobile at the rate as set from time to time for CHS staff. The Physician shall also be reimbursed for any necessary out-of-pocket expenses incurred by him/her on Center business.

X. INSURANCE

The Physician shall at his/her expense, carry automobile public liability insurance protecting him/her, and the Center against claims arising out of the use of said automobile (or any other vehicle) in the course of employment by the Center and shall keep on deposit with the Executive Director a certificate or other evidence that said insurance is in force. Said insurance shall be a minimum of $25,000 for property damage, $100,000 for the injury or death of one person, and $300,000 for injuries and death arising from one accident.

XI. TERMINATION OF AGREEMENT

A. This Agreement shall terminate immediately without notice and without action by the Center upon the conviction of the Physician of a criminal offense, a felony, or a misdemeanor involving moral turpitude or immoral conduct, or loss of professional licensure.

B. This contract may be terminated by either party upon six (6) months written notice to the other.

C. This contract may be terminated if a disability prohibits the Physician from performing his/her duties for a period of ninety (90) days or more.

D. This contract shall terminate immediately upon the death of the Physician or the dissolution of the Center.

XII. CONFIDENTIALITY

The Physician shall not during or after the termination of this Agreement reveal to any person any information which he/she received during service with the Center concerning the professional, financial, or personal affairs of the Center or the members thereof or of any servants or employees or patients of said Center except insofar as he/she may be required in the conduct or duties with the Center by law so to do, and will treat in confidence all such information.

XIII. DURATION AND REVIEW OF AGREEMENT

In consideration of the benefits to be derived by the Center and the Physician for services to be performed and compensation to be made, a review of the terms of this Agreement may be made by the Executive Director and the Physician at least two months prior to the date of the termination of this Agreement and mutually beneficial revision of terms made, if any.

XIV. ENFORCEMENT AND ARBITRATION

The Center and the Physician Mutually Covenant and Agree: That failure on the part of either party to claim a breach or seek enforcement of this Agreement by reason of a failure of performance or breach by the other party or any term or condition hereof shall not operate as a waiver of such term or condition nor prevent the enforcement hereof in the event of a subsequent breach of such term or condition.

That all disputes or differences that may arise under this Agreement, other than termination as herein above provided shall be submitted to arbitration for decision; except that no dispute shall be submitted to arbitration until all reasonable measures for an informal resolution and settlement including conferences, discussion, and mediation have been exhausted. Should a dispute require arbitration one arbitrator will be appointed by the Center, another by the Physician and the third by the two arbitrators so appointed. If the two arbitrators first selected are unable to agree within a period of thirty (30) days upon the appointment of the third arbitrator, either party may petition the Circuit Court of Denver City and County, Colorado, for the appointment of the third arbitrator. The rules of the American Arbitration Association shall govern. Each party shall be entitled to be represented by counsel. The decision of the majority of the three arbitrators shall be final. The party desiring to institute such proceedings shall select his/her appointee within 15 days of the alleged breach, dispute, or difference and notify the other party hereof. When so notified, the other party shall, within thirty (30) days, likewise select his/her appointee and give notice thereof; if he/she fails so to do, the party instituting the proceedings may petition the aforesaid Circuit Court for the appointment of such other party's arbitrator. The arbitrators shall be entitled to reasonable compensation for their services on a per diem basis as determined prior to the commencement of hearings, such compensation to be paid one-half by the Center and one-half by the Physician.

XV. ENTIRE AGREEMENT

This Agreement constitutes the entire agreement between the parties and supersedes any and all other agreements, either oral or written, between the parties hereto with respect to the subject matter hereof. The failure of either party to demand, in any one or more instances, performance of any of the terms and conditions of this Agreement shall not be construed as a waiver or a relinquishment of any right granted hereunder or of the future performance of any such term, covenant or condition.

IN WITNESS WHEREOF, the Center has caused this Agreement to be signed by its duly authorized officers, and the Physician has hereunto set his or her hand and seal on the date, month and year first written above.

CONSENT FOR BILLING

I hereby consent to and authorize CHS or its designee to bill for all services rendered by me at all sites designated pursuant to the foregoing Agreement, and hereby assign to CHS and agree to its receipt of all payment for such services.

Appendix 6: New Medical Group Employment Agreement

(The names of the parties are intended to be fictitious.)

IDENTIFICATION OF THE PARTIES:

This Employment Agreement, made and entered into as of the 21st day of January, 1999, by and between Main Street Radiologists, PLLC, a Minnesota professional limited liability corporation (hereinafter called the "Corporation"), and John Doe, MD (hereinafter called the "Doctor").

RECITALS:

WHEREAS, the Corporation was incorporated as a professional limited liability corporation organized under and pursuant to the provisions of the Minnesota Professional Limited Liability Corporation Act, and has obtained a Certificate of Registration from the Minnesota State Board of Medical examiners; and

WHEREAS, the Doctor is a Doctor of Medicine and is duly licensed to practice medicine in the State of Minnesota; and

WHEREAS, the Corporation and the Doctor desire to record their agreement with regard to the employment of the Doctor by the Corporation.

NOW THEREFORE, in consideration of the foregoing premises and of the mutual covenants and agreements herein contained, it is mutually agreed as follows:

1. Employment. The Corporation employs the Doctor and the Doctor accepts employment with the Corporation, to render medical and other services for the Corporation, as determined by the Board of Directors of the Corporation and as permitted by professional ethics and in accordance with Memorandum "A" attached hereto. The Corporation's Board of Directors shall hereafter be referred to as the "Board."
2. Duties. The Doctor agrees to devote substantially all of the Doctor's time, attention, and energies to the practice of medicine as an employee of the Corporation. The Doctor further agrees to adhere to "on-duty" and "on-call" assignments at night and on weekends and holidays, rotated in a reasonable manner by the Board, and the Doctor will adhere to such "call" demands as an integral part of the Doctor's employment dukes and responsibilities.

   The Doctor's duties shall include rendering professional patient care services, including but not limited to keeping and maintaining appropriate records relating to all professional services rendered by the Doctor under this Agreement, preparing and attending to all reports, including hospital and office charts of patients, claims, and correspondence necessary or appropriate in connection with such services (all of which records, reports, claims, and correspondence shall belong to the Corporation), and promoting the Corporation by entertainment or otherwise, to the extent permitted by law and the applicable professional ethics. The Doctor shall maintain medical staff membership and privileges at all hospitals where the Corporation practices medicine. It is agreed that the Doctor's services are not unique and other physicians may be hired to perform the same or similar services.

The Doctor will not perform professional services similar to those required or provided for herein for any other person, firm, or corporation, either as an employee of such other entity or as an independent contractor. The Doctor will not, without the express consent of the Board, become actively associated with or engage in any practice or active employment other than that of the Corporation. The Doctor may perform the duties of any public office or professional association or board office with the consent of the Board. The Doctor shall not enter into any personal service contract, oral or written, wherein a person or agency other than the Corporation has the right to designate the employee of the Corporation who is to perform the services required thereby. The Doctor shall not enter into any contract whatsoever on behalf of the Corporation except as expressly authorized by the Board.

The Doctor shall, to a reasonable extent, do all things reasonably desirable to maintain and improve the Doctor's professional skills, including the following:

(a)   Maintain membership in medical associations, hospital staffs, and other professional associations which are necessary in the normal practice of medicine and in order for the Corporation to continue to maintain its high professional reputation.

(b)   Attend postgraduate courses and professional group meetings and present professional papers and reports to medical groups.

(c)   Maintain, subscribe to, and read professional medical journals, and do each and every other reasonable thing in order to keep current with new developments in medicine.

(d)   Promote the Corporation's practice and incur reasonable expenses thereto which may be necessary and considered pertinent to the doctor's professional practice. The Doctor shall actively promote the Corporation's practice by fostering good relationships between other physicians and the Corporation, educating physicians and support staff regarding the Corporation's practice, giving seminars and speeches, entertaining, and participating in such other activities as will promote the Corporation's practice.

The Doctor's other duties shall be such as the Board may from time to time reasonably direct.

3. Term. The Agreement shall be effective commencing on February 1, 2009, and shall continue until terminated as hereafter provided.

4. Compensation. The Corporation shall pay the Doctor as compensation for services rendered during the term of this Agreement such amounts and in such manner as shall be determined from time to time by the Board, after reviewing the contribution made by the Doctor to the Corporation's practice; provided that the Doctor shall be entitled to reasonable compensation for the Doctor's services and the standards employed by the Board to determine compensation shall be applied in a fair and reasonable manner. The Doctor shall look solely to the Corporation for compensation and shall

not attempt to bill or collect any sums from the Corporation's patients for services rendered under this Agreement.

In the event of the Doctor's death while employed by the Corporation, the Doctor's compensation shall continue through the last day of the month in which death occurs.

5. Certification. The Doctor represents that he has never had restrictions placed on his license to practice medicine in Minnesota or any other state and that he currently has an unrestricted license to practice medicine in Minnesota, and will take all steps necessary to maintain said unrestricted license. The Doctor warrants that he has never had membership or privileges at any hospital restricted or revoked because of improper practice, and has never been convicted, reprimanded, or otherwise sanctioned for fraud under any State or Federal tax laws, or under any State or Federal healthcare reimbursement program, including, but not limited to Medicare and Medicaid.

6. Termination. Either party may terminate this Agreement with or without clause upon ninety (90) days written notice to the other. Upon notice of termination, the Doctor shall continue to render services and shall be paid the Doctor's regular salary through the date of termination, provided the Doctor is in full compliance with the terms of this Agreement. The Corporation may, if it desires, release the Doctor from his obligation to continue to render services but shall, in any event, continue the Doctor's salary to the stated date of termination.

This Agreement shall immediately terminate upon loss of the Doctor's license to practice medicine in Minnesota, death of the Doctor, or as provided hereafter upon the Doctor's disability.

7. Records and Files. In the event the Doctor's employment terminates for any reason, the Doctor agrees not to solicit patients of the Corporation, and the Corporation shall retain that possession of patients' records. If any patient advises the Corporation in writing that he or she wants copies of the patients' records and files delivered to the Doctor, such request shall be complied with at the patients' or Doctor's expense.

8. MMIHC Stock. The parties agree that the stock in Midwest Medical Insurance Holding Company (hereinafter "MMIHC") currently registered in the Doctor's name or in the Doctor's and the Corporation's names jointly is the sole property of the Corporation. As permitted by the MMIHC Bylaws, said stock will be held in the names of the Doctor and the Corporation jointly and in the event of the Doctor's death, the redemption price for said stock will be paid to the Corporation. To effectuate the foregoing, the parties agree to execute the Authorization of Joint Registration form. In the event the Doctor's employment with the Corporation terminates for any reason other than death, the Doctor agrees to pay to the Corporation the redemption price in effect as of the effective date of termination as determined by MMIHC. The Doctor expressly agrees that said redemption price may be offset and deducted from sums due the Doctor under this Agreement or any other agreement between the Doctor and the Corporation.

9. Disability

(a) Total Disability. In the event the Doctor becomes disabled, as determined by the Board or by a physician chosen by the Board, and cannot substantially perform all of the duties and responsibilities hereunder, it is mutually agreed that the Doctor shall be paid compensation as follows:

(1)   The Doctor shall first use his accrued but unused vacation days.

(2)   Thereafter, the Doctor will receive 50 percent of the Doctor's compensation for ninety (90) days, less the number of accrued but unused vacation days taken pursuant to (1) above.

(3)   In no event shall the number of days compensated under (1) and (2) above exceed ninety (90).

(4)   Thereafter, so long as the Doctor remains disabled, the Doctor shall receive no additional compensation.

(5)   After twelve (12) months of continuing absence, this Agreement will automatically terminate; however, the Doctor may continue to receive benefits from any disability insurance policy provided by the Corporation, but the Corporation will not be obligated to continue paying the premiums for said disability coverage. Also, if the Doctor's employment is terminated for any reason while the Corporation is making disability payments, except upon the Doctor's death, by mutual agreement, or the Corporation's insolvency or bankruptcy, the Doctor shall be entitled to receive the disability payments the Doctor would otherwise be entitled to pursuant to the provisions of this Agreement.

(6)   For the purpose of this Paragraph 9 "total disability" shall be deemed to include a Doctor's natural or adoptive maternity or paternity; provided, however, that the maximum disability periods for which a Doctor may be entitled to disability compensation shall be limited to two (2) weeks with respect to any paternity and eight (8) weeks with respect to any maternity.

In the event that the disabled Doctor recovers sufficiently from his disability prior to termination of this Agreement, and is physically able to perform substantially all of the Doctor's duties and responsibilities as determined by the Board, with the advice of a competent physician selected by it, it is mutually agreed that the Doctor may return to work at a salary to be mutually agreed upon by the parties. If the Doctor returns to full-time employment, the Doctor's compensation shall be reduced by twenty-five percent (25 percent) until such time as a cumulative amount of such reductions equals the amount of compensation the Doctor received under (2) above. In the event the Doctor does not return to work or for any reason does not reimburse the Corporation for the compensation paid under (2) above, the amount not reimbursed shall be deducted from deferred compensation due or to become due the Doctor from the Corporation.

However, if the Doctor is again disabled, the Doctor must have engaged in active full-time employment for at least twelve (12) consecutive months (exclusive of leaves of absences) immediately prior to such later disability to qualify for full continuance of the compensation authorized hereunder. In the event the doctor has not engaged in full-time employment for twelve (12) consecutive months prior to the later disability, the Doctor shall be entitled to receive as disability benefits only those amounts which come due by resuming disability payments at the point where payment for the Doctor's prior disability ceased.

To the extent the Corporation carries disability insurance on the Doctor and pays premiums therefore, the disability benefits received thereunder shall be paid over to the Doctor and shall be in addition to the compensation to be paid hereunder.

In the event of a dispute, the matter shall be submitted to arbitration in the following manner: The dispute shall be referred to arbitration upon written notice being served upon the Corporation by the Doctor. Within ten (10) days of the giving of such notice, the Doctor shall appoint one (1) arbitrator and the Corporation shall appoint one (1) and these two (2) arbitrators so selected shall appoint a third arbitrator who shall act as chairman of the board of arbitration. The appointment of a third arbitrator shall occur within fifteen (15) days of the original written notice of grievance. The arbitrators so appointed shall be specifically qualified in the particular area of medicine most specialized in the cause or result of the Doctor's disability. If the two arbitrators appointed by the parties fail to agree upon the third arbitrator within fifteen (15) days, then an application may be made by either party, upon notice to the other party, to any court of competent jurisdiction for the appointment of a third arbitrator, and any such appointment so made by the Court shall be binding upon the parties. The arbitrators selected shall hear and consult with the parties to the controversy and shall be empowered to require that the Doctor undergo such physical examinations as they deem appropriate to the controversy. Within forty-five (45) days from the original notice of grievance, the arbitrators shall give their decision in writing. The decision of a majority of the arbitrators shall be final and binding upon all parties to the controversy.

(b)   Partial Disability. In the event the Doctor is partially disabled, the Doctor may continue to be employed by the Corporation as determined by the Board upon such terms as may be mutually agreed upon. In the absence of agreement, the Doctor's employment shall be terminated upon the terms and conditions set forth above.

10. Covenant Not to Compete. The Doctor expressly agrees that during the term of this Agreement and for a period of one (1) year following termination of the Doctor's employment with the Corporation for any reason, the Doctor will not, directly or indirectly, render any medical services of an advisory nature, or otherwise become employed by or participate or engage in any business competitive with the business of the Corporation in a ten (10) mile radius surrounding the clinics where the Corporation does business without the prior written consent of the Corporation. It is further agreed that the restrictions provided in this paragraph shall survive any termination of this Agreement, except termination by the Doctor on account of breach by the Corporation.

11. Remedies for Breach Covenant Not to Compete. The Doctor and the Corporation agree that damages will not be a sufficient remedy if there is a breach of the aforesaid covenant not to compete by the Doctor, and accordingly, the parties agree that in the event of any breach of said covenant, the Corporation may seek equitable relief, monetary damages, or both, including reasonable attorneys' fees and costs. Any judicial action shall be commenced within three (3) years of the effective date of termination of the Doctor. In lieu of the foregoing, and as and for liquidated damages acceptable or enforceable at the sole option of the corporation (and to which right

the Doctor herein grants the Corporation), the Doctor shall be liable and obligated to the Corporation in the amount of fifty percent (50 percent) of any and all fees directly or indirectly billed, invoiced or otherwise generated by the Doctor within a one (1) year period subsequent to termination of the Doctor's employment with the Corporation, relative to any of the Corporation's patients within a two (2) year period prior to the date of the Doctor's termination of employment with the Corporation.

12. Facilities. The Corporation shall provide and maintain (or cause to be provided and maintained by a hospital or clinic, if appropriate) such facilities, equipment, supplies, and staff as it deems necessary for the Doctor's performance of the professional duties under this Agreement. Except as may be determined to the contrary by the Board, if the Doctor maintains an Office in the Doctor's home, the Doctor shall bear all costs of maintaining such an office.

13. Automobile. The Doctor shall maintain and use the Doctor's own automobile to the extent necessary to carry out the Doctor's duties as an employee. Except as may otherwise be determined form time to time by the Board, the Doctors shall pay all expenses incurred in connection with the ownership, maintenance, and operation of the Doctor's automobile. The Doctor shall obtain and keep in force at all times liability insurance upon such automobile designating the Corporation and the Doctor as insureds.

14. Professional Expenses. Certain professional expenses, inclusive of but not necessarily limited to continuing medical education expenses to maintain legal qualification to practice medicine, recruitment efforts on behalf of the Corporation, and normal business and professional promotional efforts, incurred by the Doctor in the performance of the Doctor's duties hereunder will be paid by the Corporation as determined by the Board. Expenses not paid by the Corporation are the Doctor's sole responsibility and will be paid by the Doctor.

15. Liability or Malpractice Insurance. The Corporation shall obtain and keep in full force and effect at all times policies of professional liability or malpractice insurance that shall afford coverage on a claims-made basis to the Doctor and to the Corporation. The Board shall determine the terms, conditions, and limits of such insurance as it deems appropriate from time to time. The Corporation shall pay the premiums for such insurance coverage while the Doctor is employed by the Corporation. The Doctor shall, upon request, be entitled to evidence of such insurance.

Upon termination of the Doctor's employment with the Corporation, a reporting endorsement ("tail") or other coverage satisfactory to the Corporation shall be purchased. To the extent that the insurer does not waive the premium, the responsibility for payment shall be as follows:

Term of Doctor's Employment	Doctor Pays	Corporation Pays
Up to 5 years	100 percent	0 percent
5 years to 10 years	50 percent	50 percent
10 years or more	0 percent	100 percent

In the event the Doctor is responsible for payment of all or any part of the tail premium, the Corporation shall have the right to offset the amount of any premium paid by the Corporation for such coverage against any funds owing to the Doctor provided, however, that if the amount owed the Doctor is insufficient to cover the premium, the Doctor agrees to pay the balance owing and to indemnify and hold the Corporation harmless for any portion of the tail premium paid by the Corporation, and any attorneys' fees and other expenses incurred by the Corporation in collecting the premium from the Doctor.

The Doctor will fully cooperate with the Corporation and its insurers and other designated agents in the investigation, negotiation for settlement, and defense of potential and reported claims under any applicable property, casualty, and liability insurance policies or coverages.

16. Additional Benefits. During the term of this Agreement, the Doctor shall (at Corporation's expense) participate in and be covered by such medical, dental disability, and life insurance programs, retirement plans, and other benefit programs as are established or provided by the Corporation from time to time, in the sole discretion of the Board. Notwithstanding any provision herein to the contrary, if for health or any other reason, the Doctor is unable to qualify for any benefit program offered by the Corporation, the Corporation shall not be required to provide the Doctor with any alternative benefit program or any additional compensation in lieu of such benefit program.

Absence from Corporation. At such reasonable times as the Board shall in its discretion permit, the Doctor shall be entitled to be absent voluntarily, without loss of pay, from the performance of the Doctor's duties under this Agreement. All such voluntary absences shall count as vacation time, provided that:

(a) The number of such paid vacation days shall be as determined by the Board;

(b) The timing of vacations shall be scheduled in a reasonable manner by the Board.

The Doctor shall not be entitled to receive any additional compensation from the Corporation on account of the Doctor's failure to take all of his vacation days, and the Doctor may accumulate unused vacation from one corporate fiscal year to the next year, not to exceed sixty (60) days;

(c) In addition to the aforesaid paid vacations, Doctor shall be entitled, without loss of pay, to be absent voluntarily from the performance of the Doctor's duties for such additional periods of time and for such valid and legitimate reasons as the Board, in its discretion, may determine.

(d) In addition to vacation days, the Doctor is annually required by the Board to continue the Doctor's medical education. The Doctor may take up to ten (10) days per year to attend medical meetings, presentations, seminars, and courses to continue the Doctor's medical education.

Confidential Information. The Doctor agrees that during the term of the Doctor's employment and after termination of the Doctor's employment with the Corporation, the Doctor will not directly or indirectly disclose, use or otherwise appropriate any confidential information of the Corporation to any person, firm, corporation, association, or other entity (other than to persons associated with the Corporation and authorized to receive such information) for any reason or purpose whatsoever. For purposes of this Agreement, confidential information shall include, but not be limited to, all information designated by the Corporation as confidential, or in the future so designated, including financial information relating to the operation of the Corporation such as books, records, and financial statements, business plans, prices and credit terms, and contract terms or other business arrangements.

17. Amendment or Assignment. This Agreement may not be amended or modified except by a writing signed by both parties. The Doctor may not assign the Doctor's rights, duties, or obligations under this Agreement without the prior written approval of the Corporation.
18. Entire Agreement. Except as otherwise expressly provided, this Agreement, including all attached exhibits, embodies the entire agreement between the Corporation and the Doctor concerning the subject matter of this Agreement, and replaces and supersedes all previous oral and written understandings or agreements concerning all or any part of the subject matter of this Agreement.
19. Notices. All notices, consent, or other communications required or permitted by this Agreement shall be deemed to be properly given if delivered personally to the other party, or sent by registered or certified U.S. Mail, postage prepaid, and sent to the Corporation at its principal office or to the Doctor at his residence.
20. Governing Law. This Agreement and the rights and obligations of the parties shall be governed by and construed under the laws of the State of Minnesota.
21. Headings. All section headings in this Agreement are provided only for convenience and ease of reference and are not to be considered in the construction or interpretation of any provision of this Agreement.
22. Waiver. The failure of either party to complain of a breach of default under this Agreement by the other party, no matter how long it may continue, shall not be construed as a waiver of a party's rights, including the right to collect damages incident to the breach or default. Furthermore, no waiver of any provision by either party shall be construed as a waiver of any other provision, or as a waiver of the same provision of any subsequent time.
23. Severability. If any provision of this Agreement is declared illegal or invalid for any reason, the remaining terms and provisions shall remain in full force and effect, notwithstanding the illegal or invalid provision, in the same manner as if the illegal or invalid provision had never been a part of the Agreement.
24. Binding Effect. This Agreement shall be binding upon the parties hereto, the Doctor's heirs and personal representatives, and upon the Corporation's successors, legal representatives and assigns.

IN WITNESS WHEREOF, the Corporation, through its proper officers, and the Doctor have executed this Agreement on the day and year first above written.

Appendix 7: Sample Concierge Medicine Practice Membership Agreement

SAMPLE DOCUMENT

MEMBERSHIP AGREEMENT

This Membership Agreement (the Agreement) specifies the terms and conditions under which, you, the undersigned member (Member) may participate in the program (Program) offered by [Practice Name]. This Agreement will become effective on the date the Agreement is signed by the Member.

I. Program

In exchange for the Membership Fee (as defined below), the Practice agrees to limit the number of members the practice serves to _____ per physician and to provide the following Amenities:

Personalized Coordinated Wellness Program including Annual History and Physical Exam

- Same-day or next-day appointments
- Appointments with minimal or no wait time
- All the time you need with your doctor
- Coordination of care, locally or worldwide
- 24/7 contact with your doctor
- Assistance in handling medical needs while traveling
- Appointments for out of town guests in need of unexpected care
- Hospital care provided locally by your personal physician

The Member acknowledges that these Amenities are not covered by insurance and are not reimbursable by Member's insurer or other health plan.

II. Annual Membership Fee

The annual membership fee for the Program is $_____ per Member. This first year's fee is due when this Agreement is signed by the Member and all subsequent years' fees are due on the anniversary of the Agreement's effective date unless prior alternate arrangements have been made in writing.

III. Renewals and Termination

The Annual Membership Fee covers a period of one (1) year. Failure to pay the renewal Annual Membership Fee before the expiration of the prior membership period may result in termination of membership.

The Practice is permitted to terminate this Agreement for any reason with thirty (30) days' prior written notice in which case the Member is entitled to a prorated refund of the Annual Membership Fee.

The Member is permitted to terminate this Agreement for any reason with thirty (30) days' prior written notice in which case the Member is entitled to a prorated refund of the Annual Membership Fee.

IV. Healthcare Services Excluded from Annual Membership Fee

The Annual Membership Fee covers only the Amenities stated herein. In the case where healthcare services excluded from the Annual Membership Fee including but not limited to services ordered by the Practice but provided by a third party, ultimately the Member will be financially responsible for these charges.

V. E-mail and Fax Communication

If the Member wishes to send email or communications to and receive email responses from the Practice or their agents or representatives, the Member should be aware that email is not a secure medium for sending or receiving sensitive personal health information. Although the Practice will take steps to keep your communications confidential and secure, the confidentiality of email communications cannot be assured or guaranteed. The Member also acknowledges and understands that email and fax are not good media for urgent or time-sensitive communications. In the event a communication is time sensitive, the Member must communicate with the Practice by telephone or in person. The Member acknowledges and understands that, at the discretion of the Practice, email or fax communications may become part of the Member's permanent medical record.

VI. Miscellaneous

This Agreement may not be assigned without the other party's prior written approval. The parties understand that this Agreement contains the entire Agreement of the parties. Nothing in this Agreement shall be deemed to influence or construed to influence or affect the independent medical judgment on behalf of the Member of [Practice Name].

VII. Change of Law

If there is a change of any state or federal law, regulation, or rule that affects this Agreement or the activities of either party under this Agreement, or any change in the judicial or administrative interpretation of any such law, regulation, or rule, and either party reasonably believes in good faith that the change will have a substantial adverse effect on that party's rights or obligations under this Agreement, then that party may, upon written notice, require the other party to enter into good faith negotiations to renegotiate the terms of this Agreement. If the parties are unable to reach an agreement concerning the modification of this Agreement within the earlier of forty-five (45) days after the date of the notice seeking renegotiation or the effective date of the change, or if the change is effective immediately, then either party may immediately terminate this Agreement by written notice to the other party.

VIII. Governing Law

This Agreement shall be governed by and construed in accordance with the laws of the State of [State].

Member Information:
   Name, Address, Phone, DOB, etc.
Billing Information:
   Annual membership fee can be paid with either a check or credit card. Please make checks payable to [Practice Name].
   Single Member Fee: $_____ Couple Fee: $_____
Payment Method: Check Enclosed | American Express | VISA | Mastercard

This Agreement accepted on behalf of [Practice Name]:

Index